The Temne of Sierra Leone

Much of the research and study of the formation of Sierra Leone focuses almost exclusively on the role of the so-called Creoles, or descendants of ex-slaves from Europe, North America, Jamaica, and Africa living in the colony. In this book, Joseph J. Bangura cuts through this typical narrative surrounding the making of the British colony, and instead offers a fresh look at the role of the often overlooked indigenous Temne-speakers. Bangura explores the socioeconomic formation, establishment, and evolution of Freetown, from the perspective of different Temne-speaking groups, including market women, religious figures, and community leaders and the complex relationships developed in the process. Examining key issues, such as the politics of belonging, African agency, and the creation of national identities, Bangura offers an account of Sierra Leone that sheds new light on the social history of the colony.

Joseph J. Bangura is Associate Professor of History and Director of the African Studies Program at Kalamazoo College, Michigan. He holds a PhD in African history from Dalhousie University, Canada, and has published widely on the colonial history of Sierra Leone and Freetown.

The Temne of Sierra Leone

African Agency in the Making
of a British Colony

Joseph J. Bangura

Kalamazoo College, Michigan

CAMBRIDGE
UNIVERSITY PRESS

CAMBRIDGE
UNIVERSITY PRESS

University Printing House, Cambridge CB2 8BS, United Kingdom

One Liberty Plaza, 20th Floor, New York, NY 10006, USA

477 Williamstown Road, Port Melbourne, VIC 3207, Australia

314–321, 3rd Floor, Plot 3, Splendor Forum, Jasola District Centre, New Delhi – 110025, India

79 Anson Road, #06-04/06, Singapore 079906

Cambridge University Press is part of the University of Cambridge.

It furthers the University's mission by disseminating knowledge in the pursuit of
education, learning, and research at the highest international levels of excellence.

www.cambridge.org
Information on this title: www.cambridge.org/9781107197985
DOI: 10.1017/9781108182010

First published 2017

Printed in the United Kingdom by Clays, St Ives plc

A catalogue record for this publication is available from the British Library.

Library of Congress Cataloging-in-Publication Data
Names: Bangura, Joseph J., author.
Title: The Temne of Sierra Leone: African agency in the making of a British
colony / Joseph J. Bangura, Kalamazoo College, Michigan.
Other titles: African agency in the making of a British colony
Description: Cambridge, United Kingdom, New York, NY: Cambridge
University Press, [2017] | Includes bibliographical references and index.
Identifiers: LCCN 2017034650 | ISBN 9781107197985 (hardback)
Subjects: LCSH: Temne (African people) – History. | Temne
(African people) – Political activity. | Temne (African people) – Ethnic
identity. | Sierra Leone – History. | Sierra Leone – Historiography. |
Sierra Leone – Colonial influence.
Classification: LCC DT516.45.T45 B36 2018 | DDC 966.4/0049632–dc23
LC record available at https://lccn.loc.gov/2017034650

ISBN 978-1-107-19798-5 Hardback

Contents

Part I

Historical Epistemology

1 Introduction: Rethinking History and Freetown Historiography

The West African territory of Sierra Leone became Britain's first colony in West Africa, in the eighteenth century. A majority of the indigenous ethnic communities of this territory lived in the interior, while a few occupied the coast. British philanthropists in 1787 and later the British government in 1808 largely restricted their relationship with Sierra Leone to the coastal area where it later established a colony for freed slaves and their descendants.

Before the British took control of this coastal territory, two prominent ethnic groups initially occupied it – Sherbro- and Bullom-speakers. John Crooks states that in the fifteenth century, the Temne invaded the coastal territory and dislodged the Bullom- and Sherbro-speakers. The invading Temne lived in the hinterland of Sierra Leone from where they made frequent forays on the coastal territory and eventually took control of it in the mid-fifteenth century.

Sierra Leone, like many other states in the Upper Guinea Coast, served as a bastion for the Atlantic slave trade whereby millions of slaves faced capture and forced transfer across the Atlantic to the Americas and Europe. However, in the eighteenth century, a gamut of agents including intellectuals, clergy, poets, economists, and freed slaves worked fervently to end the trade in slaves. Consequently, in 1807, the British government made the following declaration abolishing the slave trade in its Empire:

Be it therefore enacted ... that from and after the 1st day of May 1807, the African Slave Trade, all the manner of dealing and trading in the purchase, sale, barter or transfer of slaves, or of persons intended to be sold, transferred, used or dealt with as slaves, practiced or carried on in, at, to or from any part of the coast or countries of Africa, shall be ... utterly abolished, prohibited and declared unlawful.[1]

---

[1] Cited in Kenneth Morgan, *Slavery and the British Empire: From Africa to America* (Oxford: Oxford University Press, 2007), p. 172.

The above declaration by the British government undermined the Atlantic slave trade in the British Empire. Kenneth Morgan, among others, states that Britain abolished the slave trade in its Empire on the basis of "humanity, justice and social policy."[2] Other scholars challenge Morgan's perspective; they contend that Britain abolished the trade for controvertible reasons. Stefan Goodwin argues that the abolition of the slave trade should not be viewed from a "moralistic perspective" as Morgan and others contend. He states: "Neither the British nor any other European nation was factoring the abolition of slave trading into its national policy purely on humanitarian or moral ground. Rather they gradually began to place constraints on slave trading where it was not at variance with their larger motivational interests."[3] Goodwin's assertion ignores the complementary efforts made by British philanthropists in illuminating the ills of the slave trade and slavery. He derided policy outcomes derived from the efforts of abolitionists as "half-hearted abolitionist policies."[4] Sean Sitwell raises similar observations: he highlights the gap between the "altruistic" and "paternalistic" rhetoric of Europeans with their colonial interests in ending the slave trade. He states that "Europeans relied on slavery to help make the colonial conquest possible."[5] This observation contradicts one of the major reasons adduced by European colonialists for colonizing Africa – the abolition of the slave trade and its substitution with legitimate commerce. Europeans indeed fostered legitimate commerce and played a role in promoting significant agricultural activities in Africa. In spite of this, Sitwell states that European colonizers relied on slavery to facilitate "annexation and administration of African colonies."[6] It became evident that the British, Germans, French, Belgians, and Portuguese relied on African soldiers, African slaves, and former African slaves to conquer territories and undertake laborious tasks for the various colonial projects. He points out that some slaves "were bought on the open market or from masters by Europeans and then made into slaves."[7] In short, Sitwell, Anne Phillips, and others argue that slavery became part of the fabric of colonialism as the practice persisted well into the colonial period. However, though European colonizers encouraged and in some instances delayed abolition of the slave trade for practical and

[2] Morgan, *Slavery and the British Empire*, p. 170.
[3] Stefan Goodwin, *Africa's Legacy of Urbanization: Unfolding Saga of a Continent* (Lanham: Lexington Books, 2006), p. 127.
[4] Stefan Goodwin, *Africa's Legacy of Urbanization*, p. 127.
[5] Sean Sitwell, *Slavery and Slaving in African History* (New York: Cambridge University Press, 2014), p. 180.
[6] Sitwell, *Slavery and Slaving*, p. 180.
[7] Sitwell, *Slavery and Slaving*, p. 181.

economic reasons, they allowed African slaves to challenge their status in colonial courts, and many of them won such cases.[8]

Nonetheless, in 1807, Britain abolished the slave trade for a variety of reasons. The process partly happened through the flinty determination of a group of Anglican evangelicals, the Clapham Sect, who convinced the protagonists of the trade to abolish it. Tightly bound by a set of core moral beliefs, the Clapham Sect mounted a vociferous campaign to abolish the slave trade. Supported by American Quakers, the abolitionists quickly created the society "for the abolition of the Slave Trade."[9] In 1772, in a landmark ruling by a British judge, Lord Mansfield, the abolitionists landed an unexpected victory that helped end the slave trade and its accompanying vice of slavery in England. The judge's ruling essentially declared that English culture did not permit the practice of slavery. The ruling had far-reaching consequences. Though restrictive in its reach, the legal decision enabled slaves to escape from bondage in England and beyond. Though unparalleled, the reverberations of the Mansfield ruling likely influenced American slaves, particularly those who fought alongside British forces in the American War of Independence. After the war, fearful of the repercussion of their betrayal of their American masters, the slaves requested their freedom from Britain. In other words, the Mansfield ruling resulted in an exodus of slaves to England to gain freedom. The influx of slaves in London resulted in a raft of social problems: destitution, large-scale unemployment, and famine, among other social ills. Concerned by their plight, a Committee for the Relief of the Black Poor (CRBP), consisting of William Wilberforce (Member of Parliament), Henry Thornton, Thomas Clarkson, and Granville Sharp, embarked on a mission to find a suitable home in Africa for the freed slaves.[10] In its search, the committee envisioned a "free community based on Christian principles" for the poverty-stricken slaves.[11]

Eventually, in the mid-eighteenth century, the CRBP founded a settlement in Sierra Leone for the resettlement of the ex-slaves. This came about when members of the committee studied a positive report on Sierra Leone submitted by Dr. Henry Smeathman in 1783: "[T]he woods and plains produce spontaneously great quantities of the most pleasant fruits and spices."[12] The report stressed the rich agricultural

---

[8] Sitwell, *Slavery and Slaving*, p. 193.
[9] Morgan, *Slavery and the British Empire*, p. 155.
[10] Morgan, *Slavery and the British Empire*, p. 158.
[11] Morgan, *Slavery and the British Empire*, p. 158.
[12] Roy Lewis, *Sierra Leone: A Modern Portrait* (London: Her Majesty's Stationery Office, 1954), p. 25. The British government sanctioned the publication of this monograph, and it contained the autograph of Prime Minister Churchill.

qualities of the soil: "[I]t is not necessary to turn up the earth more than from the depth of 2 or 3 inches with a slight hoe in order to cultivate any kind of grain."[13] The report meshed with the vision of the CRBP that wanted a settlement where the ex-slaves would live independently and uphold democratic and Victorian principles. Consequently, two members of the CRBP, Wilberforce and Thornton, traveled to Sierra Leone to acquire a piece of land occupied by the Temne. On arrival in 1787, the CRBP representatives signed a lease agreement with the Temne regent of the territory, King Tham (erroneously represented as King Tom in the literature). The first batch of former slaves arrived in the new settlement, designed "for the sole benefit of the free community of settlers, their heirs and successors," soon after the lease was signed.[14] Disagreement over the terms of the lease led to another round of negotiations for a final status agreement with the local chiefs. In 1788, King Naimbana, a Temne regent of Koya, signed an obscure land deal with British philanthropists; this deal resulted in the permanent ceding of the land to Britain. Before signing the agreement, Naimbana showed his cosmopolitan character when he critiqued the Atlantic slave trade in an apothegmatic statement: "[M]any of us African rulers are not happy about the slave trade going on in our country. It brings to our country and people a lot of destruction and unhappiness. But we have found out that we cannot stop it on our own unless the white people cooperate with us."[15] The land granted by Naimbana to representatives of the CRBP became a mainstay and a refulgent scheme for the resettlement of thousands of ex-slaves. The resettlement of these freed slaves is the subject of numerous scholarly discourses; its examination here will be brief.

Between 1787 and 1864, the CRBP and the British government repatriated four sets of freed slaves to the new settlement: the Black Poor, Nova Scotians, the Maroons, and Recaptives or Liberated Africans.[16] The Sierra Leone settlement as it came to be known carried different designations – Granville Town, Sierra Leone Colony, and/or colonial Freetown; Sierra Leone Colony and colonial Freetown will be used interchangeably in this study. Founders of the new settlement wanted it "to be a beacon on the coast of savage Africa: a light to lighten the Gentiles still

---

[13] Lewis, *Sierra Leone*, p. 25.
[14] Colonial Secretary's Office, *Treaty between the Governor of Sierra Leone and King Tom* (London: 1801) and J. J. Crooks, *A History of the Colony of Sierra Leone: Western Africa.* (London: Browne and Nolan, Ltd., 1903), p. 30; *Sierra Leone Weekly News*, April 16, 1890; Colonial Secretary's Office and *Sierra Leone Weekly News* are abbreviated as CSO and *SLWN*, respectively.
[15] Adeleye Ijagbemi, *Naimbana of Sierra Leone* (London: Heinemann, 1976), p. 28.
[16] *SLWN*, January–April 1892; see also *SLWN*, June 15, 1895.

sunk in superstition."[17] The original financiers of the resettlement project administered it through the Sierra Leone Company until the British government declared it a Crown Colony, or a British overseas territory, in 1808.[18]

In the mid-nineteenth century, the colony became a hodgepodge of descendants of freed slaves from which a "hybrid" group variously described as Creole and/or Krio emerged. The group is the most intensely studied in the history of the Sierra Leone Colony; its history dominates Sierra Leone historiography. The extant historiography equates the historical and social activities of the Creoles with the history of the Sierra Leone Colony. Elites, culture brokers, the popular media, local intellectuals, ethnonationalists, and colonial authorities described members of the group as Creoles. Members of the group, however, used multiple identities stimulated by sociopolitical and economic factors to describe themselves. By equating the history of those recorded as Creoles with the history of the Sierra Leone Colony, the dominant literature constrains our understanding of the contributions of various groups in the social formation of this British overseas demesne. The historical literature thus oversimplifies the complex history of Britain's oldest and arguably most important colony in West Africa in the nineteenth century.

This study offers a different interpretation of the dynamics that shaped the history of the Sierra Leone Colony – one that breaks significantly with a long tradition of historical writing about Sierra Leone. To fully appreciate the historical trajectory of the colony, it will be useful to outline the dominant texts and interpretations of the historiography over the past half-century, for these studies, both in their methodologies and interpretation, have established a narrow, Western-centric model of colonial power dynamics in the Sierra Leone Colony. The study limns the significant contributions of disparate indigenous groups in the colony's history, particularly the preponderant indigenous ethnic group described as Temne. It departs from the approach of African historians who seek to interpret aspects of Africa's past in terms of a "transcendent tension" between colonizers and colonized. It also challenges the use of Western education as a marker of success and civilization in the colony. The study seeks to underscore the role played by non-Western-educated elites, marketers, and local intellectuals in the social formation and success of this British colonial project. The study shows the complex history of the colony, which cannot be reduced to simplistic renditions.

[17] Lewis, *Sierra Leone*, p. 32.
[18] Crooks, *History of the Colony*, pp. 107–109.

As leasers of the land that accommodated the Sierra Leone Colony, Temne-speakers, though lacking Western education in the nineteenth and first half of the twentieth centuries, developed institutions that rivalled the Creole-dominated British institutions. The study discusses the historical patterns, features, and activities of Temne-speakers such as market women, Islamic feminists, religious entrepreneurs, gatekeepers of Temne identity, community and opinion leaders, "tribal" chiefs, provincial migrants, and grassroots activists. It delineates the colony's relationship with the peninsula towns and peri-urban and nonurban communities – Funkia, Adonkia, Regent, Rokel, York, Gloucester and Waterloo – including the interaction, mobilization, and mutation of ethnic identities. The study is one of the first book-length projects to problematize and challenge the use of the term "Creole." Was Creole identity fixed or consistent? A careful analysis of the historical evidence indicates that colony residents with settler lineage referred to as Creoles in the historiography did not carry a fixed or consistent identity.

The study also explores the meaning and process of "becoming" and "being" Temne. What did "being Temne" mean? What role did Temne institutions play in the making of this British colony and why and how did these institutions become influential in the post–World War II period? Did Temne identity makers facilitate the making or construction of this British colonial project? This volume is one of the first book-length projects to probe and address these questions. It argues that identity formation in the colony, especially among the Temnes and Creoles, became rife with instrumental undercurrents, because the identities shifted from time to time for material advantage. Despite this, disparate groups contributed significantly to the growth of the colony's economy in the nineteenth and twentieth centuries; many served as cooks, domestics, hawkers, peasants, gardeners, marketers, janitors, and court bearers. The historiography pays inadequate attention to these significant contributions.

The following section outlines the major scholarly motivations, failures, and weaknesses of works on the history of the colony.

Deconstructing Sierra Leone Historiography: Trends and Praxis in History

A careful examination of Sierra Leone historiography reveals that the interpretation of the history of the colony has been ethnocentric in character. To fully appreciate this trend, it is useful to survey and deconstruct the historiography by examining the motivations and weaknesses of the major texts.

Many of the major works surveyed in this study have influenced and shaped our understanding of the history, growth, and socioeconomic development of the colony. Some of the works of scholars reviewed here, particularly Christopher Fyfe, Arthur Porter, Leo Spitzer, Akintola Wyse, Abner Cohen, Gibril Cole, and David Harris, equate the history of this British colony with the history of one of the multifarious groups that occupied the colony since the mid-eighteenth and nineteenth centuries. The images that emerge from many of the works of these scholars suggest that the history of the colony is best understood by understanding the history of descendants of ex-slaves described as Creoles. James Thayer summarizes this point ingeniously:

The repatriated Africans [Creoles] who were settled in Sierra Leone are one of the most intensely studied and well documented people on the continent of Africa, certainly in sub-Saharan Africa. Except for large ethnic groups like the Yoruba or the Asante it is hard to find a single ethnic group on which so much scholarly effort, mostly of an historical nature, has been expended.[19]

The quotation shows that the works of Fyfe, Porter, Spitzer, and others privilege the historical activities of those described as Creoles over non-settler groups in the colony. Some of these scholars used the history of the Creoles to show that Africans possessed enough capacity to thoroughly assimilate and exhibit Western civilization. Fyfe reinforces this point when he states that Creoles served as torchbearers of Western civilization "in Sierra Leone and West Africa in the nineteenth and twentieth centuries."[20] In concluding his seminal work, *History of Sierra Leone*, Fyfe states that the Creoles

Were ... indispensable, the unrecognized vehicle by which not only British rule but [also] trade, education and Christianity were conveyed to West Africa. In the churches and schools which must have closed without their ministrations, in mercantile counting-houses and government offices, dependent on their subordinate toil, these gentle pioneers bringing a European culture Europeans resented their possessing, could well look round them to see in whatever good Britain brought West Africa in the nineteenth century a plant which could never have taken root without their slighted labour.[21]

He argues that other ethnic groups in the colony looked to the Creoles as a social reference and followed their example: "[W]hatever they feel

[19] James Steel Thayer, "A Dissenting View of Creole Culture in Sierra Leone." *Cahiers D'Études Africaines* 31, no. 121/122 (1991): p. 251.
[20] *SLWN*, Freetown, April 9, 1951.
[21] Christopher Fyfe, *A History of Sierra Leone* (London: Oxford University Press, 1962), pp. 619–620.

about the Krios personally they followed their social lead."[22] He posits that given their inculcation of Western values, the Creoles influenced the identity and mode of life of indigenous non-Creole groups: "[T]he off-spring [of non-Creoles] had a choice of identity – to be Krio or (as might be) to be Temne, Limba or Mende. But whatever their choice, their upbringing was still within Krio culture."[23] This suggests that autoch-thonous groups like Temne-, Mende-, Sherbro-, and Loko-speakers in the colony had to "behave like Krios to be accepted as civilized."[24] Fyfe regarded Christianity, education and attendance at balls as hallmarks of civilized behavior.[25] For Fyfe, the Creoles did not limit their civiliz-ing mission to the Sierra Leone Colony; they undertook similar enter-prises and provided educational and religious training to non-Creole groups in the hinterland as well.[26] Though Fyfe's works on the colony stresses Creole agency, his works also cover non-Creole groups in the colony and in the interior. He states that in 1895, the colonial admin-istration allowed Temne-, Mende-, Mandingo-, and Kru-speakers the opportunity of electing a headman to coordinate their affairs in the col-ony. Subsequently, the government legitimized tribal rule in a series of Ordinances passed in 1905.[27]

Arthur Porter shares many of Fyfe's views on the role of the Creoles in the historical and social formation of the colony. He avers that Western education, dominated by the Creoles, became a "royal road" to success in the colony: "Education was thus, in Freetown, one of the important mechanisms providing for social mobility. It was and still is the royal road to success and positions of power and prestige."[28] The assimilation of Western civilization by Creoles made them the "desired reference group in Sierra Leone."[29] Porter asserts that in the post–World War II period, non-Creoles gradually acquired Western education in sufficient numbers to challenge the dominance of the Creoles in all spheres of life, especially after the introduction of drastic constitutional reforms between 1922 and

[22] Christopher Fyfe, "1787–1887–1987, Reflections on A Bicentenary" in Murray Last and Paul Richards, Sierra Leone, 1787–1987 Two Centuries of Intellectual Life (Manchester: Manchester University Press, 1987), p. 148. The term "Krio" is used interchangeably here with the term "Creole."

[23] Fyfe, "Reflections," p. 148.

[24] Fyfe, "Reflections," pp. 148–149.

[25] Fyfe, A History, pp. 403–415.

[26] Christopher Fyfe, "European and Creole Influence in the Interior of Sierra Leone before 1896." Sierra Leone Studies 6 (1956): pp. 113–115.

[27] Fyfe, A History, p. 495.

[28] Arthur Porter, Creoledom: A Study of the Development of Freetown Society (London: Oxford University Press, 1963), p. 92.

[29] Porter, Creoledom, p. 63.

1948.[30] The constitutional reforms expanded the political landscape; in other words, they created the space for non-Creole communities like the Temne-, Mende-, Limba-, Loko-, Kru-, Fula-, and Mandingo-speakers to participate unequivocally in colony politics.[31]

Leo Spitzer's work on the colony also addresses Creole agency, images, and self-aggrandizement. In his foremost work, Spitzer states: "[T]he [Creole] group was numerically small. But it included the most literate and vocal members ... of society, men with direct access to the Sierra Leone press and other vehicles of communication. Occupying the top rung of the social hierarchy, they set fashions, shaped opinions and exerted an influence far exceeding their numerical strength."[32] He opines that Creole cultural arrogance affected their relationship with non-Creoles, especially in "expression of Creole ideas about themselves, their British mentors and colonial masters and other Africans."[33] He observes that the Creoles saw themselves "as special, different from or even superior to Africans who had not experienced prolonged cultural contact with Europeans."[34] In buttressing this perspective, John Peterson affirms that "the history of Sierra Leone is a history of an acculturative process which produced a Westernized African ... the Creole chapter of this process is the first phase of this broader history." Like Fyfe, Peterson trumpets and privileges Creole cultural superiority over the culture of non-Creole groups.

Additionally, Abner Cohen's major work explores the spread of cultural ideas by descendants of settler groups he describes as Creole. Cohen states that before 1947, Christianity, balls, and membership in freemasonry became important markers of status and prestige. These markers of prestige made Creoles a secure elite in the colony and Sierra Leone as a whole until the eve of independence.[35]

Akin to the above, Akintola Wyse shares and touts similar views in his numerous works, though with a conspicuous slant. Wyse constructed the term "Krio" to describe people in the Sierra Leone Colony described as Creoles by Fyfe and others in the historical literature. He uses the term to distinguish Sierra Leone Creoles from other groups with

---

[30] Porter, *Creoledom*, p. 28.
[31] Porter, *Creoledom*, pp. 68–72.
[32] Leo Spitzer, "The Sierra Leone Creoles, 1870–1900" in Philip D. Curtin, ed., *Africa and the West: Intellectual Responses to European Culture* (Madison: University of Wisconsin Press, 1972), p. 108.
[33] Spitzer, *Creoles of Sierra Leone*, p. 3.
[34] Spitzer, *Creoles of Sierra Leone*, p. 218.
[35] Abner Cohen. *The Politics of Elite Culture: Explorations in the Dramaturgy of Power in a Modern African Society* (Oakland: University of California Press, 1981), p. 138.

similar designations in the Americas and Europe. He asserts that those he referred to as Krio "possessed a superior culture civilisation to that of the interior peoples and that they were so many distances removed from their unfortunate brethren."[36] Wyse contends that descendants of freed slaves he describes as Krio were culturally superior to non-Creole ethnic groups living in the colony because members of these groups were not exposed to Western values and education. The phrase "interior peoples" refers to indigenous residents born in the Sierra Leone Colony. He states that "the detractors of the Krio" continually assaulted their society:

> But it was at this period [the nineteenth century] when the accomplishments of the Krio sparkled with brilliance, the successful among them displaying all the attributes of a bourgeois society with its social circuit and pretensions, vocal press and reading public and being called "the Athens of West Africa," that the detractors of the Krio began to make continual assaults on their society.[37]

The above is a rehash of the views expressed by Fyfe and others on the aristocratic culture of Creoles. Gibril Cole magnifies some of Wyse's views in his recent monograph.[38] Cole describes descendants of settler groups as Krio and, tracing the etymology of the word to nineteenth-century Yoruba society in Nigeria, claims that the compellation Krio is a derivative of a Yoruba expression.[39] Like Wyse, he maintains that the Krio also comprised some kindreds of ethnic communities from the hinterland. He exalts the role and contributions of the Oku and Aku in the history of the colony. In brief, the undercurrent of Cole's work equates the history of the colony with the histories of those he describes as Krio and Muslim Krio. Analogously, David Harris' recent work also impressively examines the political history of Sierra Leone from the colonial period to contemporary times. Harris' key argument aligns with the views of Wyse and Cole on the use of the constructed term Krio as a horizontal identity to describe descendants of former slaves in the colony. In all, like others, Harris accepts the Krio claim of cultural superiority and arrogance, and gives a detailed account of the factors that led to their loss of political influence in the Sierra Leone Colony before and after independence. Though Wyse and Cole rationalize the decline of the Krio, Harris situates

---

[36] Akintola Wyse, *H. C. Bankole-Bright and Politics in Colonial Sierra Leone, 1919–1958* (Cambridge: Cambridge University Press, 1990), p. 28.

[37] Akintola Wyse, "Perspective and West African Historiography." In McGrath, Simon et al. eds. *Rethinking African History*. (Edinburgh: University of Edinburgh Press, 1997), p. 205.

[38] Wyse, *The Krio of Sierra Leone* : An Interpretive History. (Freetown: Hurst and International African Institute, 1989), pp. 20–29.

[39] See Gibril Cole, *The Krio of West Africa: Islam, Creolization, and Colonialism in the Nineteenth Century* (Athens, Ohio: Ohio University Press, 2013).

this notion in a bigger, nuanced context. Besides Cole and Harris, Sylvia Ojukutu-Macauley and Ismail Rashid's edited anthology also equates the history of the Krio with the history of the colony; the work clearly overlooks the contributions of other key actors in the making of the British colony. A careful examination of the anthology shows that some of its chapters are a replay of some of the arguments of Fyfe, Porter, Cole, and Harris. Like Wyse, Cole, and Harris, the volume uses the term Krio to refer to those described as Creoles in the historical literature.

Other scholars concerned with a different set of questions include Frances White and LaRay Denzer. White emphasizes the economic contributions of those she describes as settler women traders, while Denzer highlights their political activities in the twentieth century.[40] White states that some of the women traders ventured into the interior to buy goods wholesale for distribution in colonial Freetown, and others stayed permanently with their host communities and assimilated traditions of their hosts.[41] She claims that Creole women traders dominated one of the important centers of economic activity, the Big Market, from the nineteenth to the mid-twentieth centuries. Though other women sold goods at the market, Creole women traders dominated the sale of vegetables and garden products. The Big Market linked the local and international economies and formed an important core of Creole society. After 1950, Creole women traders lost their coveted monopoly to the rising influence of people White described as Temne and Mandingo market women traders.[42]

In her contribution, Denzer maintains that the role of women in shaping the history of the colony has been ignored. She states that in 1938 and 1951, Creole women played a substantial role in protonationalist politics as they contributed to the founding of two key organizations in Sierra Leone: the West African Youth League and the Sierra Leone Women's Movement. The founding of these organizations and the strong leadership of Adelaide Casely-Hayford and Agatha Constance Cummings-John spurred women's interest and participation in national politics in spite of the strong opposition they encountered from some of their male compatriots.

The Creole-centric approach of the historical literature also extends to our understanding of the spread of Islam in the colony. Scholars

---

[40] E. Frances White, "The Big Market in Freetown: A Case Study of Women's Workplace" *Journal of the Historical Society of Sierra Leone* 4, nos.1 and 2 (December 1980): p. 22.

[41] E. Frances White, *Sierra Leone's Settler Women Traders: Women on the Afro-European Frontier* (Ann Arbor: University of Michigan Press, 1987), pp. 13–16.

[42] E. Frances White, *Sierra Leone's Settler Women Traders*, pp. 15–16.

such as Leslie Proudfoot, Saif'ud Deen Alharazim and Alusine Jalloh assign major agency to Aku, Mandingo and Fula Muslims for the growth and propagation of Islam in the colony.[43] The term "Aku" referred to descendants of former slaves with Yoruba ancestry and those described as Muslim Creoles. The works of Alharazim and Proudfoot laud the role of the Aku in the propagation of Islam in the colony in the eighteenth and nineteenth centuries. Proudfoot, however, recognizes the contributions of other Muslim groups, such as Mandingo and Temne Muslims, in spreading Islam.[44] For his part, Alusine Jalloh assigns major agency to Fula-speakers for their role in propagating Islam in the colony in the nineteenth century.

The works of Adeleye Ijagbemi cover a variety of subjects including the precolonial social history of the Temne, in the hinterland and the Sierra Leone Peninsula.[45] His works largely focus on the social activities of the Temne and their relationships with other ethnic communities. Ibrahim Abdullah's major historical work focuses on labor relations especially working class agitation and the response of the colonial authorities to the multiple questions raised by the action of the aggrieved workers in colonial Freetown. His numerous works on other aspects of Sierra Leone's past are outside the precincts of this volume. Other works that have not been reviewed here because their focus is different include those of T. C. Anwyl, Kenneth Wylie, E. R. Langley, James Littlejohn and Vernon R. Dorjahn. Dorjahn, for example, analyzes the changing political system and functions of Temne chiefs in the "Pre-Protectorate and Post-Protectorate days."[46] Finally, the works of Michael Banton, Barbara Harrell-Bond, Allen M. Howard and David E. Skinner are so far the most comprehensive in terms of assigning agency to non-Creole groups in the history of the colony.

Banton examines tribal rule in the colony and states that colonial authorities effectively used the services of Temne, Mandingo, Limba, Kru, and Loko headmen in liaising between the administration and their local communities. He highlights the role of various communities in the

[43] See M. Saif'ud Deen Alharazim, "The Origin and Progress of Islam in Sierra Leone" *Sierra Leone Studies* 21 (January 1939); see his other work, "Mosque Building and Tribal Separatism in Freetown East," *Africa* 29 (1959).
[44] See L. Proudfoot, "Towards a Muslim Solidarity in Freetown," *Africa* 31 (1961); see his other work, "Mosque Building."
[45] See Adeleye Ijagbami, "The Kossoh War 1838–41: A Study in Temne/Colony Relations in the Nineteenth Century." *Journal of the Historical Society of Nigeria* 1, 4 (June 1971), and his unpublished work, "The History of the Temne in the 19th Century" (PhD Dissertation, Edinburgh University, 1968).
[46] Vernon R. Dorjahn, "The Changing Political System of the Temne." *Africa* 30 (October 1966): p. 431.

cultural development of the colony through the formation of dance associations from the 1930s to the 1950s; the associations served as sources of recreation, ethnic mobilization, and relaxation.[47] Barbara Harrell-Bond and others expanded the frontier of Banton's works by examining community leadership in colonial Freetown. The authors argue that the Creoles did not occupy the colony alone; that is, they shared the commercial, political, and social spaces of the colony with different ethnic groups who collectively promoted their "economic, cultural, religious and political interests."[48]

A careful examination of the works reviewed above reveals their motivations. Fyfe and others aim to show that those described as Creoles assimilated Western civilization and effectively served as its principal agents in the colony and in West Africa as a whole. Put differently, many of the scholars mentioned show that an African could be "the equal of the white in all essential matters."[49] Porter eloquently sums up this view:

Creoledom exemplified the possibility of rapid and effective social change. It argued powerfully for the speedy acceptance of Africans within the international community. The Creoles undoubtedly fulfilled the most cherished ambitions of their benefactors that, once, the chains were removed and given the opportunities, they could rise to any heights Victorian England was capable of providing. And the lesson was not lost, though their detractors were many ... This is its larger theoretical relevance. It provides a setting, a historical demonstration, for students of social change some of whom, even today, doubt the capacity, capabilities and potentialities of Africans.[50]

White expresses similar motivation for focusing on those she referred to as Creole and settler women. Her motive for focusing on women traders is to challenge the "Western-biased categories that have found their way into much of the emerging feminist canon comparing women's status across cultures."[51] Clearly, the intellectual milieu in which these scholars wrote influenced their thoughts. Shortly after many African countries obtained independence in the 1950s and 1960s, African historians and Africanists felt the need to correct the negative portrayal of African history by Eurocentric scholars, who wanted to show that Africa had a glorious and sophisticated past – a genre of postcolonial nationalist scholarship which emphasized that Western-educated Africans thoroughly

---

[47] Michael Banton, *West African City: A Study of Tribal Life in Freetown* (London: Oxford University Press, 1957), p. 150.
[48] Barbara Harrell-Bond, Allen M. Howard and David E. Skinner, *Community Leadership and the Transformation of Freetown (1801–1976)* (The Hague: Mouton, 1978), p. 16.
[49] Lewis, *Sierra Leone*, p. 33.
[50] Porter, *Creoledom*, p. 140.
[51] White, *Settler Women*, p. 13.

assimilated Western values and became agents of such values in Africa. In Sierra Leone, Fyfe et al. used the history of those recorded as Creoles to challenge Eurocentric perspectives on African culture and history. Spitzer underlines this motivation lucidly: "the history of the Creoles is an especially rich source for this kind of study."[52]

Methodological factors may have influenced the motivations behind the works reviewed here. The Creoles had almost a century of accessible history traceable in the archives. Many scholars may have found the Creoles literate in English and thus an easy group to research, as indicated by Denzer, Spitzer and White in their works. As Cohen states, the history of Sierra Leone as written by Fyfe "has indirectly come to punctuate and give basic structure to Sierra Leone."[53] He asserts that "the most authoritative academic history of Sierra Leone by Christopher Fyfe (1962), starts with an introduction of 12 pages covering the earlier history of the country of the Creoles and the Colony."[54] Thus the works reviewed here make up a substantial part of Freetown historiography, as they are very informative on the history of the colony.

Given their motivation, many of the works reviewed here ignored other aspects of the history of the colony; i.e. the works focus heavily on the European-versus-African paradigm. In light of this, many of the works fail to fully explore the contributions of other groups, particularly the pre-ponderant Temne-speakers in the making of this British colony. Though some of the works presume the existence of non-Creoles, the voices of these groups remained largely silent in the established literature. The dominant literature simply accepted Creole claims of cultural hegemony and Western education as markers of success in the colony. This study shows that other markers of success, such as community leadership, religious entrepreneurism, membership and leadership of cultural associations, existed in the colony.

In addition, Wyse's description of indigenous groups, such as Temne-, Mende-, Limba-, Loko-, Mandingo-, and Fula-speakers living in the colony as "interior peoples," consigns these communities to subsidiary status.[55] Census returns in the nineteenth and first half of the twentieth centuries indicated that those described as Creoles and Temne formed the bulk of the colony's population.[56] In the mid-twentieth century, the Temne population became the largest indigenous community in the

---

[52] Spitzer, *Creoles*, p. 3.
[53] Cohen, *Elite Culture*, p. 138.
[54] Cohen, *Elite Culture*, p. 138.
[55] Wyse, *Bankole-Bright and Politics*, p. 150.
[56] "Return of the Census of 1921," *Sierra Leone Blue Book, 1928* (London: National Archives).

colony.[57] In categorizing non-Creole groups as interior peoples, Wyse de-emphasizes their key contributions to the social formation of the colony. This also intimates that the history of the colony is the history of the Creoles.

The Creole-centric approach of the historiography extends as well to our understanding of the position of women in the colony. In an attempt to call out the androcentric literature about its marginalization of women, the feminist literature focuses heavily on the activities of those described by White as settler women; Denzer describes them as Krio. Though White acknowledges the role of Temne- and Mandingo-speaking women in the Big Market after 1950, she believes that settler women traders served as a social reference for non-settler women. She also ignores the centrality of other key markets dominated by non-settler women traders in the colony: King Jimmy, Kissy Road, and Dove Cut, among others. The microeconomic activities undertaken by many non-settler market women in these markets contributed to the development of the colony's formal and informal economies. In underscoring this fact, Osman Newland states that non-Creole women dominated trade activities at these markets.[58] Despite the fact that, Western-educated women contributed to the development of the colony, the historical documents show that non-Western educated women traders and grassroots female activists, particularly ascendant Temne women, also played a key role in giving women a voice in the colony. Like White, Denzer focuses heavily on promoting the contributions of Western-educated women in the making of this British colonial compass. She highlights the leadership of a distinguished Western-educated woman, Agatha Cummings-John, leader of the Sierra Leone Women's Movement (SLWM). Though highly educated and accomplished, Cummings-John strongly relied on the support of illiterate and grassroots women, such as Mbalu Conteh and Sukainatu Kai Bangura, to build the SLWM. Denzer overlooks the contributions of these women in her works.

The works of Proudfoot and others on the propagation and entrenchment of Islam assigns major agency to the Aku and to some extent the Mandingo and Fula communities. Although he acknowledges the Islamic activities of non-Aku Muslims, Proudfoot however understates the role played by these groups in the growth and development of the religion, especially the Temne Islamic Community, with its largest

[57] See Lamin Sanneh, *The Crown and the Turban: Muslims and West African Pluralism* (Boulder, Colorado: Westview Press), p. 175.
[58] H. Osman Newland, *Sierra Leone: Its People, Products and Secret Societies* (New York: Negro Universities Press, 1969), pp. 17–21.

agglomeration of Muslims in the colony. Added to this, the historical literature pays insufficient attention to the importance of Islamic institutions established by non-Aku Muslims, such as the Temne-dominated Muslim Reformation Council (MRC), the Temne School or *Imaniyya*, and various Temne-led ethnic associations, in spreading the tenets of Islam between 1901 and 1961.

From the foregoing, the works above show that Creoles attained the highest educational point "which the African black man can attain."[59] Some of the works reviewed here fail to ask probing questions on Creole identity and the role of others in the social formation of this hotchpotch British territory. It is discernible that in the process of redressing Eurocentric denigration of Africans and their past, many Africanists and African historians privileged Creole cultural and historical contributions in the colony over those of non-Creoles. Although the works of Banton, Barbara Harrell-Bond et al. draw attention to some of these questions, their works fail to adequately address questions on identity formation, religious entrepreneurism, class differences, and gender relations, among the disparate groups that occupied the colony. Banton's work, for example, is largely androcentric; it overlooks the activities of market women in the development of the colony's informal and formal economies. The specific questions addressed by Banton, Barbara Harrell-Bond, Allen Howard, David Skinner and the like constrained them from probing the contributions of the preponderant Temne community in the historical development of colonial Freetown.

This study uses the new social history approach advocated by Jonathon Glassman, Sean Sitwell, and Frederick Cooper, among others, to explore diverse relations among Africans living in urbanized spaces. In the context of the new African social history agenda, the book shows that Britain's relationship with the colony transcended the colonial versus colonized binary abound in African historiography.

Between the 1890s and 1940s, Temne-speakers organized around particular institutions such as tribal administration, cultural associations, mosques and microcredit schemes. By organizing around these institutions, and with the steady increase in their population due to large-scale immigration from the protectorate, the Temne community became socially, politically, economically and religiously influential and rivalled the Creoles in various spheres. The populations of other ethnic communities, such as Mende-, Limba-, Loko-, Fula-, and Mandingo-speakers, also increased over time, though not on the same scale as that

---

[59] F. W. H. Migeod, *A View of Sierra Leone* (New York: Brentano's, 1927). Cited in Lewis, *Sierra Leone*, p. 33.

of Temne-speakers. In 1905, colonial authorities integrated tribal rule in the colonial governance system.[60] The dominant Temne community established the Temne Tribal Authority (TTA), headed by the Temne Tribal Ruler (TTR).[61] The TTA consisted of native courts, local councils, civic groups, and various officials appointed by the Tribal Ruler. It should be pointed out that the Creole-dominated Freetown City Corporation frowned at the idea of tribal rule that paralleled its own authority. The Temne community, as the largest indigenous ethnic group, led other groups in confronting what they perceived as Creole cultural arrogance. The leaders of the community led the charge, because they claimed to have offered refuge to the forebears of those described as Creoles in the eighteenth century.[62]

This study is motivated by the desire to understand the struggles and contributions of local intellectuals, provincial elites, ethnonationalists, community organizers, Islamic missionaries, and market women traders living in a cosmopolitan environment. The new African social history agenda advocates understanding, interpreting, and analyzing the historical role of Western-educated as well as non-Western-educated elites in African societies. At the end of the nineteenth century, the colony became prone to class struggles and tension, conflicts over cultural and political hegemony, and clashes over the control of public spaces such as cemeteries and entrepots. Thus one of the key aims of this study is to unlade the involute history of this British overseas possession. As Cooper signalizes, historians should devote more time and energy to analyzing the "transformation of ideology and culture, the forging of vast spatial systems in which people carried out their efforts at survival, advancement and struggle."[63] He suggests that urban studies require Africanists and African historians to devote time to analyzing the lives, activities, struggles, and roles of Western-educated and non-Western-educated elites in shaping cities in colonial Africa. He highlights that the conventional approach to history that divides African history "between colonial and post-colonial African history, a division which conceals as much as it reveals," should be replaced with an approach that "bridges one of

---

[60] C.S.O. *An Ordinance to Promote A System of Administration by Tribal Authority Among the Tribes Settled in Freetown, No. 19 of 1905* (Freetown: Government Printing Office, 1905), p. 1.

[61] C.S.O. *Notes on Tribal Administration in Freetown M P/170/39: Tribal Rule 48/1915* (Freetown: 1917), pp. 1–5.

[62] C.S.O. *Notes on Tribal Administration*, pp. 4–7.

[63] Frederick Cooper, *Struggle for the City: Migrant Labor, Capital and the State in Urban Africa* (London: Sage Publications, 1983), p. 10.

the classic divisions of African history, between the 'colonial' and 'post-colonial.'"[64] This new line of historical inquiry suggested by Cooper is a useful method of probing the actions of non-Creole cultural agents in the social formation of the Sierra Leone colony. This study shifts the focus toward the major agency of the ascendant indigenous Temne community in the making of Britain's oldest West African colony. By studying the activities of Temne-speaking men and women, it is clear that disparate historical actors struggled to shape the history of this colonial cosmopolis. This shows that the history of the colony cannot be reduced to the colonizer-and-colonized binary spotlighted in the established orthodoxy. This means if the activities of the elitist Hubert Bankole-Bright and the patrician Adelaide Cromwell and Agatha Cummings-John are relevant in the making of the Sierra Leone Colony, the contributions of Haja Sukainatu Bangura, Pa Alimamy Yenki Kamara, and Yankaday Kargbo, Temne market women and local intellectuals should also be deemed relevant. Freetown historiography devotes much time and space historicizing the sociopolitical activities of Bankole-Bright, Isaac Wallace-Johnson, Adelaide Cromwell, and Constance Cummings-John, because they constituted the best that Victorian England offered in Africa. The dominant literature portrays these historical figures in a far more influential way than it does their non-Western-educated counterparts such as Gibril Sesay, Sukainatu Bangura, Mbalu Conteh, and others in the history of the colony. This study seeks to fill this lacuna in the historiography.

All in all, there is a dearth of literature on the role of non-Western-educated marketers, cultural activists, ethnic entrepreneurs, Islamic elites, tribal headmen, and community leaders in the making of the colony. In fact, the struggle for cultural hegemony, political leadership, and control over space, constitutes a significant aspect of the historical development of this British demesne.

Deciphering Meaning: Research Methodology and Analysis

Sources for this study are drawn from archives in Sierra Leone and the United Kingdom, government documents, colonial newspapers, census data, and oral interviews. Other important files on the Freetown Municipal Council could not be accessed because rebel fighters destroyed its library, which contained valuable data on the council's history. Colonial-era newspapers served as a major source of primary data on

[64] Frederick Cooper, *Africa since 1940: The Past of the Present* (Cambridge: Cambridge University Press, 2002), pp. 4–15.

various aspects of the colony's history, given that the colony maintained a vibrant press. It should be pointed out that the Creole elite owned many of the colony's leading newspapers in the nineteenth and mid-twentieth centuries. The *Sierra Leone Weekly News, Sierra Leone Times, The Vanguard, The Sierra Leone Guardian* and *The African Standard*, among others, became the most vibrant newspapers in the colony and West Africa, as these papers regularly critiqued the activities and policies of the colonial administration.[65] The government-controlled *Daily Mail*, later the *Sierra Leone Daily Mail*, served as an effective mouthpiece for the colonial government. In 1960, the SLWM launched its own newspaper, *Madora*, to promote the views and welfare of women in the androcentric colony. Many political parties, such as the United People's Party (UPP), and the Sierra Leone People's Party (SLPP), also established newspapers such as *Shekpendeh, Unity,* and *Sierra Leone Observer*, which promoted partisan interests. These newspapers proved very valuable, and many contained a trove of data relating to party activities.

Finally, because of the dearth of literature on some important past events, the study relied on oral accounts provided by participants in the events analyzed in the study. The author interviewed a significant number of people, including community chiefs, Islamic missionaries, ethnic entrepreneurs, market women, and founding members of various cultural groups, such as the *Alimania, Ambas Geda, Ariah, Nuru, Jinati* and Temne Progressive Union. The mainstream media largely overlooked the contributions of these institutions in the making of the colony. The archives in the UK and Sierra Leone did not provide meaningful data on this aspect of the colony's history. The interviews provided an opportunity to obtain firsthand information from the founders of and participants in the events described in the study. All informants for this study agreed to be interviewed in Krio or Theimne since all of them spoke one or both languages.[66] When interviewees gave conflicting accounts, the author interviewed them again to synthesize the discrepancy. However, in cases of irreconcilable inconsistencies, the author disregarded the information provided by the informants.

This study is one of the first book-length projects to unearth such a trove of valuable information on the contributions of cultural associations in the development of popular culture in the colony. It is worth pointing out that all interviewees gave permission for use of

---

[65] See *SLWN* coverage of events from 1905 to 1950.
[66] *Theimne* was the language spoken by members of the Temne community in the colony. The term Temne can be both a noun and an adjective. *Theimne* and Temne were interchangeably used to refer to the people and the language they spoke.

their names, quotations and opinions in this study. Additionally, the study is the first to gain exclusive access to the private papers of one of Sierra Leone's prominent Islamic clerics, Alhaji Gibril Sesay. These papers show Sesay's significant contribution in the propagation and Sierra Leonization of Islam in the colony between 1930 and 1961; the historical literature minimizes his immense contributions in the dissemination of the principles of Islam in a Christian dominated colony. The study also used unpublished pamphlets, typescripts, dissertations and reports, written and compiled by various scholars and colonial officials.

Organization of Chapters

Part 1

1 *Historical Epistemology*   Chapter one encapsulates the introduction, historiographical analysis, research methodology and summary of chapters.

2 *Frontiers of Identity: The Creoles and the Politics of Belonging* Chapter two critically analyzes the use of the compellations Creole and/or Krio to describe descendants of settler groups living in the Sierra Leone Colony. Many scholars state that those portrayed as Creole had a fixed identity and bound culture in the nineteenth and twentieth centuries. This chapter challenges this claim and argues that the group described as Creole carried multiple identities in the colony and protectorate for instrumental reasons. Expressed differently, a careful examination of the historical documents reveals that those portrayed as Creoles in the nineteenth century claimed different cultural traditions contrary to their portrayal in the established literature.

Over and beyond this, the chapter challenges the claims Creoles made about themselves and the impact of such claims on their relationship with non-Creole Africans. In fact, the available historical documents indicate that being Creole was not an established identity in the nineteenth and early twentieth centuries, because Creoleness proved malleable and multidimensional. That is, descendants of settler groups referred to as Creoles shifted their identities in the nineteenth and early twentieth centuries for political and economic reasons. As a matter of fact, some of the identifers used by members of this group ranged from "British subjects," "Africans," "Sierra Leoneans," and "Sierra Leonese," to "Black Englishmen" in the nineteenth century, and "Proper Creoles" in the mid-twentieth century.

Further, the study states that the socially constructed term Krio, which has gradually replaced the nineteenth century appellation Creole in the extant historiography, is conjectural and a misnomer. The works of Thomas Spear, Jonathan Glassman, Terence Ranger, and others on the invention and construction of identity in Africa are instructive. This study maintains that Creole identity in the nineteenth and mid-twentieth centuries was not primordial, as culture brokers and nationalist historians propound; Creole identity was highly instrumental. Put another way, Creole identity in the nineteenth and mid-twentieth centuries was not based on consanguinity because it was widely predicated on political, social, economic and hegemonic calculations. On this basis, this chapter disputes the exaggerated claim of Creole cultural superiority over non-Creole indigenous Africans – a concept that aristocratic Creoles and the intellectual elite in the colony bandied around and practiced.

Overall, then, chapter two indicates that the continuous use of the terms Creole and/or Krio in the literature is untenable. In other words, the use of these identifers in the literature by scholars and culture brokers to describe descendants of settlers in the colony is based on hermeneutics and scanty historical evidence. Thus, the study substitutes the use of the terms Creole and Krio for Freetonian – a designation with geographic underpinnings and focus. Simply put, the compellation Freetonian refers to those born and raised in the Sierra Leone Colony between the mid-eighteenth and mid-twentieth centuries. Freetonian is all-inclusive and avoids the cultural underbelly invoked by the use of the terms Creole and Krio to describe descendants of ex-slaves in the Sierra Leone Colony.

Part II: Beyond the Colonial Sphinx: African Agency in the Making of the Colony

3. *Realpolitik and the Boundaries of Power: The Temne in Local Administration* The chapter investigates the meaning of being Temne, and the role of the Temne Tribal Authority and other Temne institutions in shaping and manipulating Temne identity in the mid-nineteenth century. The idea of being Temne in the colony was different from the idea of being Temne in the hinterland. Numerous written and oral historical accounts show that Temne identity became instrumental and was largely shaped, determined and controlled by ethnic entrepreneurs and gatekeepers for hegemonic purposes. Put differently, Temne identity, like Creole identity, shifted over time and proved fluid and malleable; being

Temne in the nineteenth and early twentieth centuries proved different from being Temne in the late twentieth century.

Furthermore, the chapter analyzes the intersection of British rule and the role of local administration (tribal authorities), especially the TTA, in facilitating colonial rule through the application of the "indirect rule system." Through this system, colonial authorities employed and relied on the services of local officials, tribal chiefs, and religious and secular leaders in the administration of the colony. The chapter particularly examines how the leadership of the TTA influenced British policy on local administration, including its social and political ramifications. In fact, the British integration of tribal rule in its administration met with vituperative opposition from the Freetown Municipal Council, also known as the Freetown City Corporation, dominated by Creoles. The chapter examines the acerbic tension between the City Corporation and tribal authorities led by the Temne Tribal Authority. The City Corporation vehemently opposed tribal rule in the colony for a variety of reasons, not least for fear of political competition, given Britain's insistence on the majoritarian principle. Despite sustained expostulations from officials of the Corporation, colonial authorities fostered and to some extent relied on tribal rule in the colony. This collaborative experiment in local administration contributed to the success of the colonial project which to some extent influenced politics in the postcolony.

   4   *Intergroup Relations and Genealogies of Conflict: The Temne and Freetonian Dichotomy*   The chapter probes the social and economic impact of urbanization on the colony and explores the cluster of social and political relations which developed around class, ethnic, and religious identities, particularly between the two major ethnic groups – the Creoles and the Temne.

As the urban space evolved, ethnic communities became consumed by political and social conflicts between the Creoles, who saw themselves as natural heirs to British rule, and non-Creole Africans led by the ascendant Temne community. Thus palpable tension developed between the two groups over control of public spaces such as entrepots and/or marketplaces, public cemeteries, and public parks. Moreover, the chapter addresses the impact of the Creole/Temne dichotomy on British rule in the colony. How did the animus between the two major groups, the Creoles and the Temne, shape the political future of the Sierra Leone Colony? What role did colonial rule play in this conflict? To what extent did British rule enhance identity politics in Sierra Leone as a whole? Finally, how does the conflict inform politics and social relations in the postcolonial state? The chapter addresses these questions and shows that, though British rule contributed to identity politics and ethnic cleavages, hegemonic and economic factors deepened the divide between the Creole establishment and non-Creole tribal authorities in the lead-up to independence, and in the post-independence state.

Part III Ethnocentrism and New Frames of Popular Culture

5 *Temne Cultural Associations and Popular Representations* The chapter focuses on the activities and contributions of cultural associations, especially Temne cultural associations, in the development of popular culture. Temne cultural associations such as the *Alimania, Ambas Geda, Nuru Jinati,* Boys London, and *Ariah,* among others, established a popular culture that changed the indices and bounds of what mattered in a multicultural spatial milieu like colonial Freetown. While the Creole intelligentsia perceived Western education, attendance at balls, cocktail parties, and membership in freemasonry as markers of prestige and high status, local intellectuals privileged variables such as membership and leadership of cultural associations, and community leadership, as having special cachet. Consequently, the colony developed a spryly urban culture, which bolstered Temne identity and sharply increased the profile of non-Western-educated Temne intellectuals. Given this, an intriguing sets of values emerged between the virtues associated with being a freemason, and the cachet connected with membership in cultural associations. As the urban context evolved, acrimonious disputes over identity politics, and class struggles, increased.

Thus being Temne became a prerequisite for membership in the Temne associations, a process that exposed the fluidity and ductility of Temne identity. This speaks to Thomas Spear's views on the role of elites in imagining identities: "In recent times when colonial and modern elites have got to mobilize values to support their own claims to restricted resources in both traditional and modern sectors ... ethnicity then becomes instrumental capable of being invented and manipulated in the service of one goal or another."[67] The Temne community attracted admirers from other ethnic groups and boosted Temne ethnic pride through social activities. This aspect of the colony's development is important, as it speaks to the complexity of the colony as a historical process and an intriguing unit of inquiry.

---

[67] Spear, *Being Massai: Ethnicity and Identity in East Africa* (Athens, Ohio: Ohio University Press, 1993), p. 15. See also T. C. McCaskie, *History and Modernity in an African Village, 1850–1950* (Athens, Ohio: Ohio University Press, 2001).

In all, the chapter argues that the various cultural associations, particularly the ascendant Temne and other tribal associations, created a unique tradition which informed and influenced popular culture in colonial and postcolonial Sierra Leone. It situates the history of the colony within a wider system of social and political relations and analysis – a feature of the new social history agenda in African history. In his major work on the subject, Porter states that Western education served as a "royal road" to success in the colony. Spitzer reinforces this view, as he uncritically accepts Creole claims of cultural superiority. This chapter avers that the ideas of success and apotheosis in this salmagundi of a colony were dynamic and labyrinthine. It shows that the attainment of Western education and/or the assimilation of European values formed a marginal part of this potpourri of an urban space contrary to the insinuations of Ffye, Porter, Spitzer, Cohen and others. The chapter highlights that European values were not the only barometers of prestige in the colony.

6 *Islamic Triumphalism in a Christian Colony: Temne Agency in the Spread and Sierra Leonization of Islam* In this chapter, the spread of Islam in a Christian colony is set in the context of religious tension between non-Creole Muslims abetted by the Temne Islamic Community (TIC) and Muslim Creoles, or Aku, on the one hand, and Christian Creoles on the other. Though the colony originated in a protestant Christian tradition, its early inhabitants practiced other religions, including Islam. However, because Christian philanthropists and politicians established the original settlement of Freetown as a Christian experiment, non-Christian residents experienced religious bigotry from their Christian counterparts. Notwithstanding the tension between Christians and Muslims, intra-religious rancor also engulfed and rocked the Muslim community, especially between the Aku and Temne Muslims. The division led to the proliferation of community mosques and *jammats* (assemblies) in the early twentieth century. In spite of this, a complex web of factors accelerated the spread of Islam, which became dominant over time. The major works of Leslie Proudfoot, Alusine Jalloh, Gibril Cole, and others assign major agency to the Aku, Mandingo, and Fula Muslims for the growth of Islam in the colony.[68] David Skinner contends that no one ethnic community had dominated the spread of Islam in the

---

[68] See M. Saif'ud Deen Alharazim, "The Origin and Progress of Islam in Sierra Leone," *Sierra Leone Studies* 21 (January 1939); see also L. Proudfoot, "Muslim Solidarity," and his other work, "Mosque Building"; see also Lamin Sanneh, "Islamic Consciousness and the African Society: An Essay in Historical Interaction" (Freetown: Unpublished

Sierra Leone Colony since the nineteenth century. He also states that, in 1826, Mandingo-, Fula-, Susu-, and Temne-speakers constituted more than half of the population of indigenes in the colony who became ardent adherents and disseminators of Islam.[69] Added to this, the Temne became some of the largest adherents of Islam in the nineteenth century.[70]

The chapter indicates that non-Creole Muslims, such as the Temne and others, generated a new dimension of Islamic practice in this Christian colony. Temne Islamic entrepreneurs, imams, sheiks, community organizers, and marabouts used Temne institutions to propagate the tenets of Islam in and outside the precincts of the colony. As one of the largest agglomerations of Muslims, Temne Muslims gave Islam a certain demographic advantage, and thus made it a dominant force. Colonial newspapers and oral accounts reveal that the leadership of the Temne Islamic Community considerably helped increase the profile of what colony elites hitherto perceived as an exotic religion. In light of this, the Temne Islamic Community contributed to what the study refers to as the "Sierra Leonization" of Islam in the colony. Relying on the theoretical frame propounded by Roman Loimeier in his recent work, *Muslim Societies in Africa*, the study shows that the Temne Islamic Community, in collaboration with other Muslim communities, appropriated Islam to suit local customs. The chapter also challenges Rudolph Ware III's claim in his most recent work, *The Walking Qur'an: Islamic Education, Embodied Knowledge, and History in West Africa*, about the dangers of presenting African Islam as subsidiary to Middle Eastern Islam. The study states that the Sierra Leonization of Islam gave the religion a distinct stamp and attraction that accelerated its growth and propagation. As Loimeier points out, "there is no uniform and singularly 'orthodox' form of Islam, either in Africa or in the Islamic world as a whole."[71]

Paper, Institute of African Studies, University of Sierra Leone, 1975), pp. 4–7. He has expanded these ideas in his recent work, *The Crown and the Turban: Muslims and West African Pluralism* (Boulder, Colorado: Westview Press, 1997). See also Alusine Jalloh, *African Entrepreneurship: Muslim Fula Merchants in Sierra Leone* (Athens, Ohio: Ohio University for International Studies, 1999).

[69] David Skinner, Barbara Harrell-Bond and Allen M. Howard, "*Islam in Sierra Leone during the 19th Century*" (University of California, Unpublished PhD Dissertation, 1971), p. 131. See his work on "Mande Settlement and the Development of Islamic Institutions in Sierra Leone," *International Journal of African Historical Studies* 11 (1978).

[70] Skinner, *Islam in Sierra Leone*, p. 132.

[71] See Roman Loimeier, *Muslim Societies in Africa: A Historical Anthropology* (Bloomington: Indiana University Press, 2013); see also Rudolph Ware III, *The Walking Qur'an: Islamic Education, Embodied Knowledge and History in West Africa* (Chapel Hill, North Carolina: University of North Carolina Press, 2014).

This study is one of the first book-length projects to critically examine and expatiate on the concept of the Sierra Leonization of Islam, as it illumines the agency of various players who contributed to this significant aspect of the colony's religious traditions.

7 *From the Margins to the Center: The Role of Temne Market Women Traders* The chapter explores the contributions of Temne women traders in the colony between 1890 and 1961. The feminist literature, particularly key works of LaRay Denzer, Frances White, and others, focuses heavily on the activities of Western-educated female elites, such as Agatha Cummings John and Adelaide Casely-Hayford, and their roles in the socio-economic formation of the colony.[72] The works of these scholars draw attention to the androcentric literature and the denigration of the contributions of women in the colony's formation. The literature also overlooks the roles and contributions of non-Western-educated women engaged in grassroots activism, microcredit schemes, retail commerce, and politics.[73]

The chapter analyzes the activities of prominent rural intellectuals, such as Haja Sukainatu Bangura, Nana Turay, Yankaday Kargbo, and their leadership at various marketplaces: the Big Market, King Jimmy, Kissy Road and Dove Cut Markets. A careful examination of historical sources reveals that Temne women traders organized around commercial institutions – they established microcredit schemes to subsidize small-scale enterprises for Temne and non-Temne-speaking women traders. Their activities contributed to the strengthening of the informal sector of the economy. Women traders also significantly contributed to the successful formation of the Sierra Leone Women's Movement (SLWM), a feminist staple that influenced national politics in the twentieth century. In short, the chapter indicates that, contrary to the established orthodoxy, feminist ideology was not the exclusive domain of Western-educated female elites. The chapter highlights that grassroots female activists and retail politicians made significant contributions to the socio-economic formation of the colony, and therefore deserve a cardinal place in the feminist literature.

Parallel to the above, the established feminist literature fails to fully integrate the story of non-Western-educated historical actors. The oral

---

[72] Adelaide Cromwell, *An African Victorian Feminist: The Life and Times of Adelaide Casely Hayford 1868–1960* (Washington, D.C.: Howard University Press, 1992), pp. 142–144.
[73] Catherine Coquery-Vidrovitch, *African Women: A Modern History* (Boulder, Colorado: Westview Press, 1997), p. 175.

data reveal that Temne women traders became major suppliers of garden and marine products, and engaged in retail commerce, and politics.

Conclusion

8 *Nexus of Microhistory: New Perspective on the Colony's Historical Landscape* This chapter adopts a new approach to understanding the social history of the colony: it maintains that the initial impetus in Sierra Leone historiography was nationalist. Fyfe, Spitzer, Porter, Cohen, Denzer, Wyse, Cole, and others focused on Creole accomplishments to make the case that African agency, as well as colonial initiative, proved important in the making of Britain's oldest colony in West Africa. Some of these scholars left non-Creole Africans in the background, and grouped them as "non-colony peoples" or "interior peoples." Even when other groups came under inquiry, such as women and Muslims, the Creole focus remained. But colonial censuses identify a Temne population that matched the Creole, and the colonial government recognized and entrenched the Temne Tribal Authority in its governance structure. The study highlights the fact that across social spaces – mosques, cultural associations, marketplaces and local administration – the idea of being Temne not only mattered, it also clearly grew in profile and importance in the colonial period. The volume analyzes the case of Temne agency to promote an alternative view for a complete understanding of the making of this complex British colony.

Clearly, the aim of the study is not to present an exhaustive microanalysis of the contributions of all non-Creole Africans, as this would exceed the limits of this historical inquiry. The aim is to illuminate the agency of the preponderant indigenous Temne community in the colony's complex social history. Corollary to this, the book aims to amplify the voices of rural intellectuals, provincial elites, and market women traders, which have been largely overlooked in the established literature.

2   Frontiers of Identity: The Creoles and the Politics of Belonging

This chapter challenges the use of the compellation Creole, or Krio, as an identity category in Sierra Leone historiography. Creole, or Krio, broadly refers to descendants of the various ex-slaves repatriated to Sierra Leone from Europe, the Americas and Africa in the eighteenth and nineteenth centuries. In addition, Akintola Wyse and Gibril Cole state that Krio identity also comprised members of various ethnic groups from the hinterland. The historiography portrays this group as a fixed and unique community with a distinct identity.[1] Though the orthodox application of Creole is the subject of multiple scholarly discourses, this study is one of the first book-length projects to challenge and problematize the use of the register in the dominant literature. It probes the kind of perception those described as Creoles held about themselves since the time of their evolution in the Sierra Leone Colony in the eighteenth and nineteenth centuries, to the time Sierra Leone gained political independence in 1961. Did those described as Creoles maintain a fixed identity, as some scholars contend? Did their identity change over time? If it did change, why did it change? To thoroughly investigate and analyze these questions, the study explores the role scholars played in the construction of Creole, or Krio, identity, especially Africanus Horton, T. C. Luke, John Peterson, Christopher Fyfe, Leo Spitzer, Arthur Porter, and Akintola Wyse, among numerous others. Did these authors visualize the existence of this group or simply report an historical fact? Porter is credited as the first Sierra Leonean extensively to study the history and sociological structure of those he describes as Creoles. The claim he advances in his major work on the Creoles became a major source of reference on the evolution of

---

[1] The Colony of Sierra Leone comprised Freetown and the peninsula towns; the Koya Temne occupied this territory before the arrival of British philanthropists, who eventually took possession of it in the eighteenth century. When Freetown became a Crown Colony in 1808, the British government, through treaties and sometimes force, annexed all areas previously owned by the Temne, including the renamed territories of Leicester, Gloucester, Kent, Regent, and York, in the West, and Waterloo, Hastings, Rokel, Wellington, and Kissy, in the east. Thus the use of the term colony in this study refers to Freetown and the rural areas or peninsula towns.

the group. He maintains that the Creoles evolved as a special community with a distinct identity and a bound culture. This study probes the veracity of Porter's assertion. Similarly, Wyse is widely recognized as the inventor of the Krio myth. Of particular importance will be an investigation into whether the immense scholarship produced on this group played a role in the construction of Creole, or Krio, identity.

The chapter shows that those described as Creoles in the literature did not carry a linear and/or horizontal identity; they carried asymmetrical identities spurred by political, social, and economic factors in the nineteenth and early twentieth centuries. A careful examination of the historical documents indicates that multiple agents such as culture brokers, intellectual elites, the popular media, and colonial officials constructed and popularized the use of Creole as an identifier. However, the views carried by the group about themselves in public clearly belie this description. On this basis, the study shows that the persistent use of the designation Creole to describe progenies of settler groups in the Sierra Leone Colony is a misnomer. In addition, the use of the constructed ideated appellative Krio by Wyse and others to describe descendants with settler ancestry in the colony is ahistorical. There is insufficient evidence to support the view that the group of people Wyse and others referred to as Krio carried this identity in the Sierra Leone Colony in the nineteenth and early twentieth centuries. The persistent use of the Krio compellation, which has been uncritically accepted in the literature, is based on feigned evidence that is immersed in specious speculation. As Karin Berber and P. F. de Moraes state, intellectual nationalists and/ or culture brokers promote ethnic groups for political reasons, as they engage in popularizing specific ideas about particular ethnic groups via a variety of agencies. Berber and de Moraes point out that the histories of many ethnic groups in Africa become the construct of intellectuals of such historical accounts with the broad aim of embellishing the status of specific groups.[2] Spear also draws attention to the fact that "ethnicity has, thus, been continually reinterpreted and reconstructed over time in such a way as to appear timeless and legitimate, it has been deployed by contending parties in complex processes of selectivity and representation that is key at the core of peoples' collective historical consciousness and struggles for power, meaning and access to resources."[3]

---

[2] P. F. de Moraes and Karin Berber, eds., *Self-Assertion and Brokerage: Early Cultural Nationalism in West Africa* (Birmingham: University of Birmingham Center for West African Studies, 1990), pp. 1–4.

[3] Thomas Spear, "Neo-Traditionalism and the Limits of Invention in British Colonial Africa." *Journal of African History*, 44 (2003), p. 24.

Did scholars like Fyfe, Porter, Spitzer, Peterson, Wyse, and others ascribe an identity to descendants of former slaves based in the colony to promote an agenda, or did Creole, or Krio, identity naturally evolve to access power and resources? The following sections seek to address these questions.

Identity Formation and the Construction of Creole Identity, 1870–1961

Africanus Horton became the first scholar of Sierra Leone to survey the history of the descendants of settlers in the colony. In his major work, Horton uses adjectives like "Creoles," "natives of Sierra Leone," and "native-born Sierra Leonist" to describe those referred to as Creoles.[4] In recommending a political system for Sierra Leone, Horton suggested that a monarchical form of government be adopted, with an elected monarch who must be a "native-born Sierra Leonist or a citizen by constitutional adoption."[5] In defending the group against inexorable European racist vilification and denigration, Horton observed that:

The Creoles of Sierra Leone have been stigmatized as the most impertinent rogues in all the coast, even by men who know nothing of them ... But we find nevertheless that these Creoles of Sierra Leone occupy lucrative subordinate positions of trust in both military and civil service of the government in four colonies and settlements of the coast.[6]

The quotation above shows that Horton considered acculturated hinterland people as Creoles. This characterization of Creole identity is unique and belies the perspective of other scholars who view Creoles as descendants of Liberated Africans – a characterization that excludes non-descendants of settler groups living in the colony and hinterland.

Other scholars, such as T. C. Luke, expanded and used Horton's description of those he portrays as Creoles. In a detailed article, Luke expounds the perception that being Creole became a way of life:

The term 'Creole' ... as used in Sierra Leone is applied to descendants of original settlers, i.e. poor blacks, Nova Scotians, Maroons and Liberated Africans. The term implies no admixture of European blood nor any connection with the West Indies (unless it be very partial or a remote one), as it does in the West Indies and America. In fact the term was originally applied exclusively to the children of Liberated Africans; with intermarriage and the passage of time this

---

[4] James Africanus Beale Horton, *West African Countries and Peoples, British and Native* (Switzerland: Kraus-Thomson, 1970), pp. 162–206.
[5] Horton, *West African Countries*, p. 206.
[6] Horton, *West African Countries*, p. 97.

distinction came to be ignored and the term applied generally to the settlers and their descendants.[7]

He perceives members of the group as pure Africans with no trace of European blood. He also states that members of the group had little that is indigenous to Africa apart from their skin color.[8] This description denotes that those Luke calls Creoles are Africans by blood and European by orientation. Who then were the Creoles? To what extent is it true that the Creoles possessed very few African traits in their character, as stated by Luke? It is clear from his description that the Creoles became a special group with distinct features separate from other groups in Sierra Leone. In commenting on their dwindling population, he states that "according to the census returns the Creole population of the colony, the most advanced class of people native to the country, decreased from about seven-twelfths to a little over one-third between 1881 and 1921."[9] Because of their "relative educational superiority," Luke argues that the Creoles deserved to fill top positions in commerce and clerical occupations in the colonial administration.[10] This study challenges the accuracy of the above claim and shows that Western education became one of several variables the colonial authorities used in determining relevance in the colonial establishment.

Christopher Fyfe, who is widely perceived as the patriarch of Sierra Leone history, developed the view that the Creoles lived as a distinct community. A former colonial government archivist, turned scholar, Fyfe points out in his seminal work that "the colony-born children were called 'Creoles,' a name used in many countries with different connotations, but in Sierra Leone for Recaptives' descendants."[11] He states that the Creole compellation became gratifyingly defined and gleefully used "by members of the Sierra Leone Community during the nineteenth century."[12] He insinuates that children born in the colony by immigrant parents also formed part of Creole society. This statement supports Horton's perspective, and has long term implications for a fuller understanding of the

---

[7] T. C. Luke, "Some Notes on the Creoles and their Land." *Sierra Leone Studies* 21 (1939), p. 53.

[8] Luke, "Creoles," pp. 53–54.

[9] Luke, "Creoles," p. 66.

[10] Luke, "Creoles," p. 68.

[11] Christopher Fyfe, *A History of Sierra Leone* (London: Oxford University Press, 1962), p. 238.

[12] Christopher Fyfe, "The Term 'Creole:' A Footnote to History." *Africa* 50: 4, (1980): p. 422; see also Joseph J. Bangura, "Constitutional Development and Ethnic Entrepreneurism in Sierra Leone: A Metahistorical Analysis" in Marda Mustapha and Joseph J. Bangura, eds., *Democratization and Human Security in Postwar Sierra Leone* (New York: Palgrave Macmillan), pp. 23–24.

identity of this group. In discussing the extensive business interests of the group outside the colony, Fyfe maintains that numerous Creole traders travelled to the hinterland, where they settled for business and became established entrepreneurs, especially around the Bagru, Jong and Bum-Kittam areas.[13] Though he perceives the identity of the group he refers to as Creoles as fixed, symmetrical and categorical, his works did not address the identity of Creole entrepreneurs who permanently relocated to the hinterland. Did these so-called Creoles who lived in the hinterland carry a distinct identity in their new settlements?

In his contribution to the discourse, John Peterson explores in a detailed monograph the activities of Liberated Africans who constituted the core of those he describes as Creoles. Peterson states that "a Creole was an African born in Sierra Leone to parents of liberated African descent who are living outside the geographical area of their birth."[14] He asserts that the word "Creole" first appeared "during the admin-istration of Governor MacCarthy (1814–1824) which was an adapta-tion of its original meaning, a Frenchman born in the New World."[15] This statement indicates that the colonial administration helped ascribe Creole identity to progenies of settlers in the colony. By the second half of the nineteenth century, the compellation Creole generally referred to a "Europeanized African" and a "Black Englishman."[16] Creole exclusivity faded over time as the immigrant population challenged their presumed superiority.[17] In asserting the exclusiveness of Creole society, Peterson observes that:

By the 1890s, the Freetown Creole had begun to face the problem of working out his relationships with the immigrant population from the Sierra Leone interior. Fears in the Creole community led the settled Freetown population to suspect that they were no longer heard at Government House and that they were in fact becoming sacrifices to the less sophisticated African.[18]

The above implies that those described as Creoles became an established and self-aware ethnic group in the 1890s. Leo Spitzer makes a similar argument in his work on the historical activities of the descendants of set-tlers. Unlike Horton, Luke, Fyfe et al., Spitzer offers a slightly different definition of the group he also refers to as Creoles. He describes them as

[13] Fyfe, *A History*, p. 400.
[14] John Peterson, "A Study of the Dynamics of Liberated African Society, 1807–1870" (Northwestern University, PhD Dissertation, 1963), p. 340.
[15] Peterson, "Liberated African Society," p. 340.
[16] Peterson, "Liberated African Society," p. 340.
[17] John Peterson, *Province of Freedom: A History of Sierra Leone 1787–1870* (London: Faber and Faber, 1969), p. 247.
[18] Peterson, *Province of Freedom*, p. 247.

"colony-born children of liberated Africans."[19] He states that intermarriage and cultural syncretism among the various settler groups erased the distinctions which originally existed among them. Thus the Creole designation came to mean descendants of all "black-African groups" settled in the Sierra Leone settlement after 1787.[20] He observes that the "Creole community always included and still includes persons of black-African stock, usually from one of the neighboring ethnic groups of the Sierra Leone hinterland, who emulated the 'Creole way of life' by adopting the habits, standards of behaviour and outlooks with which Creole is identified."[21] Spitzer clearly believes that being Creole became a way of life because the group lived as a special community with distinct features.

However, T. F. V. Buxton, who offers a slightly different perspective, maintains that those "now known as Creoles, being drawn from many different tribes, have adopted English (among the uneducated pidgin English) as their common tongue; and as the result of missionary labours in the early part of the last century, the great majority profess Christianity as their religion."[22] Unlike other scholars, Buxton views those he records as Creoles as descendants of various African tribes in the interior of Sierra Leone who used English as their medium of communication. This implies that those he refers to as Creoles directly originated from indigenous groups in the adjacent hinterland.

The works above show that Horton, Luke, Peterson, Spitzer, and Buxton broadly agree that those they refer to as Creoles are descendants of liberated Africans with African characteristics. Fyfe on the other hand defines them as "colony-born children," without denoting their character traits.

Notwithstanding the above, the first Sierra Leonean historian, A. B. C. Sibthorpe, described as Creole by his biographer, Christopher Fyfe, did not use the term Creole to refer to himself or his compatriots in his work. In a tribute to him, Fyfe notes that: "Sibthorpe was writing the history of a 'nation,' the Creole (today Krio) people of Sierra Leone (though the ascription 'Creole' was then current – Africanus Horton used it – Sibthorpe normally used 'Sierra Leonese' for his people)."[23] Sibthorpe describes prominent citizens of settler descent, like Sir Samuel Lewis,

[19] Leo Spitzer, *The Creoles of Leone: Responses to Colonialism 1870–1945* (Madison, Wisconsin: University of Wisconsin Press, 1974), p. 12.
[20] Spitzer, *Creoles*, p. 12.
[21] Spitzer, *Creoles*, p. 12.
[22] T. F. V. Buxton, "The Creole in West Africa." *Journal of the African Society*, 12 (1913), pp. 385–386.
[23] Christopher Fyfe, "A. B. C. Sibthorpe: A Tribute." *Sierra Leone Studies*, ns 10 (1958), p. 327. The original version of Sibthorpe's *History of Sierra Leone* is inaccessible probably because it is out of print. However, the revised version used here carries most of the texts contained in the original version as indicated by the printers/publishers. His other works

as "native" but he uses "Sierra Leonese" to refer to other people. He maintains that:

The centenary of the settlement and the founding of Sierra Leone, 1887 was a great event in the history not only of the inhabitants of Sierra Leone, but for the black race everywhere ... Addresses were delivered by three native gentlemen, all born in the colony and educated chiefly on the spot: Reverend O. Moore representing the ecclesiastical, the Reverend S. Spain the Educationalist and the Honorable Samuel Lewis the Political life of the community. Then began the Sierra Leonese to play stringed instrument – guitar, violin and harp.[24]

In commenting on the achievement of Lewis, Sibthorpe states that "Mr. Lewis was the first native African in Africa who had been the recipient of such high honour and the intelligence was received in the colony with much joy and satisfaction by all classes of the community."[25] Born in 1843, Lewis became one of the most influential Africans in the colonial administration in the nineteenth century.[26] Between 1872 and 1895, Lewis became the first African to be knighted, and he acted as Queen's advocate, Chief Justice, councilor, and the first mayor of the Freetown Municipal Council.[27] Lewis did not use the term Creole as an identifier, nor did he serve as advocate for a particular ethnic group. As a barrister, he represented all parties who sought his services, whether they resided in the colony or hinterland. His biographer, John D. Hargreaves, observed that Lewis generally used the term African to refer to himself or his compatriots. In commenting on the census of 1891, Sibthorpe notes that "Freetown the capital contained 30, 000 inhabitants and over 5000 dwellings. About half of the black population consisted of Liberated Africans and their descendants, the balance being composed of the neighboring tribes."[28] Sibthorpe referred to half of the black population in the colony as descendants of "Liberated Africans"; he did not use the compellation Creole to describe himself in his work.[29] His knack for using different adjectives in describing his compatriots is exemplified by the encomium he heaped on an honoree: "the President then invested with the same order J. A. Macarthy, Queen's Advocate, a native African.

on Sierra Leone were not historical; some were on the geography of Sierra Leone. They are out of print as well.

[24] A. B. C Sibthorpe, alias Aucandu Prince of Cucuruku, Niger, F. P., *The History of Sierra Leone: Revised, Remodeled and Enlarged* (London: Elliot Stock, 1906), p. 105. Paragraph break suppressed.

[25] Sibthorpe, *History*, p. 115.

[26] J. D. Hargreaves, "Sir Samuel Lewis and the Legislative Council," *Sierra Leone Studies*, n.s., 6 (June 1956), p. 40.

[27] Hargreaves, "Sir Samuel Lewis," pp. 40–43.

[28] Sibthorpe, *History*, p. 112.

[29] Christopher Fyfe, "A. B. C. Sibthorpe: A Tribute," *Sierra Leone Studies*, p. 327.

This was the second time that the Liberian government conferred honours upon a native of Sierra Leone ..."[30] Sibthorpe uses the phrase "native African" to describe Macarthy as he did for Lewis. By the definition of Creole propounded in the historical literature Macarthy could be deemed a Creole but Sibthorpe describes him as "native African." This shows that Sibthorpe, who is the first to write the history of his country, did not use the Creole compellation to refer to descendants of settlers in the colony.

Among the notable works done on this group is the work of Arthur Porter, who is credited as the first Sierra Leonean scholar to publish a comprehensive account of those he refers to as Creoles. Porter presents the Creoles as a group with a distinct identity, a bound culture and an established way of life. He defines them as "descendants of settlers and Liberated Africans in Sierra Leone and to others who had cultivated their habits and had come to accept their way of living."[31] This definition of Creoles is open-ended, because it shows that non-descendants of settler groups in the colony also became Creole as long as they imbibed the Creole mode of life. He further asserts that, after 1870, Creole identity evolved and came to mean "settlers, liberated Africans and their descendants."[32] In commenting on the exclusivity of the group, he affirms that the Creoles had a legitimate right to provide political leadership in Sierra Leone because they "constituted an elite group (excluding the European administration) in which were conserved the high ranking positions in the economic, social and political orders until they began to be seriously challenged by the indigenous inhabitants especially after 1945."[33] Furthermore, in the late nineteenth and early twentieth centuries, the Creoles proved to be a unique and bound group whose "distinct brand of culture has given the peculiar stamp and colour to Sierra Leone."[34] Succinctly put, Porter points out that in the pre–World War II period, aboriginal tribes acknowledged Creole superiority without resentment because "both groups accepted the 19th century pattern of Creole superiority, mutually recognized social distance and differential behavior typical of tribesmen towards the Creoles."[35] Did Porter's claim reflect the true situation in the Sierra Leone Colony in the nineteenth and first half of the twentieth centuries?

[30] Sibthorpe, *History*, p. 114.
[31] Arthur Porter, *Creoledom: A Study of the Development of Freetown Society* (London: Oxford University Press, 1963), p. 3.
[32] Porter, *Creoledom*, pp. 51–52.
[33] Porter, *Creoledom*, p. 137.
[34] Porter, *Creoledom*, p. 14.
[35] Porter, *Creoledom*, pp. 66–67.

Like Porter, Akintola J. G. Wyse is widely known as the obdurate progenitor of the "Krio myth."[36] Put another way, Wyse is the first Sierra Leonean historian to perpetuate the use of the compellation "Krio" in the historical literature, followed by other historians of Sierra Leone, such as Gibril Cole and David Harris. These scholars use "Krio" as an identifier in referring to those described as Creoles by Porter and others.[37] Wyse portrays Krio not only as a noun but as an adjective. Though he agrees with Porter on the evolution of the group in the Sierra Leone Colony, he however maintains that "Krio ... [is] the only acceptable usage." He postulates that Krio is a corrupt form of the Yoruba word *Akiriyo*, meaning moving from place to place.[38] Added to this, he posits that the Creole compellation did not capture the uniqueness of the descendants of settlers that occupied the Sierra Leone Colony. In his effort to entrench the Krio designation as a historical and acceptable identity, Wyse states that scholars purposely tried to "externalize the Krio, to peripheralize them, to cast them in a svengali role in a dichotomized history of the nation, tuck them under general themes rather than see them as subject worthy of study in their own right."[39] He bemoaned the point that the dominant literature treated the Krio as "extra African, Western, an aberration, not part of the mainstream of West African history."[40] This statement betrays Wyse's motive for persistently ennobling the Krio as a group worth studying and writing about in the history of Sierra Leone. His motive for promoting the Krio myth ignores the volume of work done on "descendants of Liberated Africans" described as Creole by scholars before him. Like Fyfe and other scholars before him, Wyse equates the history of the colony with the history of those he describes as Krio.

Overall, the varied interpretations of what it meant to be Creole speak to the problematic nature of the group's identity. Peterson, Spitzer, Buxton, Porter, and others refer to descendants of settler groups as Creole, while Wyse, Cole, and Harris among numerous others identify

---

[36] Christopher Fyfe, "Akintola Wyse: Creator of the Krio Myth" in Mac Dixon Fyle and Gibril Cole, *New Perspectives on the Sierra Leone Krio* (Baltimore: Peter Lang Inc. 2005), p. 27.

[37] See Akintola Wyse, *The Krio of Sierra Leone: An Interpretive History* (Freetown: Hurst and International African Institute, 1989), and Gibril Cole, *The Krio of West Africa: Islam, Culture and Creolization in the Nineteenth Century* (Athens, Ohio: Ohio University Press, 2013).

[38] See Wyse, *Krio of Sierra Leone*; Cole, *Krio of West Africa*.

[39] Akintola J. G. Wyse, "The Krio of Sierra Leone: Perspectives and West African Historiography," in Simon McGrath et al., eds. *Rethinking African History* (Edinburgh: University of Edinburgh, 1997), pp. 201–202.

[40] Wyse, "*The Krio of Sierra Leone*," p. 201.

them as Krio. Is the description advanced by these scholars an accurate reflection of the identity of scions of settlers that occupied the Sierra Leone Colony? Did the group develop a distinct way of life, as many scholars suggest? Or did the group prove to be a monolithic entity with a bound culture and traditions distinct from other communities in the Sierra Leone Colony? Put differently, how did the group recorded as Creole use history to further its political ambitions in Sierra Leone in the nineteenth and mid-twentieth centuries? Using the extant historiography on ethnic identity, this study rethinks the claim of various scholars that being Creole became an established way of life by the nineteenth century. These scholars assume that progenies of settlers and their associates developed a symmetrical identity and remained unaffected by political and economic influences. They indicate that the Creoles evolved as a well-defined community with a common history, culture and destiny. Did generations of Creoles also imagine themselves as a special community with a legitimate right to govern Sierra Leone, as Porter contends? Ranger, Spear, Glassman, Bravman, and Cooper demonstrate in their works that ethnic identity can sometimes be driven by factors which revolve around power relations. Ranger observes that: "ethnicity it seems to me is not a given primordial identity, but an ideological assertion of [the] centrality of language and of the superiority of one language, or dialect, to another."[41]

In light of Ranger's comment, it is clear that descendants of settlers in the Sierra Leone Colony did not develop a distinct community with a bound culture and a shared ancestral history. Over and beyond this, the use of "Krio" as a semantic proxy for "Creole" is highly problematic.

All in all, it is tenable to state that, as the literature on ethnic identities in Africa shows, African elites played a role in the construction, imagination, and invention of Creole and/or Krio identity. If Creole society existed as an exclusive community with a bound culture, shared ancestral history, and primordial values, a consistent identity would have emerged among the members of the community. However, a careful reading of the available historical documents shows that the group described as Creole carried asymmetrical identities which ranged from "Sierra Leonean natives," "Sierra Leonean," "descendants of Liberated African," "British subjects," "Sierra Leonese," "African," "Black Englishmen," and "Creole."[42] As David Skinner and Barbara Harrell-Bond argue, the

---

[41] Terence Ranger, "Concluding Comments" in Paris Yeroes ed., *Ethnicity and Nationalism in Africa: Constructivist Reflections and Contemporary Politics* (London: Macmillan 1999), p. 134.

[42] *SLWN*, Freetown, September 20, 1884 and August–September 1887.

community identified as Creole by Luke, Peterson, Porter, and Fyfe, but identified as Krio by Wyse and others, did not carry a "self-conscious, self-identified" identity marker in colonial Freetown in the nineteenth century, when the community and its identity should have evolved, as Porter asserts.[43]

Trajectory of Creole Identity and the Burden of History, 1870–1961

As the colony evolved into a cosmopolitan city in the mid-nineteenth century, the identities of various groups became circumstantial and multidimensional. Descendants of settler groups described as Creole in the colony utilized, mobilized and deployed an assorted array of identity-markers based on salutary factors.[44] Sociopolitical and economic factors, such as the demographic impact of immigration on the colony population, the fight for political hegemony, and the tension over racism, largely influenced the discourse on identity.

In the late nineteenth century, the colony became a melting pot for disparate ethnic groups and immigrants from the hinterland. The increased influx of new immigrants rankled many descendants of settlers, who perceived immigrants as the exotic other, different from Europeanized descendants of former slaves. The excitability caused by the immigration discourse ostensibly led this colony resident to opine that:

Having seen that it will be futile, if any attempt were to be made tending toward their expulsion from the settlement [colony] and their further influx; the one only remedy available is for the whole body of Sierra Leoneans to wake to a sense of the danger that hangs over them and to resolutely as one man invoke the aid of the influential in making move in the form of a petition to the Governor.... If patriotic zeal for interest of all and cold and selfish indifference, fills the breast of every true born Sierra Leonean they will rise EN MASSE as one man to this glorious and laudable cause and will not rest content until they shall have gained their end.[45]

The author of the article requests the solidarity of all Sierra Leoneans against the influx of immigrants from the hinterland, who posed an economic and demographic threat to the colony. The trepidation expressed in the quote supports Spear's point that "in the face of

---

[43] David Skinner and Barbara Harrell-Bond, "Creoles: A Final Comment," *Africa* 51, no. 3 (1981): 787.
[44] *Methodist Herald and West African Educational Times*, Freetown, December 8, 1882.
[45] *The Agency*, January 8, 1887.

immigration and social changes ethnicity could be used to divide as well as to join."[46]

This appeal for unity among descendants of settlers shows that the group did not exist as a distinct community with a special mode of life; it also reveals that many different groups with settler descent lived in the colony, which triggered the appeal for solidarity within their ranks. An article in the *Sierra Leone Weekly News*, apparently written by a colony resident with settler lineage, underlines the dudgeon of immigrants, as demonstrated in the acidulous critique of the role Mandingo-speakers played in the colonial administration: "[T]he contrast between a British born subject who is entirely amenable to laws ... and a Mandingo who is not amenable and would not hesitate to ... do any unlawful act, is wide ..."[47] Another ruffled colony resident with settler lineage made a blistering observation in an article in *The Sierra Leone Times*. The author states that "many British-born subjects in this place [colony] ... can better represent [the] government ..." than Mandingo-speaking officials.[48] In both articles the description "British born subjects" is used as an identifier to illuminate the distinction between the two groups – British subjects and those referred to as Mandingos.

Other colony residents with similar backgrounds used the Creole identifier infrequently and sparsely in the same period, as revealed in this comment: "[S]ome of the Constables posted ... never carried mail packets themselves to the next Police Station but would ask or employ some passers-by – Creole or Timeneh – to perform the task for them ..."[49] The use of different registers, such as "British subjects," and "Creole," suggests that disparate factions existed among the offspring of settler groups in the colony. Further, the use of Creole in this context implicitly refers to a group with low status, as indicated by the use of the phrase "passers-by." In 1892, an unnerved colony resident wrote a letter to the editor of the *Sierra Leone Times* highlighting the following concern: "[T]he inspector general does not care to have listed any Creole in the civil branch of the Constabulary."[50] The designation Creole is again used as an identity category with a seemingly neutral characterization. Several years later, another article appeared in the same newspaper that highlighted the scarcity of laborers and porters "who call themselves Creoles – i.e.

[46] Thomas Spear, "Neo-Traditionalism and the Limits of Invention in British Colonial Africa." *Journal of African History*, 44 (2003), p. 23.
[47] *SLWN*, Freetown, April 20, 1889.
[48] *SLWN*, Freetown, April 20, 1889.
[49] *SLWN*, Freetown, October 18, 1890,
[50] *The Sierra Leone Times*, Freetown, June 18, 1892. *Sierra Leone Times* is henceforth abbreviated as *SLT*.

Sierra Leoneans ..."[51] In addition, a conspicuously indignant columnist commented that "the Creole labourer, rather than the indigent Sierra Leonean ... scorns the idea" of serving his fellow countrymen rather than serving foreigners.[52] The contrasting use of the Creole identifier contains several implications. First, it shows that "Creoles" also meant "Sierra Leonean" in this context. Second, the quotes suggest that those referred to as Creoles formed part of the labor force, and did not constitute the elite establishment, in contrast to the claims made by Fyfe and Porter. Third, it is clear that the designation Sierra Leonean did not encompass indigenes from ethnic groups like the Temne-, Mende-, Limba-, Loko-, and Mandingo-speakers, even though these ethnic communities lived in the territory before the establishment of the colony, particularly Temne-speakers, who leased the land that became the Sierra Leone Colony. Finally, the quotations indicate that the compellation Creoles refers to "descendants of the Liberated Africans ... born here [colony] ..."[53] This strengthens Skinner and Harrell-Bond's point that Creole carried "different meanings during the course of the [nineteenth] century ..."; that is, the designation "applied to different groups and that it was not adopted as a general definition of identity by one group."[54] Skinner and Harrell-Bond strongly aver that many different groups in the Sierra Leone Colony described themselves as Creoles. In other words, the term "Creole" did not apply to any particular group.

Moreover, an analysis of the demographic outlook of the colony in 1900 underscores the point that descendants of settlers did not develop a fixed community or a symmetrical identifier. The census data reveals that:

In Freetown alone are to be found representatives of over 40 such tribes and dialects – the principal of which may be said to be Eboe, the Aku, the Settler, the Maroon, the Nova Scotian, the American, the Liberian, the West Indian, Timney, Soso, Limbah, Jollofe, Mendi, Serakoulie, Mandingo, Popo, Congo, Lagosian, Fante, Bagga, Kotokori, Gallinas, Moco, Ashantee.[55]

The census does not mention the existence of any group described as Creole, though the popular media used the term spasmodically. The census report also highlights the existence of numerous languages spoken in the colony, but does not mention the existence of a Creole community:

[51] *SLT*, Freetown, August 24, 1895.
[52] *SLT*, Freetown, March 12, 1892.
[53] *SLT*, Freetown, January 23, 1897.
[54] Skinner and Harrell-Bond, "Creoles," p. 187.
[55] *SLT*, Freetown, February 17, 1900.

Our city represents one huge caravanserai made up of incongruous elements, which are bound to remain conflicting. As an inevitable result we are no nearer the obtention of one uniformed recognized language that were before. To make your self understood, you are bound to have smattering of at least five different languages. The Timiney language appears to be the only one that bids fair to outlive the others. You are nowhere if you don't know it. Our women speak it far more fluently than they do either Aku or Ebo and with the large Mercantile firms, I do not know if a clerk who has a knowledge of say Soso, Mandingo, Foulah and Timney languages, would not hold a better passport than even if he graduated at Durham and took a double-first. I mean no insult whatsoever.[56]

It is reasonable to maintain that Creole identity, as portrayed by Luke, Porter, Peterson, Fyfe, and others, did not become a bound cultural entity. Notwithstanding the fact that the census does not mention the existence of a Creole community, it also observes that this does not mean that "Creoles are dying away," rather they are "gradually making way for Sierra Leoneans" in the future.[57] The ambiguous use of Creole and Sierra Leoneans in the report suggests that the identity of colony residents with settler descent became inconstant, multiple and mutable throughout the nineteenth and mid-twentieth centuries. Clearly, prominent individuals of settler descent carried different identities based on social and political happenstance.

A. J. Shorunkeh-Sawyerr, a prominent merchant and barrister widely perceived as a descendant of liberated Africans, shifted his identity on many occasions. In a speech he gave to a forum, he states: "there was a time in the annals of the settlement when a little Sierra Leonean might kick a Timneh or Soso with impunity."[58] Added to this, in 1893, when Creole society should have been fairly well established as a cultural entity, Shorunkeh-Sawyerr again wrestled with his identity in a revealing fashion. He denotes that colony residents with settler lineage were:

Mainly the descendants of various West African tribes who were set free here [from] slavery by British philanthropy about the year 1787 and thereafter; they are products of the current century, for before then the Sierra Leone native do not form one of the constituent populations of Africa. They are Black Englishmen.[59]

Shorunkeh-Sawyerr interchangeably uses "Sierra Leone native" and "Black Englishmen" as identifiers. He asserts that "the Sierra Leonean therefore, white or black is an Englishman."[60] It is evident that he is

[56] *SLT*, Freetown, May 20, 1893. Paragraph break suppressed.
[57] *SLT*, Freetown, September 29, 1900.
[58] Christopher Fyfe, *Sierra Leone Inheritance* (London: Oxford University Press, 1964), p. 200.
[59] *SLWN*, Freetown, March 11, 1893.
[60] *SLWN*, Freetown, March 11, 1893.

stressing the historic connection between Britain and descendants of settlers and hence his use of "Black Englishmen." Aside from this, the mode
of dress adopted by descendants of settler groups reflected their ties with
Britain and/or Western culture:

We feel that of all the peoples in the British possessions none can be more loyal
than the people of Sierra Leone. And why? Because we are not a conquered
nation ... but we are a people born and fostered by the British Nation whom we
can regard and own as our parents and to whom we look for instruction, advice,
guidance and advancement in the same manner as other British subjects born
in England.[61]

Clearly, descendants of settlers believed that living, dressing, and acting
like Englishmen signified their degree of enlightenment and civilization.
Britain therefore became the focus of attention for educated progenies
of settlers, who saw it as their second home, where they completed their
education. An editorial in a widely read newspaper criticized the special
relationship between Britain and Sierra Leone: "[T]he ideas of many
in our colony are 'narrow, crabbed and confined,' and a few months'
residence in England among Englishmen will tend to round off those
angularities in our character."[62]

The available historical documents reveal that designations such as
Black Englishmen and Sierra Leonean excluded other colony inhabitants, like those the census data recorded as "Timney, Soso, Limbah
and Mendi."[63] Thus it is reasonable to conclude that the use of identity
markers like Black Englishmen served sociocultural and political intend-
ments. When colony residents of settler descent clashed with indigenous
inhabitants, they referred to themselves as British subjects, or Black
Englishmen. Analogously, when they bickered with colonial authorities
over a range of issues including discrimination, they used compellations
such as Sierra Leonean, African, and Sierra Leone natives to demonstrate a sense of African nationalism and to remind British colonialists
that, regardless of their Western orientation, they were Africans and
Sierra Leoneans – an incisive and instrumental use of identity.[64]

Other prominent colony residents with settler descent, such as Isaac
Wallace-Johnson, a firebrand pan-Africanist who launched his West
African Youth League in the colony in 1938, did not embrace the Creole
identity. Wallace-Johnson's youth league "was indeed a genuine movement of the people, or the masses ... Membership was opened to all and

---

[61] *SLWN*, Freetown, May 10, 1890.
[62] *SLWN*, Freetown, June 6, 1885.
[63] *SLT*, Freetown, February 17, 1900.
[64] *SLT*, Freetown, June 18, 1892.

sundry – Creoles and natives, learned and unlearned, rich and poor."[65] The youth league cut across ethnic barriers and appealed to a broad constituency. In fact, as the youth league became popular, Wallace-Johnson criticized and railed against ethnicists and perpetrators of divisive politics, as observed in this afflatus: "[W]e must make it clear ... that this Sierra Leone and Freetown included does not belong as of right to any class or family of people among us not even to those who are called lawyers ... Sierra Leone belongs to us all whether Christian or Muslim, whether born and bred in Freetown or born and bred in outlying villages. The country belongs to us all ..."[66] However, Wallace-Johnson nonplussed his admirers, when he shifted his position from being a fiery nationalist to being an ethnonationalist by joining the National Council of Sierra Leone (NCSL), an ethnic and political organization largely dominated by those portrayed as Creoles.

Another notable resident with settler lineage in the colony, J. C. Zizer, favored the total exclusion of protectorate representatives from colony politics. Zizer used different identifiers to refer to those recorded as Creoles in the historiography. As a descendant of settlers, he fervidly stated that the British government founded the colony "for the sole benefit of the Free Community of Settlers, their Heirs and Successors."[67] In his exposition, Zizer interchangeably used phrases like "free community of settlers" and "Sierra Leone Creoles" to describe descendants of settlers.[68] He recommended that the colonial government should divide Sierra Leone into two territories: "the one side a British territory to be known as the Colony of Sierra Leone, (even as it is known now) and on the other side a British protectorate with separate Legislatures in both colony and protectorate."[69] Ahmed Alhadi, a renowned colony resident of settler descent, supported Zizer's views when he stated that, "the 1951 constitution is repugnant to the laws of England and contrary to what the Free Settlers were led to expect when they laid down their lives for the British people. In fact the 1951 constitution is a stock-in-trade to convert Sierra Leone to another Palestine."[70] Alhadi rejected and excoriated the colonial administration's introduction of the principle of majority rule, which gave the protectorate a demographic advantage. He stated, "[S]o

---

[65] Edward Blyden III, "Sierra Leone: The Pattern of Constitutional Change, 1924–1951" (PhD Dissertation, Harvard University, 1959), p. 168.
[66] *SLWN*, Freetown, June 17, 1939.
[67] *SLWN*, Freetown, August 3, 1950.
[68] *SLWN*, Freetown, August 3, 1950.
[69] Joseph J. Bangura, "Identity Formation and Ethnic Invention: A Case Study of the Creoles, 1870–1961" (Dalhousie University, Unpublished MA thesis), 2001, p. 104.
[70] Bangura, "Ethnic Invention," p. 106.

far as we in the colony are concerned this policy is tantamount to a negative democracy tantalizing the hopes of the Free Settlers, their heirs and
successors, enshrined and raised in the Treaty of 22nd August, 1788 and
then dashed their 200 years old aspirations into nothingness."[71] Unlike
Zizer, Alhadi used the phrase "free settlers" as an identity marker, but
did not use the Creole appellative. Corollary to this, during the swear-
ing-in ceremony of Justice C.E. Wright as Chief Justice, C.D. Hotobah
During described as a descendant of settlers markedly observed that
"Mr. Wright sitting on the Bench today justifies our wish that whenever there are Africans capable of holding high positions in this colony,
they should be given the opportunity to do so;" he proclaimed himself
and the newly installed Supreme Court Judge as Africans.[72] The statement highlights the convenient use of the identifier "African," given the
nature of the ceremony which occasioned its deployment. In fact, an
ally of Hotobah-During, Dr. Herbert C. Bankole-Bright, also viewed as
a steely conservative, a medical practitioner and the head of the NCSL,
portrayed himself as a descendant of settlers. In the foreword he wrote
to Alhadi's pamphlet, Bankole-Bright stated that justice would be done
to "descendants of these settlers [before] the heavens should fall."[73] He
did not use the designation Creole to describe himself or other colony
residents of settler descent. In all, it is revealing that members of the elite
establishment, such as Shorunkeh-Sawyerr, Alhadi, Hotobah-During,
and Bankole-Bright, did not identify themselves as Creole or Krio, as
Porter, Wyse (Bankole-Bright's biographer), and others unabashedly
assert.[74]

Aside from concerns over immigration, which prompted descendants
of settlers to deploy assorted identity markers to distinguish themselves
from other residents in the colony and protectorate, concerns over racism also provoked a contentious discourse on identity. Though many
descendants of settlers capriciously and alternately portrayed themselves
as Black Englishmen and British subjects, many suffered discrimination from the colonial authorities. This is because they realized that their
demonstrated absorption of Western values did not shield them against
racist discrimination.[75] Such auto-reflective efforts resulted in the formation of the Reform Movement in 1887, with the sole purpose of inculcat-
ing and promoting their lost African identity. To entrench the principles

---

[71] "Ethnic Invention," p. 107.
[72] *SLWN*, Freetown. April 5 1947
[73] Bangura, "Ethnic Invention," p. 107.
[74] See Wyse, *H. C. Bankole-Bright.*
[75] Leo Spitzer, "Sierra Leone Creole Reactions to Westernization, 1870–1925"
(Unpublished PhD Dissertation, University of Wisconsin, 1969), p. 166.

of the movement, the inaugural president, William J. Davis, changed his European-sounding name to an African-sounding one – Orishatukeh Faduma – a name derived from his Yoruba ancestry.[76] Following Davis's lead, A. E. Metzger became Kufileh Tuboku-Metzger, while Claude George assumed the name Esu Biyi, and Isaac Augustus Johnson became Algerine Kefallah Sankoh. The movement partially failed due to internal dissension: "[U]nless these names had been given to Mr. Davis by his parents and despised in his ignorance, but valued in his intelligence he may be regarded as guilty of great indiscretion in his selection."[77] In rejecting the criticism, Kufileh Tuboku-Metzger states:

Those who censured Faduma for changing a name by which he had been known from his birth should remember that every one of our Liberated Negro Parents had a name given him in the land of his nativity … with full meaning. When transported through the baneful traffic of the Slave Trade to this land, that name was exchanged for a foreign one as void of meaning and insignificant to him, as his native name full of meaning and significance.[78]

To complement the reform movement, some of its members established the Dress Reform Society. Founders of both movements believed that a change in name must be accompanied by a change in the manner of dress. Therefore, some male members changed their dress from the "European waist-coat, collar and tie" to an African "gown and under-tunic," and "*agbada*." On the other hand, female members of the movement changed their apparel to *lappa* and *bubu*.[79] The change in the names and dress culture of members of the Dress Reform Society and Reform Movement speak to what J. D. Y. Peel refers to as "cultural imperialism" adopted by the Yoruba in the late nineteenth and twentieth centuries. Peel asserts that in response to "racial discrimination and social exclusion as well as to the disparagement of their culture and collective achievements, educated or 'bourgeois' Africans reasserted their dignity as a race/nation by a new insistence on the worth of what was distinctive of them."[80] Like descendants of settlers in the Sierra Leone Colony, the Yoruba also "changed their European names to Yoruba ones" in response to European discriminatory tendencies.[81] The Dress Reform Society, like the Reform Movement, faced withering opposition from some of their more conservative compatriots.

[76] Moses N. Moore, *Orishatukeh Faduma: Liberal Theology and Evangelical Pan-Africanism, 1857–1946* (London: Scarecrow Press, 1996), p. 40.
[77] *SLWN*, Freetown, August 13, 1887.
[78] *SLWN*, September 24 1887.
[79] Spitzer, *Reactions*, p. 176.
[80] J. D. Y. Peel, *Religious Encounter and the Making of the Yoruba* (Bloomington: Indiana University Press, 1999), p. 279.
[81] Peel, *Religious Encounter*, 279.

Many critics questioned the virtue of abandoning the waistcoat for the "country cloth." Despite the momentariness of the two movements, their impact lingered, as some liberal and reform minded colony residents of settler descent decided to syncretize tradition and modernity by adopting a hybrid culture – they combined European and African cultures. The hallmark of this hybridity led to the simultaneous adoption of European mystical institutions, such as the freemasons and esoteric African societies such as *Ogoogoo*, represented as *Egungun* in the literature, *Gunugunu, Hunters' Societies and Geledeh*.[82] These social institutions and/or associations, particularly the *Ogoogoo*, captured the imagination of admirers and aspiring members. The admiring public became besotted with the serape worn by the association's coryphees as captured in this comment: "[T]he images, dressed in their long robes with a net or wooden mask over the face, parade the streets, jumping about, uttering sentences in an artificial voice and accompanied by friends who keep the bystanders at a distance with their long wands. They are treated with great respect ..."[83] This development flustered colonial authorities, especially the acting governor, Lord Moyne, who proposed an ordinance to "declare certain societies to be unlawful societies and to provide for matters connected therewith."[84] The conclusion to draw from the ambivalence experienced by members of the Reform Movement and Dress Reform Society speaks to the inherent difficulty descendants of settlers faced in carving out a vertical cultural path.

The declaration of a protectorate over the hinterland of Sierra Leone in 1896, and the subsequent adoption of various constitutional provisions that entrenched the principle of majority rule, also strongly influenced the discourse on identity in the colony. It is noteworthy that the colonial administration declared a protectorate over the hinterland at the instigation of descendants of settlers. Hargreaves states that many colony residents clamored for the declaration of a protectorate over the hinterland, because they believed that "the colony could only prosper if its trade was assured of dependent markets among the interior peoples," and the delay by the British in declaring a protectorate led some to believe that "had its settlers been Europeans, this would have been secured long before."[85] The declaration of a protectorate over the hinterland resulted in uniting the two erstwhile different territories under one administration.[86] The

[82] Colonial Office 267/683 6/21/1941 32336 (London: National Archives).
[83] CO267/683 1941.
[84] CO267/683 1941.
[85] Hargreaves, *Sir Samuel Lewis*, p. 47.
[86] See Joseph J. Bangura, "Ethnic Entrepreneurism and Constitutional Development in Sierra Leone: A Metahistorical Analysis" In Marda Mustapha and Joseph J. Bangura, eds., *Democratization and Human Security in Postwar Sierra Leone* (New York: Palgrave Macmillam, 2016), pp. 13–34.

declaration of a protectorate heartened business-minded colony residents with settler descent to travel to the protectorate to trade. Though many protectorate inhabitants welcomed and hosted traders from the colony, others responded to them with circumspection and trepidation. Hargreaves notes that when colonial authorities imposed a house tax (erroneously referred to as Hut Tax) on property owners in the protectorate, many of those taxed unfairly blamed those described as Creoles, albeit the latter vehemently opposed the tax. The refusal of colonial authorities to reconsider the imposition of a tax on owners of property in the protectorate resulted in the outbreak of the House Tax War. During this time, many visiting colony traders encountered problems of diverse proportions: they faced murder, molestation, and physical assault from their hosts, who blamed them unjustly for colluding with the colonial administration. Some colony traders also blamed their compatriots for complotting with angry mobs, who targeted their fellow traders. In all these instances, colony traders demonstrated and invoked various identities in the protectorate. This came to the fore with the murder of a colony trader in the protectorate, as sympathizers referred to the murdered man as "a native of Sierra Leone born of Liberated African parents," and further commented that:

From all that we have as yet learnt of any reliable character it appears that the murder took place in a town named Mongray by the command of the chief ... and through the instigation of certain malicious Sierra Leoneans residing in the same town ... But be that as it may, the stern facts remain, SAMUEL GEORGE METZGER, a native of Sierra Leone, born of Liberated African parents who were located at, Kissy to all intents and purposes a British subject, educated at Missionary Society for Great Britain among a heathen tribe to labour for its conversion to the Christian faith has been murdered; his own countrymen, British subjects like himself, participating in, if not originating, the murder ..."[87]

It is interesting to note that the use of "Sierra Leonean" in this context excludes non-descendants of settlers such as the Temne-, Limba-, Mandingo-, Mende-, Loko-, and Fula-speakers, who also lived in the colony and protectorate. The author of the article assumed that all colony residents with settler genealogy should stand united against people in the protectorate because, as "Sierra Leoneans," "British subjects" and "natives of Sierra Leone" they all belonged on the same side. In another instance, colony traders in the protectorate bemoaned what they depicted as the "Massacre of Sierra Leoneans by Mendi war boys" and further noted the brutality and inhumanity of Mende-speakers, who the

[87] *SLWN*, Freetown, August 26, 1899.

author criticized for "their desire to kill all Sierra Leoneans whom they suspect as having lent aid to the government in the collection of the Hut Tax."[88] Closely related to this, an article in the *Sierra Leone Times* stated that: "[W]hereas except in self defence, the Timinis killed only two of three British Subjects, and were severely dealt with by Bai Bureh for so doing, the Mendis with less excuse or without any excuse, killed hundreds."[89] Parallel to the grievous picture portrayed about the victimization of Sierra Leoneans, a colony resident who probably witnessed the murder of his compatriots observed that: "[N]otwithstanding the prejudicial feelings exhibited against our race and country ... I am glad to say that we are loyal British subjects and no one can induce us in vain words to do anything that is contrary to law and order."[90] In light of this, it is tenable to point out that if those described as Creole had a homogenous identity, the self-image they depicted about themselves in the colony and protectorate would have been linear and less shifty.

With the merger of the colony and the protectorate into one administrative entity, colonial authorities established two separate categories of citizenship. The administration designated colony residents with settler descent as de facto British citizens, while inhabitants of the protectorate became de jure "British Protected Persons."[91] The colonial administration also enacted a series of constitutional provisions for administrative and political purposes between 1863 and 1961. The various constitutions established legislative and executive councils with considerable African representations on both councils. Representation on the legislative council resulted in persistent caviling between descendants of settlers who became key political players and protectorate elites.[92] The adoption of the various constitutions ergo influenced the incessant debate on identity, as squabbling over the eligibility of protectorate representatives on both the legislative and executive councils continued unabated.[93] Editorials in colony-based newspapers carried captious vilifications of the constitutional provisions that allowed traditional chiefs to represent their chiefdoms on the legislative council. Shorunkeh-Sawyer, in his opposition to the appointment of chiefs as representatives on the legislative council, argued that "the power wielded in the protectorate by the District

88 *SLWN*, May 7, 1898.
89 *SLT*, Freetown, February 25, 1899.
90 *SLWN*, Freetown, June 18, 1898.
91 See Bangura, "Ethnic Entrepreneurism."
92 Gershon Collier, *Experiment in Democracy in an African Nation* (New York: New York University Press, 1970), pp. 10–11.
93 John Cartwright, *Politics in Sierra Leone, 1947–1967* (Toronto: University of Toronto Press, 1970), p. 43.

Commissioner is great; in the protectorate, the District Commissioner is a Governor; being such a Governor, it seems to me that to bring him ... is simply to muzzle the chiefs as to their real feelings and wishes ... I am concerned that the chiefs come to this council, but they should come under healthy auspices."[94] Similarly, E. S. Beoku-Betts, a colony elite perceived to have settler ancestry, vehemently rejected the idea that chiefs should sit on the same council with colony representatives: "[F]rom a constitutional point of view an anomaly has been created, for so long as the protectorate remains such, the Paramount Chiefs are aliens and not British subjects; and it is contrary to the fundamental principle of the British Constitution for aliens to legislate for British subjects ..."[95] This quotation reinforces Edward Wilmsen's observation about ethnic identities in Africa: "[E]thnicity appears to come into being most frequently in just such circumstances when individuals are persuaded of a need to confirm a collective sense of identity in the face of threatening economic, political or social forces."[96] The colonial administration established constitutional rule in Sierra Leone against opposition from colony-based politicians with settler genealogy. In 1947, Governor Hubert Stevenson, who replaced Governor Slater, implemented the principle of constitutional and majority rule by expanding the number of African representatives on both councils. His determination to adopt a new constitution, with expanded legislative and executive councils, angered colony-based elites, who took every chance to flay the idea. In upbraiding the constitutional provisions, Hotobah-During asserted that, "I am again to call the attention of my people that as British Subjects it is not a question of protectorate majority or equal minority entering our legislative council and vote with us in any matter pertaining to the colony proper and vice versa nor can we ... vote in any matter pertaining to the protectorate."[97] Hotobah-During's argument was that the protectorate and the colony are separate, as they were culturally distinct, which nullified the rationale of the constitutional provisions. Apart from Hotobah-During's reprobation of the constitution, groups with settler ancestry, such as those referred to as the Nova Scotian and Maroon Descendants Association (NSMDA), also objurgated the constitutional provisions Governor Stevenson introduced. In a resolution they adopted at a meeting, the members stated that they felt "alarmed at the proposals contained in Sessional Paper No.2 of

---

[94] *SLWN*, August 24, 1924.
[95] *SLWN*, August 23, 1924.
[96] Edward Wilmsen and Patrick McAlister, *The Politics of Difference: Ethnic Premises in a World of Power* (Chicago, Illinois: University of Chicago Press, 1996), p. 5.
[97] *SLWN*, Freetown, August 5, 1950.

1950 whereby the legislative council, a British colonial institution is to be dominated by foreign elements from the protectorate of Sierra Leone who differ from the colony inhabitants in culture, outlook and legal status."[98] Like Hotobah-During, the members of NSMDA believed that the colony and the protectorate were separate entities and therefore representatives of both territories should not share the same political space. It should be pointed out that the criticism by members of NSMDA ran contrary to the hand of friendship they extended to the governor when he assumed office. In 1948, in a visit to the governor, the leaders of the association stated that, "we the undersigned representatives of the Nova Scotian and Maroon Descendants Association, the descendants of the original Colonists, brought here by British Philanthropy in the eighteenth century, take this opportunity of extending to Your Excellency ..." a warm welcome.[99] They also averred that "the association, the membership of which is strictly limited to those who are able to prove their descent, was founded in 1947, is fully registered and governed by rules ..."[100] Although the members of NSMDA claimed to be "descendants of the original colonists," they identified themselves as the Nova Scotian and Maroon Descendants Association, rather than Creole, which undermines Porter's claim that "by the 1870s the term [Creole] had come to mean Settlers, Liberated Africans and their descendants."[101] It is thus plausible to assume that Porter and others merely imagined the idea of being Creole, because the people they described as such never consistently identified with the designation ascribed to them.

In response to the astringent criticisms directed at the provisions of the constitution he introduced, Governor Stevenson audaciously vociferated that "the Creoles have no firm roots in the country outside the colony peninsula," and he dauntlessly criticized their condescending view that protectorate inhabitants belonged to "an inferior race."[102] Though critics of the constitutional provisions did not use the Creole appellative, the governor used it to broadly refer to the various descendants of settlers. The Reverend R.W. Sorenson, MP, expressed similar sentiments about those he depicts as Creoles. He observes that: "The Creoles of the colony, descended from African Settlers from America and with over 150 years of contact with European culture and tradition, have inevitably exercised an influence in Sierra Leone out of all proportions to their numerical

[98] *SLWN*, Freetown, August 26, 1950.
[99] *SLWN*, Freetown, October 9, 1948.
[100] *SLWN*, Freetown, October 9, 1948.
[101] Porter, *Creoledom*, 1963, p. 63.
[102] CO 267/683, 32375/1943.

strength."[103] Sorenson's characterization of the Creoles is markedly different from their depiction in the historical literature.

Homologous to the above, the colony-based NCSL also exposed the asymmetrical identity of descendants of settlers. Members of the NCSL claim that they established the organization because of "the failure of Colony groups to alter materially the substance of the 1947 constitutional proposals."[104] This quotation acknowledges the fact that descendants of settlers belonged to disparate groups in the colony, which also undermines the view perpetuated in the historiography that descendants of settler groups described as Creoles developed a unique community with a homogenous culture. The NCSL served as the mouthpiece of colony politicians; it excluded indigenous communities based in the colony, such as the Temne-, Limba-, Mende-, and Loko-speakers. The NCSL also rejected the merger between the colony and the protectorate:

Owing to the present Political Crisis in which the people of the Colony (The Descendants of the owners by purchase and conquest of this Settlement) find themselves consequent on our local Government attempting to infringe on our prescriptive Rights by endeavouring [sic] to bring into Force a New legislative Council which is to have foreign majority to pass Laws for the British Colony.[105]

To bolster its finances, the NCSL implored "all Sierra Leoneans and their friends ... for contribution towards a National Council Fund."[106] Some members of the NCSL perceived protectorate representatives as foreigners "[p]repondering in our Legislative Council" who had no right to do so.[107] These comments elicited pungent backlash from protectorate elites or their apologists.

In a sharply worded letter to the editor of the *Weekly News*, the thunderstruck author, M. O. Allen, observed that, "we do not mean to adopt an unfriendly attitude to you in return but ... we shall very much loathe to associate with a community which imagines itself to be superior to us and in that respect we would very much welcome a separate legislative council provided our revenue is not being utilized in the colony ..."[108]

---

[103] CO 267/698 1950.
[104] Martin Kilson, *Political Change in a West African State: A Study of the Modernization Process in Sierra Leone* (Cambridge: Harvard University Press, 1966), p. 225.
[105] CO 267/698, 32810/9/4/51 "To All Sierra Leoneans and Friends at Home and Abroad" (London: National Archives, 1951).
[106] CO 267/698/8, 32810/9/4/51, "To All Sierra Leoneans."
[107] Kilson, *Political Change*, p. 226. See also Bangura, "Constitutional Development and Ethnic Entrepreneurism."
[108] *SLWN*, Freetown, October 16, 1948.

The de facto leader of protectorate politicians, Dr. Milton Margai, also responded to the controversy provoked by the proposed constitution and strongly objected to the patronizing comments from the leadership of the NCSL. He passionately stated that:

Sierra Leone, which has been the foremost of all the West African colonies, is still saddled with [an] archaic constitution with official majority. The reason for this backwardness is evidently due to the fact that our forefathers, I very much regret to say, had given shelter to a handful of foreigners, who have no will to cooperate with us and imagine themselves to be our superiors because they are aping the Western mode of living and have never breathed the true spirit of independence.[109]

Alarmed by the prospects of losing political hegemony and relevance in an urbanized colony, descendants of settler groups in the colony increasingly gravitated toward a symmetrical identity – Creole. As the identity became vertical in the 1950s, colonial officials, African intellectuals and culture brokers continued to attach meaning to it, and phrases like the "Creoles of Sierra Leone" became inveterately used, as shown in the following acclamation, "the visible evidences of the loyalty of the Creole exist today in the War medals on the breast of our Creole countrymen ... for the defence of the city of Freetown" against the rebellious Mendes.[110] The use of the compellation Creole, wrapped in adulation, reinforces Spear's point that "when colonial and modern elites have got to mobilize values to support their own claims to restricted resources in both traditional and modern sectors ... ethnicity becomes instrumental capable of being invented and manipulated in the service of one social goal or another."[111] Despite the regular use of Creole as an identity category at this time, its overall use remained desultory and inconsistent; this shows that the process of constructing an identity that defined people with settler lineage in the Sierra Leone Colony proved spasmodic, spotty and dialogic throughout the colonial period. Put differently, the available historical documents show that Creole identity remained malleable, multi-dimensional and oscillatory, because several groups of settler descent used multiple identity markers to designate themselves, as demonstrated by the NSMDA in the mid-twentieth century.[112]

---

[109] C.S.O. *Proceedings of the Seventh Meeting* (Freetown: Government Printer, 1950), pp. 27–32.
[110] *SLWN*, Freetown, October 30, 1909.
[111] Thomas Spear and Richard Waller, eds., *Being Massai: Ethnicity and Identity in East Africa* (Athens: Ohio University Press, 1993), p. 15.
[112] *SLWN*, Freetown, August 24, 1924.

In fact, even when the Creole identifier assumed a linear pattern, gate-keepers of the identity scrutinized people who claimed to be Creole. Given this, the gatekeepers delineated two sets of Creoles – proper Creoles and factitious Creoles. An article written by a concerned resident decried those who claimed to be Creole for instrumental reasons: "There is no doubt that some hooligans of the Creole set took away Palmoil … but I stand against those who propound that the Creoles, the proper Creoles took away fancy goods and other markets besides those for food. A good many of the people in Freetown who claim to be Creoles are Mendis."[113] It can be assumed that factitious Creoles referred to people who claimed to be Creole for instrumental reasons, such as those the article described as Mendis. Did "proper Creole" denote people born to parents who claimed to be Creole? Or did it mean people with shared historical experience? The article did not explain what "proper Creole" meant. This underscores Bill Bravman's point about identity in colonial Kenya, particularly Taita identity, which proved malleable and muta-ble. To preserve their dominance over the community, old men defined Taita identity "as a community of affective belonging that simultaneously pressured lineage members to adhere to a body of 'proper' beliefs and behaviors."[114] Those who failed to comply with the edictal requirements of proper Taita ways incurred a penalty: they suffered ostracization from Taita society. In the Sierra Leone Colony, it is unclear if those perceived as factitious Creoles faced consequences for not being proper Creoles. Parallel to this, while the educated Yoruba embarked on cultural imperi-alism to consolidate Yoruba identity, descendants of settler lineage in the Sierra Leone Colony flocked in and out of multiple identities throughout the nineteenth and mid-twentieth centuries; their identities ranged from Creole, Sierra Leonean, Sierra Leonese, Sierra Leone natives, African, and British subjects, to Black Englishmen.

In view of the above, it is justifiable to assert that Creole or Krio iden-tity did not develop a fixed community with primal values, in spite of the fierce determination by African elites, colonial authorities, the popular media, and culture brokers to ascribe a vertical identity to them; the iden-tity continually shifted, based on social, political, and economic motives. Historical sources show that when the relationship between groups of settler descent and the British became cordial, the former used identi-fiers like British subjects, and Black Englishmen, to demonstrate their assimilation and mastery of British values. The use of British subjects as

---

[113] *The Sierra Leone Guardian*, Freetown, August 22, 1919.
[114] Bill Bravman, *Making Ethnic Ways: Communities and their Transformations in Kenya, 1800–1950* (Portsmouth, New Hampshire: Heinemann, 1998), p. 253.

an identity category indicates that the carriers of this identity wanted to show their cultural superiority over indigenous communities in the colony. By the same token, when those described as British subjects visited the protectorate to trade, they invoked nationalist fervor by referring to themselves as Sierra Leoneans, or Sierra Leone natives, to demonstrate their African ancestry to their host and to British expatriates in the protectorate, such as the District Commissioners. On other occasions, when the colonial administration discriminated against them, they formed the Dress Reform Society and the Reform Movement.

Conclusion

In his work on colonial Zanzibar, Jonathon Glassman shows the contingent nature of ethnic identities in Africa. He states that: "Swahili-speakers simultaneously perceive themselves as Arab, Persian and/or Indian as well as African," based on happenstance.[115] Glassman effectively illustrates that Swahili identity, like other ethnic identities in Africa, shifted continuously over time according to the players involved in the process.[116] Like Glassman, the literature on ethnic identities in Africa indicates that identities can be primordial, constructed and/or instrumental. On account of this, instrumentalists show that ethnic identities in Africa can be mobilized in specific circumstances for fluky and propitious reasons. That is, instrumentalist literature "has been central to demolishing the fallacy that ethnic identities are primal and inborn."[117] Primordialists, per contra, explain identities in terms of ancestral lineage and connate values. The works of Fyfe, Porter, Wyse, and others discussed in this chapter can be situated within the ambit of the primordialist discourse. These scholars portray Creole identity as primal and predicated on a common history, bound culture, and shared experience. This is why Porter asserts that colony residents of settler descent he describes as Creoles "developed a group solidarity and class consciousness and this unifying force meant that there was no unnecessary dissipation of potential and that all worked for the development of society. Their compactness and concentration, mostly in Freetown made them increasingly conscious of group interests."[118] This study has shown that the group portrayed as Creoles did not develop group solidarity, as Porter contends. His claim that the

---

[115] Jonathon Glassman, *War of Words, War of Stones: Racial Thought and Violence in Colonial Zanzibar* (Bloomington: Indiana University Press, 2011), p. 5.
[116] Glassman, *War of Words*, pp. 5–6.
[117] Glassman, *War of Words*, p. 23.
[118] Porter, *Creoledom*, p. 15.

Creoles developed group solidarity is further undermined by the formation in the mid-twentieth century of the Nova Scotian and Maroon Descendants Association, whose members portrayed themselves as descendants "of the original colonists"; they never identified themselves as Creoles. Aside from this, the lack of group solidarity among descendants of settler groups also became conspicuous during the House Tax tohubohu in the protectorate, when colony traders with settler lineage passionately appealed for solidarity among those they perceived as their compatriots.

By the same token, the use of the extant compellation Krio, constructed by Wyse to describe groups delineated by some scholars as Creole, is a misnomer. Wyse states that Krio, a purported derivative of the Yoruba word *Kiriyo* and/or *Akiriyo*, is a corrupt form of Creole. He postulates that the Yoruba word *Akiriyo*, which denotes the movement of people from place to place, captures some of the characteristic features of scions of settler groups, who became accustomed to the act of visiting relations and associates after Sunday worship. On the basis of this, he and others contend that Krio, rather than Creole, best captures and represents the shared history and pristine values of people with settler lineage and others who lived in the Sierra Leone Colony.[119] Historical records clearly contradict this claim; the records show that no community in the colony used the appellative Krio either as a horizontal and/or vertical identity in the nineteenth and mid-twentieth centuries. It is therefore reasonable to assume that Wyse substituted Krio for Creole to distinguish the so-called Creoles of Sierra Leone from other Creole communities in former slave-holding territories in the Americas and other parts of the world. His determination to construct the Krio designation as the true identity of those delineated as Creoles won him admiration among many people who claimed to be descendants of settlers in Sierra Leone and the diaspora. Many of his admirers hailed him as a hero, in spite of the scraggy evidence he adduces to support his Krio myth. Furthermore, a careful analysis of the works of imaginers and constructionists of the Krio compellation indicates that they carefully supplanted historical evidence with hermeneutics. This is particularly evident in the title of Wyse's first major work, *The Krio of Sierra Leone: An Interpretive History*. The work is based largely on strenuous interpretation of analogical evidence or secondary

---

[119] See Akintola J. G. Wyse, *The Krio of Sierra Leone: An Interpretive History* (Washington, D.C.: Howard University Press, 1990); David John Harris, *Sierra Leone: A Political History* (London: Oxford University Press, 2014); and Gibril Cole, *The Krio of West Africa: Islam, Creolization, Colonialism in the Nineteenth Century* (Athens, Ohio: Ohio University Press, 2013).

sources. This is why Ranger warns that "the greatest strength of ethnicity as an ideology is that once it has been invented or imagined it becomes virtually impossible to imagine any other basis of human association."[120] Ipso facto, it is instructive to draw attention to the acuminous comment of Fyfe, who observed that, "over a brief, period he [Wyse] firmly outlawed the time-honoured 'Creole' and 'Creoledom' and established instead 'Krio' and 'Kriodom.'"[121] He clairvoyantly forewarned that, "if Kriodom does survive, it will be thanks to the creator of its myth."[122] Clearly, Kriodom survived and is replete in the extant historiography despite the use of blotch-laden evidence by its proponents. Added to this, Skinner and Harrell-Bond also make clear that many of the traits Wyse attribute to those he refers to as Krio are found in other groups in West Africa. Simply put, the use of the Krio compellation is a myth, and its persistent deployment in the literature is grossly misleading! In sum, it is evident that African intellectuals played a primary role in the construction of ethnic identities: "African intellectuals filled ethnicity with real imagination and moral content."[123] Put another way, the use of the Krio designation in lieu of the problematic appellative Creole is baseless; it is not supported by the available historical evidence. Hence, Spear's bon mot is in order here:

Ethnicity has, thus, been continuously reinterpreted and reconstructed over time in such a way as to appear timeless and legitimate and it has been deployed by contending parties in complex ways of selectivity and representation that lay at the core of peoples' collective historical consciousness and struggles for power, meaning and access to resources.[124]

Against this backdrop, it is essential that historians use evidence to engage the past, regardless of whether the evidence supports a furtive or overt motive. In other words, good history is about *what happened, when it happened and how it happened.* In succinct terms, history is about "what," "when," and "how." Good history is not about *what may have happened* or *what could have happened* or *what should have happened.* Some historians often speculate on why events happened in contradistinction to the available historical evidence. That is, in the face of deficient evidence, some

---

[120] Terence Ranger, "Concluding Comments" in Paris Yeroes ed., *Ethnicity and Nationalism in Africa: Constructivist Reflections and Contemporary Politics* (London: Macmillan 1999), p. 134.

[121] Christopher Fyfe, "Akintola Wyse," p. 27.

[122] Christopher Fyfe, "Akintola Wyse," p. 32.

[123] Terence Ranger, "The Nature of Ethnicity in Africa: Lessons from Africa" in Edward Mortimer with Robert Fine, eds., *People, Nation and State: The Meaning of Ethnicity and Nationalism* (London: C. Bianis, 1999), p. 20.

[124] Spear, "Neo-Traditionalism," p. 24.

historians choose to fill in the gaps with speculation, particularly in support of an objective. However, such speculative analysis undermines the tenet of good history, because good history is based on valid evidence; it is not predicated on imagined or analogous evidence. As a matter of fact, Joseph Miller quotes Robin Blackburn, who warns about the danger of the "idols of origins" whereby some historians search for elements in the past assumed to have been known by makers of history, "but in fact usually imagined by the historian."[125] Promoters of the Krio myth imagined that the key players involved in the creation of Creole identity – the mainstream media, colonial authorities, ethnonationalists, culture brokers, and African intellectuals – misconstrued it for Krio identity. By connoting that Creole should have been Krio, the progenitors of the Krio myth reason by analogy – a violation of one of the fundamental principles of good history. Frederick Cooper reinforces this perspective in his article on the African past and its historians. Cooper underlines the distinction between professional and academic history. He states that professional history can be diverse and plural in engaging historical topics, whereas academic history can be effective in blunting predilection, gatekeeping the profession, and drawing on "the variety of conceptions of the past among different publics which is what gives them an audience beyond their peers."[126] He also makes the point that "Historians often write history backwards – from the present to the past ..."[127] Wyse's numerous works on those he calls Krio is speculative and interpretive; he reconstructs the past through the lens of the present, particularly when the historical evidence he adduces is fragmentary and elusive. Such an approach to doing history is anachronistic because "projecting communities of different sorts back is ... fallacious."[128] The substitution of Creole for Krio is an example of doing history backwards. This study is therefore a major step in debunking the Krio myth and its persistent use in the prevailing literature.

All in all, the study shows that residents of the Sierra Leone Colony with settler lineage did not develop a fixed community, nor did they carry a horizontal identity in the colonial period. In fact, an observer points out that: "[W]e do hear much of the term 'Creole' now-a-days and perhaps it is reasonable that we don't, for the 'Creoles' are not in it, the Freetown of to-day."[129] The author of this article highlights the

---

[125] Joseph C. Miller, *The Problem of Slavery as History: A Global Approach* (New Haven, Connecticut: Yale University Press, 2012), p. 6.
[126] Frederick Cooper, "Africa's Past and Africa's Historians." *Canadian Journal of African Studies* 34 (2) (2000), p. 307.
[127] Cooper, "Africa's Past," p. 307.
[128] Cooper, "Africa's Past," p. 326.
[129] *SLT*, Freetown, September 29, 1900.

fact that no community used the Creole appellative as an identifier. This statement is in line with Skinner and Harrell-Bond's point that "no self-conscious, self-identified Creole community" emerged in the nineteenth century.[130] Expressed differently, a careful examination of the available historical records shows that no self- identified Krio community developed in the nineteenth and mid-twentieth centuries.

In light of the foregoing, this study proposes the use of the compellation "Freetonian" to refer to people defined by residence that some called Creole and others Krio in the dominant literature. Roy Lewis describes them as "Freetownese"; however, we believe Freetonian is the more appropriate appellative to use. The available historical documents indicate that residents in the colony with settler ancestry used other identity-markers both in the colony and protectorate. Based on the above, Freetonian is a geographic, not a cultural term and more open-ended and inclusive than any definition of Creole or Krio so far related. An examination of the historical documents reveals that since its founding in the eighteenth century, various groups settled in the Sierra Leone Colony with different identities. Harrell-Bond and others state that "exactly who is a Creole is still open to some question, as all who call themselves Creole would not necessarily be recognized as such by the Creole elite."[131] T. C. Luke's candid observation underscores the point that "the Creole, unhappily lacks cohesion and is sadly lacking in the virtue of co-operation. This defect may largely be due to certain facts in his past history: the difference in outlook and the distinctions existing formerly between various sections of the community, i.e. poor blacks, Nova Scotians, Maroons and Liberated Africans."[132] Further, various religious sects inhabited the colony: the Akus or Mohammedan Creoles and Christians who frequently referred to themselves as Black Englishmen or British subjects. These people had settler lineage, but portrayed themselves differently in public. Since they all lived in colonial Freetown, and most of them used Freetown as their major base in asserting their self-image, it is fitting that we describe them as Freetonians. In other words, this study has shown that the term Creole became one of possible ways of describing Freetonians.

---

[130] Skinner and Harrell-Bond, "Creoles," p. 187.
[131] Barbara Harrell-Bond, David Skinner and Allen Howard, *Community Leadership and the Transformation of Freetown (1801–1976)* (The Hague: Mouton Publishers, 1978), p. 2.
[132] T. C. Luke, "Some Notes on Creoles and their Land," pp. 60–61.

Part II

Beyond the Colonial Sphinx

African Agency in the Making of the Colony

3   Realpolitik and Boundaries of Power: The Temne in Local Administration

The chapter explores the agency of the Temne in local administration, and how they organized themselves around various symbols of authority in the colony. This aspect of the colony's history is significant, because the history of local administration is extensively viewed through the prism of the Municipal Council, or Freetown Corporation/Freetown City Council, run by Freetonians. By equating local or native administration with the Municipal Council, the historical literature downplays the role indigenous ethnic communities played in fostering local governance in this hodgepodge British territory. The chapter shows that local administration and community governance in the colony contributed to the success of the British colonial project in Sierra Leone.

In the mid-nineteenth century, the colony evolved into a cosmopolitan urban space occupied by different ethnicities. In fact, in the early twentieth century, migration to the colony from the protectorate, especially from adjacent towns, increased steadily. Because of this, the colony experienced a rapid surge in its population, which prompted colonial authorities to devise a suitable administrative structure for many ethnic communities incapable of grasping the intricacies of the English legal system. To redress the lacuna, colonial authorities encouraged local administration to foster and maintain the rule of law, by authorizing the election or selection of headmen to administer their ethnic communities. To fully grasp the significant contributions of these local authorities, particularly the dominant non-Freetonian tribal authority described as the Temne Tribal Authority (TTA), it is useful to examine the identity of those recorded as Temne and delineate the process which accompanied the construction of the identity.

Culture Brokers and the Formation of Temne Identity, 1885–1961

Historical sources show that Temne identity became fluid and circumstantial in the late nineteenth century. Oral sources reveal that the term generally referred to speakers of *Theimne* – a Niger-Congo language widely spoken in Sierra Leone and some parts of Guinea. Informants for this study comment that the compellation Temne is a derivative of *Theimne*, which can be a noun or an adjective, depending on the context. However, by the mid-fifteenth century, a group of Temne-speakers migrated to the coast from the hinterland. The migrants quickly attacked, conquered and dislocated Bullom- and Sherbro-speakers – the earliest occupants of the coast. By the mid-nineteenth century, culture brokers, local intellectuals, local elites, religious entrepreneurs and impresarios, among others, conspired to construct a glossy image of being Temne on the territory that later became the Sierra Leone Colony. Oral sources show that being Temne in the colony differed to some extent from being Temne in the protectorate, though the two regional groups remained relatively united with no overt tension between them. Temne elites in the colony used different magnetic variables to help shape and construct Temneness (being Temne and its way of life); these variables included the display of cultural symbols in public, cultural associations such as *Alimania, Ambas Geda*, Temne Progressive Union, *Ariah*, Boys London, and others, financial incentives, and a raft of social programs to lure young men and women from other ethnic communities.[1] In other words, the competition for resources and political power, and the desire for hegemony, led gatekeepers to construct a burnished Temne image in the nineteenth century. The daedal process gave extensive meaning to what it meant to be Temne in the colony, in contrast to what it meant to be Temne in the protectorate. Thus in the Sierra Leone Colony, Temne identity became vertical and symmetrical and was associated with cultural hegemony, pride, a warrior-like persona, a gutsy demeanor, consanguinity, and hereditary claims (imagined or real) to the territory that became colonial Freetown. Added to this, being Temne in the colony also meant bona fide membership of Temne cultural associations. Over a period of time, being Temne transmogrified and broadly meant speakers of *Theimne*. Consequently, gatekeepers became obsessed with the notion of making Temne identity influential and culturally hegemonic. Because local elites and culture brokers deliberately helped shape Temne identity, it became particularly difficult to distinguish between a congenital Temne and a factitious Temne; that is, informants note that over a period of time the distinction between congenital and faux Temne disappeared. Faux Temne constituted those who had a primordial identity, but passed themselves off as Temne, due to their ability to learn and speak *Theimne*.

---

[1] Chief Adikalie Gbonko, interview by Joseph J. Bangura, Freetown, October 5, 2003.

This means that gatekeepers determined those who became Temne particularly in the mid-twentieth century. As a matter of fact, by the mid-twentieth century, Temne identity became a tool of mobilization and coalescence, and proved political, contingent, and circumstantial. Spear reinforces this point about ethnic identities in Africa. He states:

Ethnicity has, thus, been continually reinterpreted and reconstructed over time in such a way as to appear timeless and legitimate and it has been deployed by contending parties in complex processes of selectivity and representation that lay at the core of peoples' collective historical consciousness and struggles for power, meaning and access to resources. It is, then, simultaneously, constructed, primordial and instrumental and therein lies its essential problematic.[2]

Additionally, Spear states that "in recent times when colonial and modern elites have got to mobilize values to support their own claims to restricted resources in both traditional and modern sectors ... ethnicity then becomes instrumental capable of being invented and manipulated in the service of one goal or another."[3] In all, in contrast to Temne identity in the protectorate, which remained largely primordial with dialectal variations, Temne identity in the colony proved instrumental. On account of this, it is worthy to point out that the construction of Temne identity by indigenous elites and local intellectuals in colonial Freetown became one of the few instances where colonial authorities did not influence the invention of an ethnic identity, compared to other historical contexts in Africa.

The available historical records indicate that, since the conquest of the coastal territory, the Temne remained the dominant indigenous group until the arrival of British philanthropists and colonialists. In fact, the Temne continued to be the preponderant non-Freetonian ethnic community in the colony and peninsula towns in the nineteenth and twentieth centuries. Figure 1 gives a picture of the population distribution in the colony in ethnic and gender terms.

Figure 1 shows that, between 1890 and 1931, the Temne became the largest ethnic community in the colony, after the Freetonians. The ascendance of the Temne gave them a social and political advantage.

As indicated in Figure 2, the Temne constituted 29.9% of the population, while Freetonians comprised 20.5%, in the peninsula towns in 1947. Figure 2 also shows that Temne women outnumbered other

[2] Thomas Spear, "Neo-Traditionalism and the Limits of Invention in British Colonial Africa." *Journal of African History*, 44, (2003), p. 24.
[3] Thomas Spear and Richard Waller, eds., *Being Massai: Ethnicity and Identity in East Africa* (Athens, Ohio: Ohio University Press, 1993), p. 15. See also T. C. McCaskie, *History and Modernity in an African, Village, 1850–1950* (Athens, Ohio: Ohio University Press, 2001).

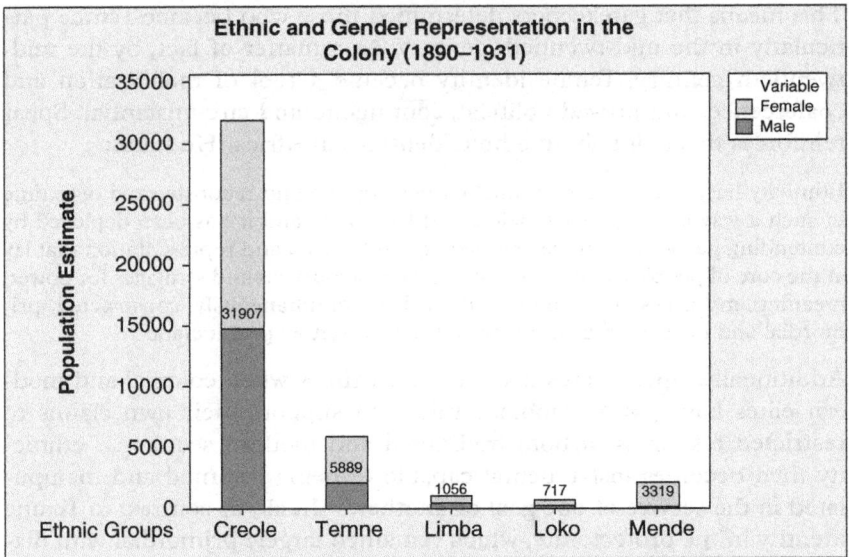

Figure 1 Population Analysis 1890–1931.
Source: *SLWN*, Freetown, October 10, 1931.

women in the same locale in 1947 and 1950. Akin to this, while Temne women constituted about 37.2% of the female population, Freetonian women constituted 27.9%.[4] Oral sources show that Temne women traders worked collectively to optimize their business potential and maximize interests from expenditures, etc.[5]

Table 1 gives the population distribution of Temne and Non-Temne residents in the colony and surrounding areas, before 1931 and in 1947. That is, a simple chi-squared test produced a value of 5796.04 with 1 degree of freedom and a p-value of 0.0. This suggests that the proportion of Temne within the colony and its surrounding areas was significantly different for pre-1931 and for the year 1947. Based on the values, we note that this difference is positive, which supports the claim of the preponderance of the Temne population due to increased migration during the indicated period of time. This further suggests that Temne tribal rulers had significant influence in shaping local administration and fostering good governance in the colony.

[4] Richardson and Collins, *Economic and Social Survey*, pp. 82–85. The report was completed in 1950.
[5] Interviews, Sukainatu Bangura and Adama Kamara.

Table 1 *Population Distribution of Temne and non-Temne in the Colony and Its Environs*

	Temne	Non-Temne
Pre-1931	5889	36999
Year-1947	15651	27582

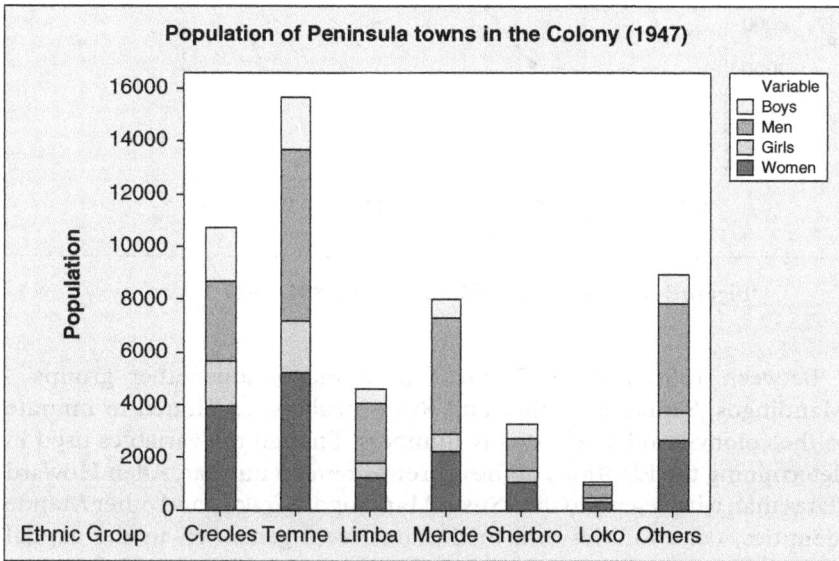

Figure 2 Population of the peninsula towns in the Sierra Leone Colony in 1947.
Source: E. M. Richardson and G. R. Collins, *Economic and Social Survey of the Rural Areas of the Colony of Sierra Leone* (London: Colonial Office Research Department, Unpublished Report, 1951), p. 39.

Figure 3 shows a line graph representing the demographic makeup of the rural areas between 1881 and 1947.[6] It clearly shows the dominance of the Temne ethnic community, in terms of numbers in the rural areas.

[6] E. M. Richardson and G. R. Collins, *Economic and Social Survey of the Rural Areas of the Colony of Sierra Leone* (London: Colonial Office Research Department, Unpublished Report, 1951), pp. 38–39.

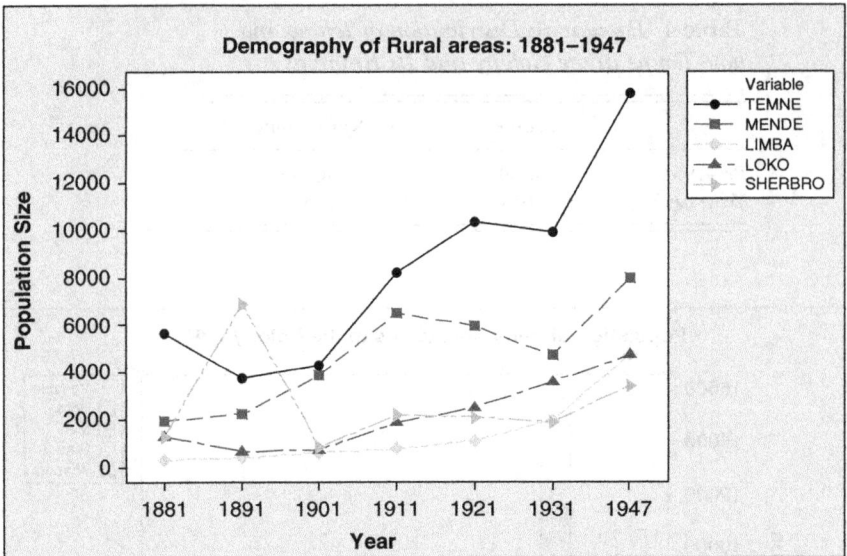

Figure 3   Demography of Rural Areas: 1881–1947.

Between 1890 and 1947, the Temne and various other groups –
Mandingos, Serakules, Fulas, and Susu-speakers, continued to migrate
to the colony in relatively steady numbers. Though the variables used in
determining the identities of these groups remain unclear, Allen Howard
states that, with regard to the "Susu, Mandingo, Serakuli and other Mande
identities, communities and institutions were generated in the capital
of Sierra Leone [Freetown] during the nineteenth and twentieth centuries through negotiations within communities, among communities and
between communities and the British authorities."[7] Against this background, the population of the colony included Freetonians and those the
study describes as indigenous communities – Temne-, Mende-, Limba-,
Loko-, Susu-, Mandingo-, and Fula-speakers. Freetonians densely occupied the central and western regions, while the Temne and others primarily occupied the east-central region, such as Bambara Town, Susan's
Bay, Kissy Village, Ro Kupr, Wellington, Waterloo, Hastings and Kissy
Road, among other places.[8] It should be pointed out that some Temne-,

---

[7] Allen M. Howard, "Mande Identity Formation in the Economic and Political Context
of North-West Sierra Leone, 1750–1900" *Padeuma* 46 (2000), p. 14.

[8] *SLWN*, September – November 1892. The paper contains reports about the different groups in the colony, in their analysis about crimes in Freetown and its environs

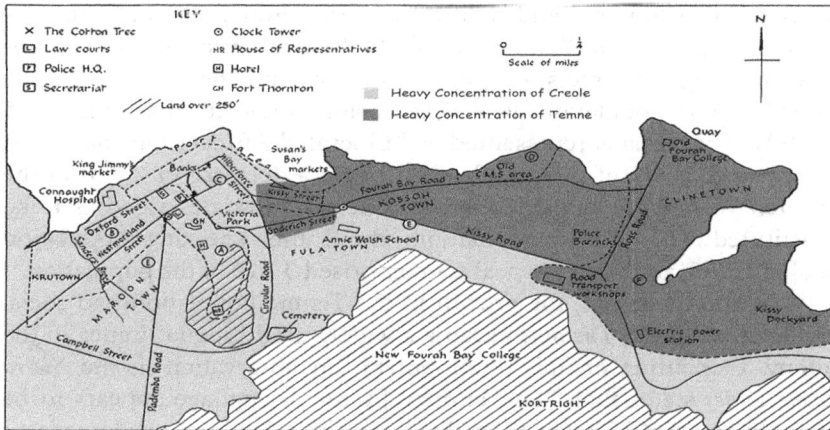

Map 1 Demographic Representation of colonial Freetown.
Source: K. G. Dalton, *A Geography of Sierra Leone* (Cambridge: Cambridge University Press, 1965), p. 13.

Mende-, and Loko-speakers, in particular, lived in parts of the western region of Adonkia, Leicester, Gloucester, Lakkah, Regent, and the like.[9]

Map 1 indicates sections of the colony occupied by different communities before 1961.

The dark gray areas marked "F" show the east-central section of the colony, with the dense population of Temne and other ethnic communities. On the other hand, sections with light gray markings highlighted as areas "A," "B," "C," "D," and "E," depict heavy clusters of Freetonians. In his report on the division of the colony, Lord Hailey states that indigenous people comprising the original inhabitants and owners of the land, the Temne, constituted a substantial portion of the colony's population.[10]

A significant number of migrants who flocked to the colony from the Protectorate between 1890 and 1892 came from northern Sierra Leone, especially from Temne strongholds.[11] Clearly, many of these immigrants

in the nineteenth century. See also Milton Harvey, "Implications of Migrations to Freetown: A Study of the Relationships Between Migrants, Housing and Occupation." *Civilisations* 18, no. 2 (1968) and John I. Clarke, *Sierra Leone in Maps* (London: University of London Press, 1969).

[9] Ernest G. Ingham, *Sierra Leone after a Hundred Years* (London: Cass Library of African Studies, 1968), pp. 5–15.

[10] Lord William, Malcolm Hailey, *Native Administration in the British Territories* (London: His Majesty's Stationery Office, 1951), p. 286.

[11] *SLWN*, January 17, 1892.

migrated for economic and political reasons, among others.[12] An article in the *Sierra Leone Times* noted that "7 out of every ten pedestrians moving along the streets are pure aborigines and the cry is 'still they come.'"[13] The population data of the colony indicate that, from 1895 to 1901, Freetonians represented as "Liberated Africans" in the report comprised 31,907 of the population, "being a decrease of 2,218 in the past ten years"; the Temne constituted 5,889; those described as Loko constituted 717 of the population; the Limba-speaking population totaled 1,056, and Mende-speakers comprised 3,319 of the population.[14]

From the foregoing, the growth in the Temne population had social implications. First, *Theimne* became a widely used Lingua Franca in the colony. Lamenting on this development, an observation in the *Sierra Leone Times* states that "The Timney [Temne] language appears to be the only one that bids fair to outlive the others. You are nowhere if you don't know it. Our women speak it far more fluently than they do either Aku or Eboe ..."[15] Second, the Temne community became one of the first ethnic groups to elect a headman, described as "tribal headman" in this British colonial sphere.[16] John Hargreaves maintains that local conditions triggered the use of chiefs in Britain's administration of the protectorate 1896.

The exponential upsurge in the colony population accelerated the need to recognize and encourage tribal governance. As with the establishment of the Freetonian-dominated Municipal Council in 1893, colonial authorities allowed similar micro-institutional systems to exist among non-Freetonian groups through the adoption of the famous indirect rule system.[17] Indirect rule and its monocentric system of governance embodied the principles of subsidiarity, and it involved a wide swath of agents to make it effective and productive: tribal chiefs, African elites, laborers, African soldiers and constables. Spear states that indirect rule "was premised on the existence of cultural homogenous territorial tribes ruled by chiefs."[18] Historical sources show that the British colonial administration first adopted the indirect rule system in the colony before they introduced it in the protectorate; this contradicts the view that colonial

---

[12] Harvey, "Implications of Migrations to Freetown," pp. 248–253. See also David Skinner, Barbara Harrell-Bond, Allen M. Howard, "A Profile of Urban Leaders in Freetown, Sierra Leone (1905–1945)." *Tarikh* 7 1 (1981).

[13] *SLT*, Freetown, June 14 and 17, 1893.

[14] *SLWN*, January 4, 1902.

[15] *SLT*, Freetown, June 14 and 17, 1893.

[16] *SLT*, Freetown, February 2, 1895

[17] See John D. Hargreaves, *A Life of Sir Samuel Lewis* (London: Oxford University Press, 1958), pp. 15–19, on the history of the municipal council.

[18] Thomas Spear, "Neo-Traditionalism," p. 16.

authorities initiated the system in the protectorate.[19] Some believe the system worked because "the rule of the Chief is deeply rooted … the people have a real attachment to their Chief and the system of tribal government to which they belong."[20] Thus local intellectuals and traditional elites supported the indirect rule system, especially the leadership of the TTA, while the Freetonian establishment vehemently opposed it. Simply put, tribal administrations helped the colonial government "deal with matters outside the range of everyday administrative machinery; the better enforcement of law and order" in the colony.[21] Expressed another way, the Temne became one of the first non-Freetonian communities to receive permission from the colonial establishment to constitute a Tribal Authority – the TTA in the colony. The Temne and their institutions organized around the TTA, which became a symbol of authority and coalescence. The leadership of the TTA also became preoccupied with boosting the profile of Temneness.

The Temne Tribal Authority and Local Administration in the Colony, 1890–1961

In the late nineteenth and early twentieth centuries, the TTA embarked on a carefully contrived process to glitz up, increase, entrench, and spread the influence of Temne identity and its institutions across time and space.

Historical sources indicate that the Temne community appeared to have been the only ethnic group to experience a slight bump in population during this period, while the Freetonian population suffered a slight decline.[22] By 1901, the Temne population was estimated at 13,370, and the population of Mende-, Mandingo-, Susu-, and Limba-speakers remained fewer than 14,000.[23] The criteria used by the compilers of this report in determining such ethnic categories remain unclear. It is reasonable to assume that they relied on the responses of those polled at the time of the research. R. R. Kuczynski observes that, in the course

[19] J. D. Hargreaves, "The Establishment of the Sierra Leone Protectorate and the Insurrection of 1898." *Cambridge Historical Journal*, Vol. XV11 (1956), pp. 56–80; see his other work, "Western Democracy and African Society: Some Reflections from Sierra Leone." *International Affairs* (*Royal Institute of International Affairs 1944*) 31, No. 3 (Jul., 1955), pp. 327–334.
[20] Donald Cameron, "Native Administration in Nigeria and Tanganyika," cited in Spear, "Neo-Traditionalism," pp. 3–27.
[21] Michael Banton, *West African City: A Study of Tribal Life in Freetown* (London: Oxford University Press, 1953), p. 11.
[22] C.S.O. *Sierra Leone Blue Book, 1901* (Freetown: Government Printing Office, 1901), p. 1.
[23] C.S.O. *Sierra Leone Blue Book, 1901*, p. 1.

of conducting population censuses in the British Empire, enumerators made basic assumptions about people polled in their findings. In West Africa, including Sierra Leone, census-taking proved difficult because of mass illiteracy, which forced colonial officials to classify people into ethnic categories on largely ethno-linguistic grounds.[24] In the Sierra Leone Colony, it is clear that census officers in particular adopted the same tools used in other British colonies to identify the Temne and those recorded as Mende, Limba, Mandingo and Loko. Clearly, the numerical strength of the Temne implies that the head of the TTA had a high level of responsibility in terms of governance and the provision of local services.

In 1895, the Temne selected Alimamy Bobo as their first de facto tribal headman, in conformity with the permission granted the community by the colonial administration. Like that of other tribal headmen, the method of Bobo's selection is unclear. A decade after the recognition of tribal rule in the colony, the colonial administration formally integrated the system, in what is widely known as the 1905 Ordinance. The ordinance states that:

When it is represented to the Governor by petition or other means that any tribe in Freetown possesses a recognized Chief, Alimamy, or Headman, who with other Headmen or representatives of the sections of the tribe, endeavours to enforce a system of tribal administration for the well-being of the members of the tribe, resident in or temporarily staying in Freetown, it shall be lawful for the Governor, subject to the provisions of sub-sections 2 and 3 hereof, to recognize such Chief, Alimamy, or Headman as the Tribal Ruler of such tribe for the purposes of this Ordinance.[25]

The quote above is one of the hallmarks of the indirect rule system designed to minimize British participation in the governance of tribal communities in the colony. Others argue that the indirect rule system proved economical for the British government, by making Africans take control of their affairs, which saved British tax payers lots of money. They state that because Britain, like other European powers, relied on indirect rule, the colonial government did not have the resources to staff native courts and, hence, tribal headmen filled that role. The Temne community rallied around their newly recognized headman, who liaised between the community and the government. His principal functions included the adjudication of civil disputes, and of issues relating to witchcraft, fornication, and adultery. He presided over the various native courts

---

[24] R. R. Kuczynski, *Demographic Survey of the British Colonial Empire* (London and New York: Oxford University Press, 1948), pp. 9–10.

[25] C.S.O. *An Ordinance to Promote A System of Administration by Tribal Authority Among the Tribes Settled In Freetown, No. 19 of 1905* (Freetown: Government Printing Office, 1905), p. 1.

directly or through his subordinates, since the English-based colonial courts proved incapable of adjudicating these specialized cases.[26] This dovetails with the idea that "making customary law was not a simple process of colonial invention"; sometimes it involved the syncretizing of African customs and European laws.[27] Alimamy Bobo levied corporal punishment on defaulters and culprits found guilty in any Temne native court. Customarily, when a complainant reported a matter of theft or abuse, he or she paid a fee to the tribal headman or his subordinate, who summoned the accused. The feuding parties involved attended daily sessions of the court until a verdict was reached on the case. The guilty party paid the court costs, and other fines to the plaintiff and his or her associates. Appeals of such decisions could only be accepted if Bobo did not directly adjudicate the matter. In instances like these, the aggrieved party reserved the right to appeal directly to Bobo.[28] If the tribal headman presided over such appeal-cases, his final verdict on the matter could not be questioned or challenged. Bobo's tenure turned out to be uncharacteristically ephemeral, which led to the installation of his successor, Alimamy Momo, in 1895.[29] Like his predecessor's, Momo's responsibilities included seeking and protecting the welfare of Temne subjects. He liaised between the colonial authorities and his subjects by serving as the representative and conveyor of the dictates of colonial policy to his community. He also assisted in law enforcement, and helped the police track down fugitives and other criminals.[30] As headman, Momo also coordinated intercommunity and intra-community activities, promoted the welfare of indigent immigrants, and provided temporary housing, employment, and other social services to new immigrants.[31] For instance, he recommended suitable candidates for menial jobs when government officers put such requests to him. On other occasions, the headman approached government departments or private companies for employment opportunities for his subjects.[32] One of the valuable services the TTA provided to the community involved the provision of funerary assistance to the family or associates of deceased paupers.

---

[26] C.S.O. *Local Administration, Policies and Notes* (Freetown: Government Printing Office, 1940), p. 12.

[27] Spear, "Neo-Traditionalism," p. 16.

[28] C.S.O. *Local Administration*, p. 12.

[29] T. J. Alldridge, *A Transformed Colony: Sierra Leone: As It Was and As It Is: Its Progress, Peoples, Native Customs and Underdeveloped Wealth* (London: Seeley, 1910), pp. 46–47.

[30] Banton, *West African City*, pp. 16–17.

[31] Barbara Harrell-Bond, Allen M. Howard and David Skinner, *Community Leadership and the Transformation of Freetown (1801–1978)* (The Hague: Mouton Publishers, 1978), p. 195.

[32] C.S.O. *Local Administration, pp.* 13–14. See also SLWN, Freetown, February 1898.

Though the 1905 tribal ordinance turned out to be relatively success-ful, colonial authorities renewed and expanded it, with the promulgation of the 1906 Ordinance. The ordinance conferred certain powers on sectional headmen answerable to the tribal headman. It also granted various communities in the peninsula towns the right to elect tribal headmen. In the case of the Temne, the tribal ruler remained the overall head of various Temne communities in the colony and the peninsular suburbs. The ordinance broadly stated that:

It shall be lawful for a Headman, after consultation with the Committee, with the approval of the Governor from time to time to make, alter or rescind regulations requiring the residents in the town to perform certain work in or near the town on not more than eighteen days in any one year and prescribing the manner in which such work is to be performed.[33]

Under the new ordinance, headmen collected taxes and market dues and supervised the cleaning of cemeteries in their various jurisdictions. They ensured the proper maintenance of bridges, roads and streets, "when not repaired by the colonial government."[34] They also had the authority to probe suspicious deaths within their jurisdictions, through the institution of commissions of inquiry, and the deployment of other judicial instruments.

The adoption of the 1906 ordinance gave some Temne headmen in the peninsula towns the tools to assert their authority, though some head-men exceeded the scope of their authority by imposing their rule on residents outside their jurisdictions. A case in point is Morlai Kamara, Temne headman in the peninsula town of Adonkia. Kamara, apparently a junior chief answerable to the tribal ruler based in the colony, moved swiftly after his appointment to assert his authority over Temne and non-Temne subjects in Adonkia, by making the following proclamation: "All residents in the district of Adonkia who are not exempted as aforesaid shall, whenever called upon by the Headman or by any person be appointed by him for the purpose, perform work in such manner as may be directed by such Headman."[35] He also required all residents

---

[33] C.S.O. *An Ordinance to Confer Certain Powers on the Headmen of Towns in the Colony of Sierra Leone, No. 31 of 1906* (Freetown: Government Printing Office, 1906), pp. 1–2.
[34] C.S.O. *An Ordinance to Confer Certain Powers*, p. 2.
[35] C.S.O. *Regulation Made By the Headman of Adonkia Under Section 4 of "the Headman Ordinance of 1905" (No. 38 of 1906)* (Freetown: Government Printing Office, 1906), pp. 2–4. According to Christopher Fyfe, the Temne heavily populated Adonkia in the nineteenth and twentieth centuries. The Bullom originally occupied it, before the Temne dislodged and possibly assimilated them. The Temne eventually assumed control of the settlement in the eighteenth century. Adonkia later became a lucrative fishing community.

to comply with his directives, such as "cleaning the Adonkia cemetery, cleaning, maintaining and repairing the streets in Adonkia and the public roads in the district other than the road maintained by the colonial government."[36] The proclamation reveals the breadth of Kamara's mandate, which had multiple implications: First, it shows that he had authority to maintain and repair streets, cemeteries and bridges. It is not clear how he generated funds to meet these responsibilities. Second, it is apparent that he asserted his authority beyond the jurisdiction of the Temne community. It remains unclear if colonial authorities sanctioned his assumed extra-jurisdictional powers. Nonetheless, Kamara proved to be a powerful and revered headman in Adonkia, since he presided over a fairly significant Temne population in the town. The census report indicated that the Temne population in Adonkia during Kamara's tenure comprised 2,137, while Mende-, Mandingo-, and Limba-speakers remained at fewer than 1,000 people.[37] Historical documents indicate that non-Temne-speakers in Adonkia did not protest the powers assumed by Morlai Kamara over them, nor did colonial authorities challenge him on the issue.[38] In 1911, a similar trend prevailed in the peninsula town of Waterloo. Waterloo served as the district headquarters for surrounding precincts. The Freetonian and Temne population estimates in Waterloo stood at 6,573 and 5,916, respectively, while the combined populations of those reported as Mende, Limba, Loko and Mandingo rose to slightly more than 6,000.[39] Like the Temne tribal headman in Adonkia, the Temne tribal headman of Waterloo also exercised jurisdictional authority over Loko, Mende and Limba ethnic communities and adjudicated cases involving the same.[40]

In short, as in Adonkia, the Temne headman adjudicated cases involving non-Temne complainants in Waterloo. His administrative staff included a coterie of junior officials, such as the *Pa Rok* (deputy headman), *Ya Bom* (senior wife of the headman), and a court messenger. The headman served as the chief justice in the local court, and his verdicts on cases went for the most part unchallenged. However, litigants dissatisfied with a particular ruling reserved the right to appeal directly to the tribal ruler based in colonial Freetown. In cases where litigants launched

---

[36] C.S.O. *Regulation by Headman*, pp. 2–3.
[37] C.S.O. *Sierra Leone Blue Book, 1911* (Freetown: Government Printing Office, 1914), p. 1. This document contains a record of census reports from the late nineteenth century to the early twentieth century. The same is true for the census report of 1921, which has records of earlier census reports.
[38] C.S.O. *Regulation by Headman*, p. 2.
[39] C.S.O. *Blue Book, 1911*, p. 2.
[40] C.S.O. *Report on Tribal Administration*, pp. 6–8.

appeals against particular rulings, the tribal ruler dispatched his personal assistant, or *Pa Kombrabai*, to review the decision before making his final ruling.[41] Like the Temne local administration, Freetonians also had a separate local administration in Waterloo. In fact, like non-Freetonian groups, the Freetonians in Waterloo took complaints and concerns to the Freetonian headman.[42] Unlike other jurisdictions, Waterloo clearly operated a dual administrative system – Freetonian and Temne local administrations. It is plausible to argue that the existence of a Temne tribal administration gave non-Freetonians an alternate system of justice in Waterloo.

Alimamy Momo Kamara became the first tribal ruler to be elected under the 1906 Ordinance. His election received strong support from the colonial administration. The colonial commissioner of police supported Kamara's appointment, as illustrated in a memo he sent to the governor:

I am of the opinion that Momo Kamara is well qualified to act as [Tribal Ruler] of the Temne in Freetown. I have personally known him for many years and can testify to his ability and intelligence, I have always found him loyal to the government; he has great influence among his people and is firm with them.[43]

It is unclear how the commissioner verified Kamara's Temne identity. It is highly likely that he relied on the fact that no one opposed or challenged Kamara's candidacy, either on ethnic grounds or on grounds of legitimacy. The colonial administration published his selection as Temne tribal headman in the government's official gazette.[44] In 1908, a leadership vacuum among Loko-speakers prompted colonial authorities to put Kamara temporarily in charge of overseeing the affairs of the community.[45] In his new role, Kamara assigned some responsibilities to sub-chiefs and other administrative staff in the Loko community. He, however, presided over contentious issues such as witchcraft, divorce, infidelity, and intercommunity clashes. As general overseer of Loko affairs, Kamara's decisions on cases brought before him went unchallenged, and litigants accepted them as final.[46] Though the Loko community appreciated Kamara's leadership and his handling of contentious issues, the community elected Kangbe Sesay as its tribal headman in the

[41] C.S.O. *Local Administration.*
[42] C.S.O. *Local Administration in Waterloo District,* MP 234/18 PC 22 1/18 112/10 (Freetown, 1911.)
[43] C.S.O. *Report on Tribal Administration,* p. 8.
[44] C.S.O. *Report on Tribal Administration,* p. 8.
[45] C.S.O. *Report on Tribal Administration,* p. 8.
[46] C.S.O. *Report on Tribal Administration,* pp. 8–9.

colony in 1908. In spite of Sesay's election, many Loko-speakers continued to report cases to the Temne tribal ruler. In addition, some sections of the Loko community asked that the post of Loko headman be subsumed under the TTA. Though the colonial government briefly toyed with the idea, it rejected it and insisted that Sesay's authority be recognized.[47] To have subsumed the authority of Sesay under the TTA would have established a terrible precedent, in terms of community governance and inter-community relations. On the governor's advice, Kamara ceased to receive complaints from some members of the Loko community. Why did the colonial government temporarily put the Temne tribal ruler in charge of the Loko community? This suggests that the TTA served as an alternative local authority to the Freetown Municipal Council. Second, it shows the relative efficacy of local administration in the colony. Third, the phenomenon indicates that the colonial administration's effective use of the indirect rule system and the principle of subsidiarity worked, at least to some extent. Finally, it is reasonable to assume that the colonial government encouraged an alternative system of local administration to create healthy political competition between Freetonians and non-Freetonians. In sum, it shows the significant contribution of the TTA in the governance of the colony. The TTA provided avenues for Temne residents in the colony to seek resolution of civil and criminal cases. This principal function of the TTA and its constituent branches proved effective and economical for the colonial administration.

In 1911, Alimamy Sillah succeeded Momo Kamara as head of the TTA. During the Sillah administration, the Temne population rose to 13,370, while the combined populations of Mandingo-, Mende-, Limba-, and Loko-speakers remained fewer than 11,000 in total.[48] As tribal ruler of one of the ascendant Temne ethnic groups, Sillah's responsibilities increased over time. Apart from overseeing the welfare of Temne subjects, he advised the colonial administration on policy relating to his constituents. Colonial authorities regularly called on him to resolve intercommunity issues involving the Temne and other non-Freetonian communities. During a political impasse in Waterloo, the police commissioner in colonial Freetown asked Sillah to mediate in the dispute and find a solution. In correspondence to the District Commissioner in Waterloo, the police commissioner stated that: "Alimamy Sillah is the Timinee Chief in Freetown and is asked to settle a dispute at Waterloo

[47] C.S.O. *Report on Tribal Administration*, pp. 8–9.
[48] C.S.O. *Report and Summary of the Census of 1921* (London: Waterloo and Sons Limited, 1922), p. 10.

which seems only natural as evidently they cannot settle it themselves."[49] Sillah and a number of sub-chiefs visited Waterloo, and met with Major R. H. K. Williams, the Acting District Commissioner, and other parties to the conflict. The conflict involved an electoral dispute between two contestants for the post of Temne headman in Waterloo, with both candidates trading accusations of vote-rigging. After listening to the contending parties, Sillah and his team declared one of the candidates, Alimamy Turay, the legitimate winner of the election, and subsequently declared him the Temne headman of Waterloo. While supporters of the losing candidate expressed frustration at Sillah's ruling, many in the Temne community in Waterloo accepted the ruling.[50] Sillah's resolution of the Waterloo dispute speaks to the bigger issue of maintaining law and order in colonial settings.[51] This is reinforced by the view that "were it not for the controlling influence of the Tribal Headmen, [disputes] would be more frequent and the accompanying social disorder greater."[52]

Sillah also contributed to the religious life of the Temne ethnic community: he expanded a mosque begun by his predecessor Momo Kamara in 1902, although he did not live to see the completion of the project.[53] Though incomplete, many in the Temne Islamic Community used the mosque to worship. Historical sources indicate that, by the mid-1940s, Temne owned and controlled numerous mosques relative to other groups, save for those described as Muslim Freetonians, or Aku.[54] The mosques became an integral part of the Temne Islamic Community in the colony; the various mosques served as a place of worship, hosted weddings, and also served as rendezvous for business transactions and meetings. The symbolic and practical importance of the Temne mosques is analyzed in Chapter Five.

In 1919, Alimamy Sillah's tenure came to a mysterious end, resulting in a leadership vacuum until Alimamy Suri took over the mantle of power in 1923.[55] Shortly after he assumed leadership of the TTA, Suri confronted the same issue which his predecessor had experienced – the outbreak

---

[49] C.S.O. *Commissioner of Police to District Commissioner, Head Quarter District, Waterloo*, MP/F No. 238, 1911 (Freetown: 1911).

[50] *SLWN*, August 23, 1911. See also, C.S.O. *Appointment of Kandeh as Timni Alikali of Waterloo*, MP 1681/21 LM 34 3/11 109/23 (Freetown, 1911).

[51] *Sierra Leone Mail and Guardian*, Freetown, September 14, 1912.

[52] Banton, *West African City*, p. 150.

[53] Harrell-Bond, et al., *Community Leadership*, p. 131.

[54] Aku is a derivative of Yoruba that describes a section of Creole society that practiced Islam as a religion. The media interchangeably referred to them as Muslim Creoles and/or Mohammedan Creoles.

[55] C.S.O. *Alimamy Suri, Tribal Ruler of the Timnies*, Minute Paper 107/2211/1923 (Freetown: 1923).

of pandemonium in Waterloo over the election of a Temne headman. The colonial governor, Governor Rowe, based in the colony, "asked the Timne Tribal Ruler of Freetown to go to Waterloo and assist the people of the town to become unanimous as to the selection of a Tribal Ruler."[56] The two camps bickered over identity issues as supporters on either side of the divide accused each other of not being authentic Temne. These allegations meant that both candidates doubted the qualifications of the other party.[57] Because of Waterloo's strategic location and size, the tribal headmen of its preponderant groups, in this case, Freetonians and Temne, carried considerable clout. This may partly explain why the leadership contest became heated, bitter, and full of rancor. Moreover, the TTA paid the tribal headman a decent stipend, because of the breadth of his responsibilities. His stipend came from taxes and other income-generating sources undertaken by the leadership of the community. After extensive deliberations with the feuding parties, Suri proclaimed Alimamy Lamina winner of the election – all contending factions accepted the ruling, which Suri then transmitted to colonial authorities.

The colonial administration and the Temne Authority officially declared Lamina headman of Waterloo.[58] It is not clear what criteria were used to resolve the dispute surrounding Lamina's Temne credentials. Since the colonial administration and the Temne Authority upheld his appointment, it is reasonable to assume that they accepted Lamina's version of events. Notwithstanding the determinant used in verifying the identity of Lamina, the issue speaks to a broader phenomenon – the situational nature and fluidity of ethnic identities in Africa, as highlighted by Glassman and Spear. In spite of this observation, the resolution of the Waterloo dispute reveals the colonial government's reliance on the leadership of the TTA to resolve intra-community and customary disputes. Like his predecessors', Suri's responsibility increased because of a steady growth in the Temne population, triggered by a surge in migration from Temne strongholds in the protectorate. The census returns of 1921 showed that "the Temnes are the most populous of the tribes in the colony; their population rose from 13,370 to 18,843 ... That the native of the colony, or Creole, is slowly but steadily decreasing in numbers cannot be gainsaid."[59] As a matter of fact, the Freetonian population declined, from 31,078 in 1911, to 28,222 in 1921.[60] Due to inadequate data, it is difficult to calculate the percentage of the Temne population

---

[56] C.S.O. *Tribal Ruler of the Timnies*, p. 10.
[57] C.S.O. *Tribal Ruler of the Timnies*, pp. 10–11.
[58] C.S.O. *Tribal Ruler of the Timnies*, p. 10.
[59] C.S.O. *Report and Summary of Census, 1921*, p. 11.
[60] C.S.O. *Report and Summary of Census, 1921*, pp. 10–11.

over the percentage of the colony population. Suffice it to state that large-scale immigration occurred largely from towns with dense Temne populations.[61] Given this, it can be assumed that the economic benefits offered by the TTA to people claiming Temne identity perhaps contributed to the rise in the Temne population at this time.

It should be pointed out that female officials, such as the *Bom Wara*, formed part of the political hierarchy of the TTA, and they performed a range of functions, particularly orientation programs organized for new immigrants, including job placements for the unemployed. In Kroo Bay and Susan's Bay, both major ports of entry into the colony, the *Bom Wara*, as representative of the TTA, offered protection and guidance to Temne women traders. When Temne women traders arrived at these ports with assorted goods from the protectorate, for example, they reported to a local official, usually the *Bom Wara*. As part of her responsibilities, the *Bom Wara* levied taxes on the goods of traders, provided temporary accommodation, and resolved petty disputes.[62] Howard states that many of the commodities transported to the colony came from Temne-dominated areas in the hinterland: "For example in 1885 a member of the chiefly family in Tane, Bombali, led seven canoes down the river Rokel, reportedly carrying 500 bushels of palm nuts plus other produce; he exchanged them in a river factory ... and went to Freetown with £ 90, to buy tobacco."[63] Many of the traders that anchored at Susan's Bay spoke Theimne and Bullom.[64] The *Bom Wara* ensured that traders obeyed established trade rules. Junior chiefs from other ethnic communities, such as Mandingo- and Fula-speakers, also offered similar protection to traders who publicly assumed such ethnic identities.[65] It is unclear if sub-chiefs from non-Temne communities had representatives at Susan's Bay, or Kroo Bay, like the *Bom Wara*.

In 1925, the colonial administration modified the 1905 and 1906 ordinances with increased powers for the head of the TTA. The new

[61] *The West African Mail and Trade Gazette*, January 2, 1926.
[62] Hassan Kamara, "Temne and Their Chiefs" (Freetown: 1976); this is an unpublished typescript sold in Freetown by the author himself. Widely perceived as an organic historian, Kamara served as a radio commentator on Temne issues at the Sierra Leone Broadcasting Cooperation. The Bom Wara was the senior wife of the tribal ruler and served as a junior and sectional chief.
[63] Allen Howard, "The Role of Freetown in the Commercial Life of Sierra Leone" in Christopher Fyfe and Eldred Jones, eds., *Freetown: A Symposium* (Freetown: Sierra Leone University Press, 1968), p. 43. Bombali is the headquarters of the Northern Province of Sierra Leone. It was and continues to be a Temne stronghold.
[64] Allen Howard, "Contesting Commercial Space in Freetown, 1869–1930: Traders, Merchants and Officials." *Canadian Journal of African Studies* 37 (2003), p. 260.
[65] Banton, *West African City*, p. 160.

ordinance revised the duties of the Temne tribal ruler. The ordinance states: "[A]ll members of the Temne Tribe resident in Freetown shall be subject to the Tribal Ruler of the Temne Tribe. Every member of the Temne Tribe arriving in Freetown from the Protectorate or elsewhere shall within seven days report his arrival to the Ruler."[66] This means the TTA reserved the right to deport illegal immigrants, such as petty criminals and other felons.[67] To avoid deportation, new immigrants were required by the ordinance to report to TTA officials and obtain signed passes as verification of their legal status. Additionally, the ordinance required new Temne immigrants to secure work authorization from the TTA.[68] It further stresses that: "[A]ny member of the Temne Tribe who contravenes any of the foregoing sections shall pay to the Tribal Ruler such penalty, not exceeding five pounds, as may be adjudged by the Temne Ruler."[69] Nonetheless, the new immigration policy failed to curb the flow of immigrants from Temne strongholds, which steadily increased. It is clear that immigration proved beneficial to immigrants, who flocked to the colony, despite the measures put in place by the colonial administration to curb the practice. In fact, a substantial number of new immigrants "participated in Freetown-based trade in bulky products and foods than did members of other groups."[70] Others worked as constables and domestic servants in rich Freetonian households.[71] Historical sources show that between 1923 and 1927 the Temne formed the bulk of the police force, constituting about 31% of the total force. The statistical data show that Freetonians and Mende-speaking officers comprised 4% and 16% of the force respectively.[72] The content of the 1925 ordinance reveals that the Temne wielded more influence, because of their numerical strength.[73]

All in all, immigration proved to be a contentious issue, with the Freetonian elite vehemently demanding stricter curbs on patterns of immigration to the colony from the protectorate. The debate on immigration speaks to Anne Phillips' observation that the mass exodus of laborers leaving the hinterland dismayed the chiefs "and caused consternation to the Sierra Leone government which found itself with stagnant production

---

[66] C.S.O. *The Laws of the Colony and Protectorate of Sierra Leone.* (Freetown: Government Printing Office, 1925), p. 560.
[67] Harrell-Bond et al., *Community Leadership,* p. 143.
[68] C.S.O. *Laws of the Colony and Protectorate,* p. 562.
[69] C.S.O. *The Laws of the Colony,* p. 562.
[70] Harrell-Bond et al., *Community Leadership,* p. 77.
[71] *SLWN,* Freetown, February 5, 1898.
[72] C.S.O. *Employment and Administrative Report, 1923* (Freetown: Government Printing Office, 1924), pp. 1–6.
[73] C.S.O. *The Laws of the Colony,* pp. 565–567.

in the protectorate and a swollen city in Freetown."[74] As Phillips shows, immigrants continuously realized that a "Mendi or Timani will produce a bigger profit if he leaves the Sierra Leone Protectorate for regular work [in Freetown] than if he remains in it to cultivate the soil."[75] The colony certainly provided the ambiance for upward mobility and other opportunities for industrious immigrants. Successful immigrants to the colony led economically and socially better lives; they gained prestige and status, compared to their compatriots in the protectorate.

Alimamy Koroma became head of the TTA under the new tribal ordinance of 1925.[76] On the assumption of office, Koroma introduced new policies relating to income generation, meant to increase the authority's revenue base. He strictly enforced tax rules, and enjoined registered members of the authority to pay their monthly subscriptions on time. All incomes generated on behalf of the TTA were deposited at the "Post Office Savings Bank in the names of the Tribal Ruler and two principal headmen."[77] Signatories to the account included two junior chiefs and the head of the TTA.[78] The TTA used the funds strictly for "relief of the poor and sick; burial of the poor having no relatives at time of death; relief of any member of the Temne Tribe in distress."[79]

Koroma's tenure as head of the TTA became one of the longest in the history of the TTA. In fact, his successor, Momo Tanka, served for only two years, before he handed [power] over to the highly influential Kande Bureh in 1944. During his tenure, Bureh obtained "an influence far greater than that of any of his predecessors although they had wider legal powers."[80] Born as Saidu Bai Kamara, in 1908, in the north of Sierra Leone, he migrated to the colony at a young age.[81] Though largely secularist in character and tone, "he sponsored the Ahmadiyya Muslim Movement in Freetown and also helped the Movement secure lands at Rokupr, Bo, Boajibu ..."[82] As the first Western-educated Temne chief, he had the distinction of being the first tribal leader to expand the structure of the TTA, and increased the number of women chiefs

---

[74] Anne Phillips, *The Enigma of Colonialism: British Policy in West Africa* (Bloomington: Indiana University Press, 1989), p. 34.
[75] Philips, *Enigma of Colonialism*, p. 35.
[76] Harrell-Bond et al., *Community Leadership*, Appendix 1.
[77] C.S.O. *Laws of the Colony and Protectorate*, p. 561.
[78] C.S.O. *Laws of the Colony and Protectorate*, pp. 561–562.
[79] C.S.O. *Laws of the Colony and Protectorate*, p. 561.
[80] Banton, *West African City*, p. 160.
[81] *Sierra Leonean Heroes: Fifty Great Men and Women Who Helped Build Our Nation* (Great Britain, 1988), p. 84. In this study, the name Kande is used interchangeably with Kandeh.
[82] *Sierra Leonean Heroes*, p. 84. The Ahmadiyya Movement was a Muslim sect from Pakistan that engaged in the propagation of Islam Sierra Leone in colonial Sierra Leone.

Temne
Tribal Ruler
Kandeh Bureh

Section 1
sub-chief: Pa Alikali
Assistant: Bom Wara

Section 2
sub-chief: Pa Alimamy
Assistant: Ya Bom Posseh

Section 3
Sub-chief: Pa Santigi
Assistant: Bom Kapr

Sections 4 and 5
Sub-chiefs
Pa Alimamy and Pa Santigi

Sections 6 & 7
Sub-chiefs;
Bom Wara and Bom Posseh

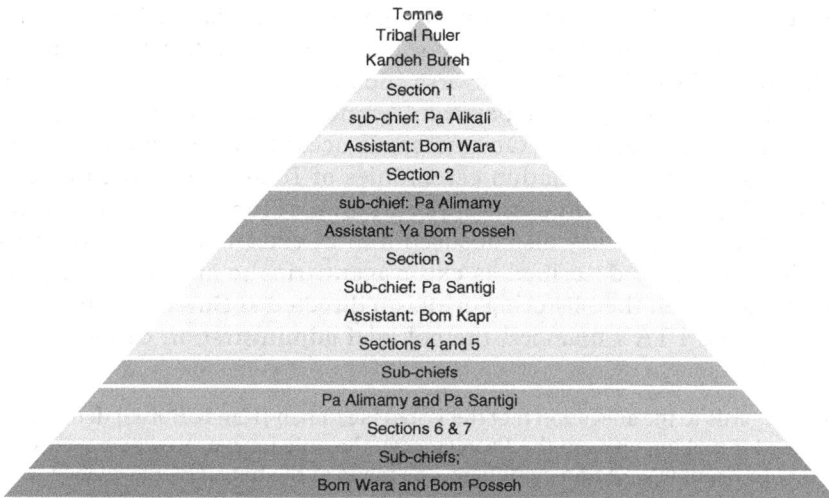

Figure 4 Temne Tribal Administrative Structure in the Colony.

in his administration.[83] In utilizing the principle of subsidiarity, Bureh divided his jurisdiction into seven sections, with each section headed by an *Alikali* and a *Bom Wara*; that is, male and female sub-chiefs.

The *Alikali* headed the first section assisted by the *Bom Wara*, while *Pa Alimamy* headed the second section, assisted by his most senior wife, *Ya Bom Posseh*. Additionally, *Pa Santigi* headed the third section, supported by his female counterpart, *Bom Kapr*.[84] Other *Alikalies* and *Santigies* headed the fourth and fifth sections, while female chiefs headed the sixth and seventh sections. Figure 4 gives a graphic representation of the governance structure Bureh established as head of the TTA.[85]

As head of the TTA, Bureh charged his junior chiefs with the basic functions of resolving disputes such as domestic abuse, sexual harassment, rape, impotence, desertions of households, divorce, infidelity, and the like. They had the right to levy paltry fines on convicts. Beyond this, in their capacity as junior chiefs, they also reserved the right to collect monthly dues, as an income-generating measure to help the TTA function effectively.

Moreover, Bureh presided over cases dealing with intra-ethnic and interethnic conflicts, such as loan disputes, property and kinship

[83] Interview, Chief Adikalie Gbonko, Freetown, November 3, 2003.
[84] Banton, *West African City*, p. 151.
[85] Interview, Chief Adikalie Gbonko, Freetown, November 3, 2003.

relations, and leadership feuds. Litigants dissatisfied with the out-
come of cases adjudicated by junior chiefs appealed directly to Bureh,
who maintained the right to reverse such rulings by lower courts.[86] He
served as the principal link between Temne residents in the colony and
those in the protectorate. On numerous occasions, he visited the protectorate to grace coronation ceremonies of Temne Paramount chiefs.
His critics accused him of misappropriation of funds belonging to the
Temne authority. They also accused him of extra-budgetary practices
during what they described as extravagant trips to and from the protectorate. Given the blistering criticism directed at Bureh over his handling of the TTA's finances, the colonial administration defended his
actions:

With regards to the allegation that the Tribal Headman [Kande Bureh] demanded
money for making visits to the Protectorate, the only journey to which you refer
is that to Kambia ... As no complaint was made at the time, His Excellency cannot but feel that it was regarded at that time as a reasonable contribution by the
Temne Community for expenses into the Protectorate to take part in the crown-
ing of a Temne Chief.[87]

Aside from participating in coronation ceremonies in the protectorate,
Bureh accommodated and entertained Temne chiefs visiting the colony
from the protectorate for business, official, personal, and/or familial reasons. Thus he "vigorously championed the rights of Protectorate peoples
in the Colony."[88] He used TTA funds to establish a vocational school for
Temne adults and children in 1949 – a unique feat for a tribal ruler and
for the Temne community as a whole.[89] Bamikole Sawyer, a resident with
a Freetonian background who admired Bureh's leadership qualities and
style, observed that: "The Tribal Headman of the Temnies is one of the
progressive and educated representatives of the indigenous natives of this
country."[90]

In evincing his progressive side, as observed by Bamikole-Sawyer,
Bureh expanded the influence and reach of Temneness in the colony.
Consequently, he became a central figure in national and local pol-
itics when colonial authorities permitted the start of party politics in

---

[86] Interviews, Mohamed Sorie Kamara, Freetown, November 2, 2003, and Ambassador
Sorsoh Conteh, Freetown, December 10, 2003. Both informants were interviewed
separately.
[87] C.S.O. *Complaint, T2/6/5, MP 1158/1/1/16, 4/10/49*, pp. 7–8.
[88] Barbara Harrell-Bond et al., *Community Leadership*, p. 199.
[89] Interviews, Chief Adikalie Gbonko, Lamin Kamara and Santigie Turay, Freetown,
November 3, 2003. The author interviewed all three informants separately. All claimed
to have attended this evening school.
[90] *The African Standard*, Freetown, August 19, 1949.

earnest in the 1950s. Though Bureh headed a tribal authority, he quickly became famous and well respected in many political circles, especially as he worked hard to bridge the gap between protectorate politicians, colony elites, and politicians on numerous occasions. He became one of the founding members of one of Sierra Leone's oldest political parties, the SLPP. In spite of his contributions to local governance and national politics, which helped Sierra Leone achieved self-determination, the dominant literature overlooks Bureh's role in the colony's historical, social and political development. That is, the historical literature focuses heavily on the contributions of Dr. Bankole-Bright, Ottobah-During, Sanusie Mustapha, and other Freetonians.

Conclusion

Oral sources show that the TTA rivalled the Municipal Council in different spheres, particularly in the domain of local administration. The authority played a major role in upholding and maintaining the rule of law in the colony. In brief, the TTA helped establish order in the largest ethnic community by providing local services for its largely non-Western-educated subjects in the colony. However, it is worth noting that local administrations in the colony, including the TTA, proved to be largely androcentric, because men held many of the top-level leadership positions throughout the colonial period. Notwithstanding the inherent weaknesses of the local authorities, the colonial administration to some extent relied on them to enhance the colonial project. This speaks to Spear's salient point that the colonial establishment relied on local authorities to make colonialism work: "[C]olonial authorities depended on local authorities to effect and legitimate their rule ..."[91] It is clear that the TTA cooperated with the colonial government for a number of reasons, not least to make itself relevant in the affairs of the colony and to carve out a political and social niche, in order to achieve political hegemony and the entrenchment of Temneness as a cultural and political force in a cosmopolitan environment. The long line of Temne tribal headmen strenuously pursued this blueprint, and the colonial government directly or indirectly contributed to the process that accomplished it. In sum, the TTA to some extent contributed to the success of the British colonial project in Sierra Leone.

The next chapter examines the tension over space between the TTA and the municipal council. The Freetonian intelligentsia, also referred to as the "coastal intelligentsia," opposed the establishment of local

---

[91] Spear, "Neo-Traditionalism, p. 9.

authorities on the grounds that they duplicated the functions of the municipal council. They argued that colonial authorities devised tribal rule as part of a scheme to divide and rule Africans. Despite the fact that, colonial authorities dismissed such criticisms, they continuously refined the functions and relevance of local administrations until their final and complete abolition in 1932.

4 Intergroup Relations and Genealogies of Conflict: The Temne and Freetonian Dichotomy

This chapter assesses the contextual relevance and significance of the TTA, and its role in mobilizing ethnic identity for political and social gain. Supporters of the TTA believed it played a big role in uplifting Temne catchet, and providing local services for constituents, such as giving financial assistance to indigent subjects, providing temporal accommodation for impecunious immigrants and impoverished subjects, and performing juridical functions. In spite of this, like other tribal administrations, the TTA failed to provide tangible benefits for the Temne community. Clearly, the TTA failed to provide educational opportunities, such as elementary and middle schools, vocational or tertiary training centers, and institutionalized healthcare facilities and community centers. Despite the fundamental weakness of the TTA and other tribal administrations, it is reasonable to note that local administrations in the colony served as auxiliaries to the colonial establishment, and they all engaged in activities that promoted colonial governance.

In fact, in the early twentieth century, two principal views emerged about the relevance of local administrations in the colony. The Freetonian establishment condemned tribal rule as nothing short of a sophisticated and elaborate artifice designed by colonial authorities to subvert African unity and effectiveness in claiming the right to self-determination. They passionately argued that tribal administrations like the TTA duplicated the functions and services of the municipal council, although the council largely served Freetonian interests. On the other hand, members of indigenous ethnic communities believed that local administrations created the avenue for their participation in the decision-making process on issues that affected them directly. They collectively advanced the case that tribal administrations gave them the opportunity to determine their own interests and concerns. The different perspectives on the relevance of local administration produced tension between the two sides – the Freetonian establishment, and the tribal authorities. In addition to sharp disagreements over the need for tribal rule, both sides haggled over issues relating to the control of public spaces: public markets, commercial centers, taxation, the legality of public holidays, and the control of necropolises. The available historical sources show that the TTA challenged the municipal council's efforts to abolish local administration in the colony.

In the post–World War II period, a steady increase in the Temne population continued to strengthen the position of the TTA, which became one of the foremost tribal administrations, with expanded jurisdictional responsibilities. The TTA thus became the symbol of authority for the Temne community in the Sierra Leone Colony. However, its activities and appeal went beyond the province of the Temne community. In 1946, at a ceremony marking the establishment of the multiethnic Muslim Association, the TTA donated £11.00 "on behalf of the Temne tribe."[1] The membership of the Muslim Association included Ahmed Alhadi (Registrar of the High Court), and I. B. Sanusi, both members of the Aku community; Councilor Metcalfe Cole (Justice of the Peace), and G. Spillsbury, legal counsel.[2] The aims and objectives of the association included serving "Sierra Leone by opening the children of Sierra Leone to a sound training in Arabic, English, etc. so that they could organize their own people in the manner the prophet of Islam has prescribed."[3] In the same year, the association launched its first school in an elaborate ceremony. The head of the TTA chaired the ceremony and received the following encomium: "Kande Bureh who might be regarded as typical of the progressive elements in Freetown and of the Temnes whose Tribal Head in Freetown he is, held the audience by his flow of eloquence and the aptness of his illustrations."[4] Though he served as head of the TTA, Bureh regularly acted as chair of the Muslim Association during its general meetings.[5] Despite such a display of multiculturalism, tension engulfed various interest groups, particularly during their adrenalized clamor for self-determination, a debate that progressively turned ugly and rancorous in many ways. As the process of decolonization took an expeditious turn, British colonial authorities insisted on adopting and practicing the principle of majority rule, which gave power to the mass of the people through their elected officials, as discussed in Chapter One.

In all, the decolonization debate led to persistent tension, which also affected local administrations, especially the TTA and the

---

[1] *SLWN*, Freetown, March 4, 1946.
[2] *SLWN*, Freetown, November 26, 1946.
[3] *SLWN*, Freetown, March 4, 1946.
[4] *SLWN*, Freetown, March 4, 1946.
[5] *SLWN*, Freetown, November 26, 1946.

Freetonian-dominated municipal council. However, the Temne tribal headman showed leadership in the midst of this political tension: as the gulf between the Freetonian intelligentsia and the TTA widened, Bureh joined forces with revered members of the Aku community, and together they formed a political but neutral organization, the East End Political Group (EEPG), with the sole aim of bringing together feuding political parties.[6] Bureh, who became inaugural chairman of the group, maintained that the issue of the "re-constituted legislative council and the building of a Community Center for the East Ward was to be resolved by all means necessary."[7] He promised to use his position as chairman to bridge the divide between the Freetonian community and indigenous tribal groups in the colony. A number of conclusions can be drawn from Bureh's leadership of the EEPG, and his role in conflict management. First, though a tribal headman, Bureh played the role of a statesman and national leader. Second, his role as the Temne tribal headman showed the influence the TTA commanded in this multiethnic British territory. Finally, the action of the EEPG proved to be one of the first major steps in fostering intercommunity and intergroup cooperation and relations in the colony. Notwithstanding the overtures of the EEPG, tensions between the various dissenting political groups remained irreconcilable and irresolvable. Freetonians feared the political drawbacks of majority rule; this fear galvanized them into action as they coalesced around the NCSL "following upon the failure of Colony groups to alter materially the substance of the 1947 constitutional proposals."[8]

They continued to believe that protectorate representatives had no "legal rights as foreigners to be represented" in the legislative council and "vote with us on any matter pertaining to the colony."[9] On the other hand, protectorate elites supported the principle of majority rule; they used the SLPP as a vehicle to achieve this goal. Simply put, the two major political parties – the NCSL and the SLPP – became dominant representative parties of the two groups at this time. The SLPP had a certain advantage, due to its widespread appeal in the protectorate and among some Freetonian and non-Freetonian residents. Because it claimed to represent protectorate interests, it commanded a bigger following than the colony-based NCSL.[10] Given his gravitas as the leader of the largest tribal authority, Bureh played a huge role in popularizing the SLPP and

---

[6] *SLWN*, Freetown, September 11, 1948.
[7] *SLWN*, Freetown, September 11, 1948.
[8] Kilson, *Political Change*, p. 225.
[9] *SLWN*, Freetown, August 5, 1950.
[10] *West Africa*, June 11, 1960.

its political philosophy in the colony and protectorate. The leadership of the SLPP appreciated Bureh's membership and his role in canvassing for the party in the Temne and other ethnic communities. Members of other political parties admired the stature of the Temne leader, as demonstrated in the following comment: "Kande Bureh has two strongholds: East Freetown where he is the idol of the illiterate and a fair tract of the Northern Province [in the protectorate]. He has a strong appeal to 'poor boys.' If there should be real popularity for the United Front he is necessary."[11]

The battle for political hegemony heated up with the use of inflamed rhetoric on both sides of the political divide. While the Freetonian intelligentsia heaped scathing opprobrium on colonial authorities for introducing the principle of majority rule, which gave the protectorate a demographic advantage over the colony, the protectorate's educated elites countered with poignant language accusing the Freetonian establishment of ingratitude. The TTA and others argued that they leased the land that made it possible for descendants of settlers or Freetonians to live in the colony.[12] In his criticism of the colonial administration, Dr. Hubert Bankole-Bright, the head of the NCSL, observed: "The Protectorate came into being after the butchering and massacre of some of our Fathers and Grandfathers and their blood streamed in the streets of Mendi Land because they were described as Black English Men ... and after only fifty years of their treacherous and villainous act Loyal Sierra Leone is asked by the British Government to vacate her seats in their British Legislature (this is what it tantamount to) for the descendants of the murderers of our ancestors."[13] The political divide between the two sides degenerated further into ethnic conflicts, as a majority of Freetonians aligned themselves with the NCSL, while a majority of non-Freetonians coalesced around the SLPP. Ahmed Alhadi, who previously worked with Bureh in the EEPG, joined forces with the Freetonian intelligentsia in opposing the idea of a single legislative council for the colony and protectorate. Like Bankole-Bright, Alhadi excoriated colonial authorities for adopting the Beresford Stooke constitution proposed in 1947. Alhadi describes the new constitution "as repugnant ... and a stock-in-trade ..." because it betrayed the interests of the "free settlers."[14]

---

[11] *West Africa*, June 25, 1960.
[12] *SLWN*, Freetown, October – November 1950
[13] *SLWN*, Freetown, August 5, 1950.
[14] Ahmed Alhadi, "The Re-Emancipation of the Colony of Sierra Leone" (unpublished pamphlet, Freetown: 1956), p. 2.

Not only that, Isaac Wallace-Johnson also joined forces with his former political rival, Dr. Bankole-Bright, becoming a member of the NCSL.

With the realignment of political forces, Bureh practically became a national politician whose influence suffused the length and breadth of Sierra Leone. As political tensions deepened the divide between the two regions, a nationwide riot broke out, instigated by the demand by members of the Artisan Workers Union (AWU) for a pay raise.[15] Uproarious riots quickly spread to the protectorate, where they rapidly gained steam.[16] In colonial Freetown, representatives of the AWU refused to drop their demands, prompting the government to engage the services of Bureh and A. B. Magba-Kamara as interlocutors.[17] The two men met with the secretary general of the AWU, Marcus Grant, to negotiate a way out of the crisis. At the end of the meeting, both sides failed to come to an agreement, until the government instructed Bureh and Kamara to appeal directly to the striking workers. Using his eloquence and genial charm, Bureh persuaded the workers to end the industrial action while negotiations continued.[18] As the riots became widespread and destructive, he travelled to every nook and corner of the colony to address striking workers. His visits took him to various communities dominated by Freetonians and non-Freetonians. One of the striking workers, Chief Adikalie Gbonko, recalled in an interview for this study that he agreed to "return to work after Bureh addressed and appealed to some of them directly in *Theimne*."[19] When the impasse between the workers and the colonial administration was finally resolved, all parties to the conflict acknowledged the collaborative efforts of the mediators of the conflict, Bureh and Magba-Kamara, for their "praiseworthy" commitment to resolving the impasse.[20]

As the pace of the decolonization process increased, colonial authorities continued their policy of the devolution of powers to local administrations, by adopting the Rural Area Council Ordinance in 1949. The uniqueness of the ordinance is that it allowed the creation of village

---

[15] *Daily Mail*, April 7, 1955.

[16] *The African Vanguard*, February 25, 1955.

[17] C.S.O. *Report of Commission of Inquiry into the Strike and Riots in Freetown, Sierra Leone During February 1955* (Freetown: Government Printing Office, 1955), pp. 29–30.

[18] C.S.O. *Proceedings of a Commission of Inquiry into the Freetown Strike and Riots in February 1955* (Freetown: Government Printing Office, 1955), pp. 3–6.

[19] Interview, Chief Gbonko, Freetown, November 2, 2003. Hajj Bangurah corroborated this information and noted that he empathized with the workers as a private citizen. He claimed to have attended some of the meetings convened by Bureh and others to undermine the strike.

[20] C.S.O. *Report of Commission of Inquiry*, p. 31. See also *The African Vanguard*, February 1955.

committees and councils for the coordination and provision of local
services. The ordinance stipulated that committee members and coun-
cilors must be popularly elected by the people resident in the relevant
electoral wards. Furthermore, it required that aspirants for council seats
must meet property qualifications and be citizens in good standing.[21]
This development added another layer of tension in the already politically charged atmosphere in the colony. During the elections for coun-
cilors, the TTA strongly supported and sponsored Temne candidates.
The first election conducted in a rural area under the 1949 Ordinance
pitted candidates supported by the NCSL against candidates funded
by the TTA. This is significant, because the TTA became one of the
few tribal authorities – if not the only tribal authority – effectively to
sponsor local council candidates, by challenging the dominance of the
Freetonian establishment. The election returns show that in Waterloo,
Alimamy Kabia and E. Turay, both Temne candidates, won the two open
seats, while W. A. K. Williams, Festus John, and Marcus Roberts won in
the heavily Freetonian-dominated wards of Hastings.[22] A fourth candidate, Alimamy Kargbo, also supported by the TTA, won the open council seat in Hastings.[23] In Tasso Island, a peninsula town, Gbassay Kargbo
and Alimamy Kamara, both strongly supported by the TTA, and Charles
John (recorded as a Freetonian), won open council seats as well. Overall,
candidates supported by the NCSL and the TTA dominated the election
results. It remains unclear whether Mende-, Limba-, and Loko-speaking candidates contested the elections, but lost. It is also worth noting
that the parameters used to determine the ethnic identities of candidates
remained nebulous. The TTA did not only meddle in local council elections, it also fully immersed itself in national politics, as it put up and
funded Temne candidates for national office.

In 1957, when the colonial government opened municipal council
elections to non-Freetonians, the TTA fielded a number of candidates.
The elections proved important because, for the first time in the history
of the municipal council, non-Freetonian candidates received the official
imprimatur to contest council seats – part of the colonial authorities'
slant toward devolution. In spite of this, the qualification-requirements
for candidates participating in the council elections as set by the electoral

[21] C.S.O. *The Rural Area Council Ordinance No. 11 of 1949 MP 13764/23* (Freetown:
Government Printing Office, 1949), pp. 3–7. See C.S.O. *Review of Government during
the Year From November 1952 to November 1953* (Freetown: Government Printing Office,
1953), p. 4.

[22] C.S.O. *Ministry of Internal Affairs and Development 137/64/23/1/52* (Freetown: Elections
Organ Office, 1957), p. 8.

[23] C.S.O. *Ministry of Internal Affairs*, p. 8.

commission proved very challenging for some candidates; i.e. to qualify to run for a council seat, candidates had to own property worth at least £20 or more and had to be literate in English.[24] In 1944, the government reviewed the property qualification for the municipal council, and concluded that the qualifications needed to run for council seats disqualified a substantial number of voters and seekers of electoral offices from participating in elections: "[T]he large Protectorate-born population of Freetown is left without direct representation on the Council."[25] To remedy the situation, colonial authorities swiftly reformed the powers of the municipal council in a new ordinance promulgated in 1945. The ordinance lowered the qualification for the right to vote or be voted for in municipal elections. It stated:

Every person whether male or female shall be entitled to be registered as a voter for any one ward and when registered to vote at the election of a member of the Council for such Ward who ... had attained the age of twenty-one years ... and in the last six months the owner and occupier of a property (jointly or severally) of any house, warehouse, counting-house, shop, store or other building (in this Ordinance referred to as qualifying property) in the City, of which the estimated annual value is not less than six pounds.[26]

The above represented a big change in the property qualification for voters and seekers of electoral offices, at least at the municipal level. Despite these reforms, the number of voters who met the new requirements remained insignificant. Because the reforms did not increase voter participation, the colonial administration made additional changes to the law, by lowering the property qualification to £3. Barbara Harrell-Bond and others suggest that additional changes in the property qualification dramatically increased voter participation by 1956. The lowering of the electoral requirements enabled the TTA to sponsor many aspiring Temne candidates. Some informants for this study reminisce about voting "for Temne candidates in city council elections in 1957."[27] The changes in the municipal ordinances helped non-Freetonians to challenge the Freetonian dominance of municipal politics effectively.

As head of the TTA, Bureh's political clout continued to increase, which culminated in his appointment as Minister of Works by the SLPP-dominated administration in 1957.[28] Notwithstanding, his national

---

[24] Harrell-Bond et al., *Community Leadership*, p. 169.

[25] *The African Standard*, Freetown, August 5, 1949.

[26] C.S.O. *An Ordinance to make Provision with respect to Municipal City of Freetown No. 1 of 1945* (Freetown: Government Printing Office, 1945), p. 9.

[27] Interview, Ambassador Sorsoh Conteh, Freetown, December 10, 2003.

[28] David Skinner, Barbara Harrell-Bond and Allen Howard, "A Profile of Urban Leaders in Freetown, Sierra Leone, (1905–1945)." *Tarikh* 1981 7 (1), pp. 11–19.

portfolio, he meddled in local politics and continued surreptitiously to support Temne candidates. Some sections of the media criticized him for stepping over the line when he campaigned for Temne candidates who were vying for municipal council seats. His critics drew the attention of the reading public to the code of ethics, which barred government ministers from actively participating in electioneering activities.[29] Bureh's political activities also drew reprobation from Wallace-Johnson, a former firebrand activist–turned–politician. Though Wallace-Johnson's popularity had ostensibly ebbed at this point, he continued to be an important political voice. In berating Bureh's covert political support for some candidates, Wallace-Johnson bleated his objection to the government about "the Temne Tribal Ruler's open involvement in politics."[30] The government, however, dismissed such criticisms and noted that Bureh had the right to offer support to candidates in a measured and "moral way."[31] At the conclusion of the first set of municipal council elections, Ahmed Conteh and Ibrahim Sesay, both candidates funded by the TTA, won seats for the east and west wards.[32] In addition to these candidates, the government nominated the Chief Imam of the Temne Central Mosque, Alhaji Gibirl Sesay, to the City Council.[33] In short, the TTA's influence went beyond the confines of its traditional functions, as it helped change the municipal electoral map arguably far more than other tribal administrations in the colony.

The foregoing analysis suggests that, between the 1890s and the post–World War II period, Temneness assumed a steady degree of significance, propelled by one of its quintessential institutions – the TTA. Given the influence it commanded, the TTA created a foundation that boosted the rise of other Temne institutions, such as cultural associations and various Islamic institutions. Oral accounts show that Temne cultural associations contributed to the acculturation of new immigrants into colony life, while Temne Islamic institutions, especially mosques, contributed to the propagation and entrenchment of the principles and teachings of the Islamic faith. Nonetheless, the rise of Temne institutions, and the steady influence and to some extent the gravitas of Temneness, frequently became a source of tension between Temne elites and the Freetonian intelligentsia. Added to the political tension between the two communities, they also

[29] *Shekpendeh*, Freetown, October–November, 1958.
[30] C.S.O. *Complaint from I. T. A. Wallace-Johnson about the Temne Tribal Ruler to the Governor, 134/11, 1957* (Freetown: 1957).
[31] C.S.O. *Colonial Secretary to Isaac T. A. Wallace-Johnson, March 25, 1957* (Freetown: 1957).
[32] *Sierra Leone Royal Gazette*, November 1957, quoted in Harrell-Bond et al., *Community Leadership*, p. 200.
[33] Sesay Private Papers, *Appointment to the City Council, November 1957* (Freetown: 1957).

clashed over a number of other hot-button issues, such as control over public spaces, the recognition and declaration of public holidays, and the right to levy taxes on various constituents.

The next section examines intercommunity relations between the Freetonian and Temne communities. It surveys the degree and range of contention between the two local administrative institutions – both representatives of major communities in this multiethnic British overseas sphere of interest.

Community Relations in a Pluralistic Colony: The Municipal Council and Temne Tribal Authority

The Municipal Council, later named the Freetown City Council, established in 1893, consisted of fifteen elected and appointed members, and had the distinction of being the oldest municipality in British West Africa.[34] Its first mayor, Samuel Lewis, elected in 1895, strongly advocated self-rule for Africans.[35] In lending support to strengthening the structures of the municipal council, the erudite Lewis passionately argued that the objective "should be to train the inhabitants [of the council] to all methods of self-help and how to deal with their own affairs."[36] The mandatory duties of the council included the cleaning and lighting of streets, provision for sanitized market spaces, and the cleaning of cemeteries. It also had mandates to collect taxes, market dues, and cemetery and property taxes from residents, among other functions.[37] It is not surprising that the council continually opposed the existence and operation of tribal authorities in the colony. With such broad mandates and functions, the council and tribal administrations faced off on a number of issues. The tension between the municipal council and tribal authorities revolved around the legitimacy of tribal rule, and the council's mandate to collect taxes and control public spaces. The municipal council believed it was the body authorized by statute to oversee the use of public facilities and other public spaces. In challenging this perspective, the TTA executive argued that the municipal council did not have legal jurisdiction over the Temne community in the colony. It particularly argued that the council did not have legal authority to collect taxes from Temne residents. In light of these ill-disposed

[34] Thomas Joshua Alldridge, *A Transformed Colony, Sierra Leone, As It Was, And As It Is, Its Progress, Peoples, Native Customs and Underdeveloped Wealth* (London: Seeley, 1910), p. 62.

[35] Alldridge, *A Transformed Colony*, p. 62.

[36] J. D. Hargreaves, *A Life of Sir Samuel Lewis* (London: Oxford University Press, 1958), p. 68.

[37] Hargreaves, *Sir Samuel Lewis*, p. 69.

exchanges, the leadership of the council appealed to the colonial admin-istration for tribal administrations to be subsumed under the council's jurisdiction.[38] Akin to this, some key members of the council advocated an end to immigration from the protectorate, to curb the persistent flow of ethnic immigrants. The calls from these members persisted, which impelled the colonial administration to take action; it took steps to mod-ify and consolidate tribal authorities. The administration argued that the changes made the tribal administrations much more effective. It is legit-imate to state that colonial authorities reformed the system to appease members of the municipal council. Withal, the attempt to consolidate tribal rule did not appease some members of the council, as reflected in this comment:

It seems ironical that whilst efforts are being made to end the colony/Protectorate distinction, there should at the same time group be sets up … within the City, which in effect would mean division of the people instead of welding them into one … [The Municipal] Council is strongly opposed to the setting up of Tribal Council and Board in Freetown, as they are considered to be unnecessary, inim-ical to the interest of the people and derogatory to the status of the Mayor, Aldermen and Councillors.[39]

Supporters of tribal rule in the colony strongly advocated for a contin-uation of the heavily abridged system.[40] Kande Bureh and other tribal heads launched counterattacks on what they perceived as Freetonian cultural arrogance and hegemony. In spearheading the position of tribal chiefs, Bureh argued that tribal rule gave the colony the stability it enjoyed. He charged: "[W]ithout tribal administration, Sierra Leone government would find it difficult to administer justice in the country and the social life of the tribes in the colony would severely be dis-rupted."[41] Bureh and other community leaders took strong exception to what they perceived as Freetonian obstructionism on the issue of tribal administration. The tit-for-tat response continued, with tribal leaders reminding their critics that the colony belonged to all ethnic communi-ties. Bureh, as de facto leader of the various local authorities, articulated the following position:

Mr. Beckley suggests that Protectorate people should be restricted from making visits or staying in Freetown. Does he want to make Freetown a Reservation for

[38] C.S.O. *Legislative Council Debates, Sessions 1925–1926* (Freetown), pp. 146–148.
[39] CS MP 2008/5, 3.7. 1956: 336–7, cited in Harrell-Bond et al., *Community Leadership*, p. 151.
[40] Michael Banton, *West African City*, pp. 143–146.
[41] *Sierra Leone Daily Mail*, October 1953 cited in Harrell-Bond, et al. *Community Leadership*, p. 153.

Freetonians? How can he succeed in preventing the aborigines from staying in their homeland? Let him go to Creole-land and make such fantastic suggestions.[42]

Bureh and other leaders reminded council members that, when immigrants visited the colony, they relied on support from tribal leaders. They also argued that many immigrants spoke *Theimne and* other languages sometimes understood by their hosts. The migrants therefore needed some orientation from their tribal authorities, who effectively performed this task better than the Freetonian-dominated municipal council. The leaders stated that the municipal council lacked the requisite proficiency to perform such functions. Parallel to this, Bureh and other apologists of tribal rule stated that, when fugitives fled to the colony, tribal headmen tracked them down and returned them to face justice.[43] Despite the eloquent arguments advanced by the leaders, colonial authorities eventually abolished local administration in the mid-twentieth century; however, the TTA continued to wield considerable influence within the Temne community.

Tax collection and control over commercial spaces became additional sources of tension between the municipal council and local authorities. Howard asserts that control over commercial spaces, in particular, triggered persistent wrangling because "small-and middle-scale African traders fixed themselves in places where they found commercial gain and in so doing asserted their right to be there."[44] In 1945, the TTA and municipal council clashed over legal control of the King Jimmy, Bombay Street and Kissy Road markets. Historical sources show that Temne and Freetonian women traders dominated these markets because the two group of women traders owned numerous stalls in the markets mentioned above. Temne market women refused to pay market dues to officials of the municipal council, on grounds that the officials did not have legal authority to collect such taxes. The council insisted to the TTA that market women traders using city markets must pay dues to its officials. The colonial authorities in support of the council's position maintained that officials of the municipal council had the right to collect taxes within its jurisdiction. The council inflamed the situation, when it proposed a ban on all petty and wholesale trading on Sundays – the council considered Sunday a Sabbath Day for all Christians. The Mayor, and head of the municipal council, proclaimed that "the City Council has not at any

---

[42] *The Sierra Leone Daily Mail*, 23. 10. 1953, cited in Harrell-Bond et al., *Community Leadership*, p. 153.
[43] Michael Banton, *West African City*, p. 143.
[44] Allen Howard, "Contesting Commercial Space in Freetown, 1860–1930: Traders, Merchants and Officials." *Canadian Journal of African Studies* 37: 2–3 (2003), p. 261.

time encouraged Sunday trading."[45] It is clear that the hawking of goods on Sundays disconcerted a segment of the population, as highlighted in this comment: "[W]hen it spreads to hawking about, this aspect of Sunday's trading demands absolute stopping. It is surprising ... that the Tribal Authorities are unable to stop it."[46] Christian missionaries and secular supporters of the ban railed against street hawking, particularly during church services on Sundays.[47] A letter sent to the editor of the *Sierra Leone Daily Mail* stated that "[T]here may be nothing justifiable against selling and buying within [and] around the vicinity of the markets, either for foodstuffs or throughout the day, but what needs to be prohibited is hawking through the streets and shouting the articles with obvious jests and derision ... "[48] In fact, the author appealed to the municipal council and "the various Tribal Chiefs Headsman [sic] or Imams to consider" drafting legislation and forwarding it to the government for adoption.[49] The proposal to ban hawking or trading on Sundays meant that the municipal council perceived the colony as a Christian settlement. In tandem, this also means the council considered colony residents with different political persuasions irrelevant to the debate.

The TTA, on behalf of other local authorities, denounced the proposal as insensitive and unjustifiable. They stated that the colony consisted of various religious groups, and that the council's declaration banning street hawking and other forms of commercial transactions on Sundays violated the rights of non-Christians, including Muslims, free thinkers and animists.[50] In reaction to the council's declaration, some members of the TTA clamored for the adoption of countermeasures to undermine the ban on Sunday trading. In spite of the objections of members of the Islamic community and other religious groups, the municipal council outlawed trading on Sundays.[51] To counter this blanket ban, the membership of the TTA suggested to its leadership that it should also institute a similar ban against street trading on Fridays. The proposer and advocate of the ban against Friday trading urged Temne Muslim adherents and other leaders of local authorities to recognize the ban in order to preserve the sanctity of the Muslim Sabbath: "Mr. Abu Mansaray from the House of Jama Kandeh Bureh at Elk Street told the Mail that it was not necessary for all Muslims to trade on the Sabbath, it was desecrating

[45] *SLWN*, Freetown, November 5, 1949.
[46] *Sierra Leone Daily Mail*, Freetown, November 11, 1952.
[47] *Sierra Leone Daily Mail*, Freetown, November 11, 1952.
[48] *Sierra Leone Daily Mail*, Freetown, November 25, 1952.
[49] *The Sierra Leone Daily Mail*, Freetown, November 25, 1952.
[50] Interview, Hassan Kamara, Freetown, October 5, 2003.
[51] *The Sierra Leone Daily Mail*, Freetown, March 21, 1953.

to trade on that day, he said."[52] Bureh initially deplored the idea of a ban against commercial activities of any kind, noting that Muslim adherents must recognize and respect the religious plurality of the colony. He stated further that Muslims must respect Christians, and members of other faiths, and vice versa. To underscore his opposition, Bureh "invited all the section leaders with their people to a meeting. In the course of the meeting I was made to understand that Muslims and all members of the various tribes engaged in market trading were not pleased with the City Council's Order stopping Sunday trading within markets."[53] The proposal to ban trading on Friday specifically appealed to the numerous Temne Muslim adherents. It remains unclear if Bureh eventually endorsed the proposal. An informant for the study reminisced that the TTA unofficially enjoined its officials to ensure that Temne Muslims observed the ban, which came into force after the council implemented its ban on street hawking on Sundays.[54] It is not clear if non-Temne Muslim traders obeyed the TTA (informal) order, or if colonial authorities gave the ban any official imprimatur. What is clear, however, is the fact that the two sides maintained their positions; trading on Sundays remained officially banned by the council, while members of the TTA enforced a ban on Friday trading within its community. A very prominent Temne market woman, Haja Sukainatu Bangura, recollected that, according to the order handed down by the TTA, a first violation of the order by Temne traders met with a fine and the confiscation of the culprit's goods on a second violation.[55] It is reasonable to assume that the ban on Friday trading, instituted by the TTA and others, did not have the full backing of the colonial government. Thus, enforcement of the informal ban may have been contingent on cooperation within the Temne and other tribal communities in response to the ban on Sunday trading. Nonetheless, observers and participants of this episode recount that the implementation of the ban against trading on Fridays in the Temne Islamic Community undermined the colony's economy, given the preeminence of the Temne population. Moreover, they posit that the economic impact of the ban underlined the range and reach of the TTA, and its contagious influence in Britain's first overseas domain in West Africa. Due to the dearth of documentary data, it is very difficult to accurately

---

[52] *The Sierra Leone Daily Mail*, Freetown, March 28, 1953.
[53] *The Sierra Leone Daily Mail*, Freetown, November 11, 1952.
[54] Interview, Chief Gbonko, Freetown. Hassan Kamara and all informants also corroborated this information. They noted that, because the Temne headman barred Temne from selling their goods or open their markets on Fridays in colonial Freetown, that practice has continued to this day.
[55] Interview, Haja Sukainatu Bangura, Freetown.

measure the impact a ban on Friday trading had on the overall economy of the colony. The absence of documentary data also makes it difficult to corroborate the reflections and/or utterances of informants, who claim to be observers of this episode.

Corollary to this, the TTA and the municipal council clashed over the control of public spaces, such as cemeteries, national parks, and the like. The municipal council claimed and exercised legal authority over the use of these public spaces. The executive of the TTA persistently challenged these claims, and refused to comply with the dictates of the council's command: the TTA insisted that its subjects had the right to use public facilities as they deemed fit. It should be pointed out that the council had jurisdiction over the Freetown municipality, as it clearly reserved the right to generate funds through the collection of taxes and other dues to run the affairs of the colony.[56] An informant for this study recalled that in the late 1940s and early 1950s, the municipal council stipulated that the TTA needed prior authorization before its members inhumed their dead in any of the following: Kissy Road, King Tom, Race Course and Ascension Town cemeteries.[57] The council referenced the Municipal Council Ordinance of 1945, which authorized the council to regulate the use of cemeteries, to buttress its position: "[I]t shall be lawful for the Corporation to provide and regulate the use of Public Cemeteries in the City and notwithstanding anything contained in the Public Health Ordinance of 1924, to close any such Public Cemeteries in accordance with bye-laws [sic] made under the Ordinance."[58] However, in 1947, the council and the TTA reached a tacit agreement; that is, the leadership of the council offered land for use by ethnic communities in the colony

[56] Banton, *West African City*, p. 143.
[57] Interview, Chief Adikalie Gbonko, Freetown, November 2, 2003. There is not much documentary or archival information here on the Temne-Freetonian tension, with respect to the use of public space in the colony. During field research for this study in Freetown in 2003, the author visited the Freetown City Council to obtain information on the Council and its operations in the colonial period. The Town Clerk emphatically noted that the council's archives suffered a devastating loss when rebels believed to be members of the Revolutionary United Front burned the Council's library during the 1999 rebel invasion of Freetown and its environs. Given the dearth of documentary data, the study heavily relied on oral testimonies obtained from people who claimed to be participant-observers, such as Chief Gbonko, in some of the events analyzed in the study. Chief Gbonko claimed to have been an active and enlightened young Temne man in the 1940s and 1950s, when the events described in this volume occurred. Hassan Kamara, a raconteur who described himself as a local and organic historian, claimed to have authoritative knowledge on the Temne-Freetonian tension in the 1950s. The author located newspaper articles that speak to the conflict between the Temne community and Municipal Council run by Freetonians. The drift of the articles broadly supports some of Kamara's assertions.
[58] C.S.O. *An Ordinance to Make Provision*, p. 18.

to entomb their deceased. The agreement between the two administrative groups led to the establishment of the *Rukpr* necropolis in the *Rukpr* suburb – a Temne stronghold. Further, the council offered the Temne community and other ethnic communities alternative burial sites in Circular Road, Kissy, and Wellington; some of these alternative burial sites were located in areas with dense Temne populations.[59] The clash over the control of necropolises exposed the continued fight over social and political hegemony between the two ascendant communities in this pluralistic society.[60] The Temne leader persistently challenged the rights of the municipal council to control shared public spaces, in disregard of the municipal council ordinance.

Conclusion

On account of the above, it is logical to maintain that tribal administrations served as effective partners in advancing the objectives of the British colonial project, at least in the colony. This chapter reveals that the essential feature of indirect rule implemented through tribal administrations effectively utilized the skills of tribal headmen "as an integral part of the machinery of the [colonial] administration. There [were] no two sets of rulers – the British and native – working either separately or in co-operation, but a single Government in which the native chiefs have well-defined duties and an acknowledged status equally with British officials. Their duties should overlap as little as possible."[61] The activities of the TTA and other local authorities show that the history of local administration cannot be fully understood through the lens of the municipal council, as insinuated in the historical literature. It is clear from the available historical evidence that tribal administrations enhanced the activities of local and municipal governance in the colony.

The preceding analysis also indicates that the social activities of the TTA and its ethnonationalists increased the influence of the Temne community in the colony. The pan-Temne activities of the venerable Kande Bureh and his coterie of officials assiduously uplifted Temne prestige beyond the confines of the Temne community; that is, the influence of Temneness became far-reaching. Edward Blyden III states that when

---

[59] *SLWN*, August 2, 1947.
[60] See Howard, "Cities in Africa"; See also Allen Howard and Richard M. Shain, eds., *The African Spatial Factor in African History: The Relationship of the Social, Material and Perceptual* (Leiden: Brill, 2005).
[61] Frederick Dealtry Luggard, *The Dual Mandate in British Tropical Africa* (London: William Blackwood and Sons Ltd., 1926), quoted in Robert O. Collins, ed. *Documents from the African Past* (Princeton: Markus Wiener Publishers), 2001, p. 291.

Isaac Wallace-Johnson established his National Youth League in 1939, he used a Temne slogan to garner grassroots support: "[F]or the first time in the country's long history, all of the people were literally brought together under a common slogan SABARNOH (a Temne language term meaning, DIS KONTRI NA WE YONE (Krio) or this land belongs to us, the people."[62] The implications of the use of the phrase are twofold. First, it shows Wallace-Johnson's determination to make his organization appear multiethnic and all-inclusive. Second, it reveals the amplitude of Temneness and its propagators in the colony. Put another way, why did Wallace-Johnson not use an Aku, Freetonian, Mandingo or Mende phrase in touting the inclusiveness of his organization? It is valid to assert that he used a Temne phrase to construct a slogan for his grassroots organization because of the preponderance of the Temne community and possibly because *Theimne* became one of several languages widely spoken in colonial Freetown. Additionally, in the lead up to independence, Sir Milton Margai, the first Prime Minister of Sierra Leone, used Temne proprietary claims to counter Freetonian animadversions on the presence of protectorate representatives in the legislative council.[63] A careful look at the historical documents suggests that Margai's line of attack effectively undermined the Freetonian position, though this did not end the back and forth between the parties.

The next section describes the role cultural associations played in augmenting Temneness. Historical sources show that gatekeepers of Temne identity used a broad range of parameters to determine Temne identity, as already mentioned. It shows that Temne identity to some extent relied on one's declarative statement, particularly in the absence of a veritable litmus test to adjudge the authenticity of such claims.

[62] Edward Blyden III, "Sierra Leone: The Pattern of Constitutional Change, 1924–1951" (Harvard University Press, PhD Dissertation, 1959), p. 168.
[63] *Sierra Leone Observer*, Freetown, May 6, 1950.

Part III

Ethnocentrism and New Frames of Popular Culture

5   Temne Cultural Associations and Popular Representations

The previous chapter shows that the TTA became one of the most influential local authorities between 1890 and 1961. As a matter of fact, the TTA offered such services to its subjects as the provision of temporal housing for new immigrants, the provision of employment opportunities, and funding for Temne candidates in municipal elections, which to some extent cushioned the challenges faced by underemployed members of the Temne community. Ergo, the TTA became a symbol of authority and influence in a multiethnic environment. It contributed significantly to the establishment of other Temne institutions, such as cultural associations and Temne Islamic institutions.

This chapter explores the rise of Temne cultural associations and their role as instruments of coalescence and mobilization. It also evaluates the role of the associations in constructing Temne identity, and uplifting Temne image in a competitive colonial space. The chapter specifically interrogates the fluid determinants used to evaluate candidates for membership in the associations. Oral sources indicate that Temne cultural associations became attractive to lots of ethnic communities – Mende-, Limba-, Loko-, Mandingo-, Aku-, and Fula-speakers. New applicants seeking membership strictly followed prerequisites laid down by the leadership of the various Temne associations; new applicants publicly "became" Temne by learning and speaking *Theimne*, brazenly singing songs in *Theimne* during public performances, and wearing customary dress that symbolized Temne values and traditions. It is not clear if the new members shed their primordial identities before they joined the associations, or if they maintained their previous identities even after they joined the associations.

The preeminent Temne associations among the many established included: *Alimania, Ambas Geda,* Endeavor, Temne Progressive Union (TPU), Boys London, *Nuru Jinati* and *Ariah.* This study departs from previous works, which focus on the historical and sociological trajectory of dance associations, such as the Mandingo *Tarancis, Yankadee,* and Aku

Ogoogoo, among others. Michael Banton's work, for example, focuses heavily on the anatomy of voluntary associations in colonial Freetown. However, Banton's work overlooks the role cultural associations, such as the various Temne cultural associations, played in the construction of ethnic identities.

Oral data and historical documents reveal that Temne identity did not just exist in the social landscape; it was continuously shaped and reshaped through the process of enculturation and acculturation. Leaders of the associations used specific symbols to create a sense of being Temne. Succinctly put, ethnic entrepreneurs and culture brokers helped determine and shape the process of becoming Temne, especially when flaunting Temneness proved socio-economically and politically beneficial. Oral sources show that the Temne community established more associations than did other ethnic communities in the colony. The relative success and enthrallment of the Temne associations resulted in the establishment of auxiliary associations in Mende-dominated towns and cities in the protectorate.[1]

In his examination of the Temne *Alimania* and *Ambas Geda*, Banton states that the formation of both associations stemmed from the need to halt the flight of young Temne men and women to Mandingo and Aku ethnic communities. He states that, in the 1920s, Mandingo-speakers established the *Yankadee* and *Tarancis* – both dance associations – as means of boosting Mandingo culture and pride. The associations adopted exclusive policies that restricted membership to Mandingo-speakers and/or non-Mandingo-speaking members who adopted Mandingo identity.[2] Similarly, members of the Aku community established the *Ogoogoo* society and restricted its membership to Aku members.[3] These policies resulted in "a growing proportion of ambitious young Temne join[ing] the Mandinka and Aku societies, often learning the language and seeking to pass as members of these tribes."[4] Since the Temne and others lacked cultural associations of their own, young men and women flocked to the Tarancis, Yankadee, and Ogoogoo, after adopting Mandingo or Aku identities respectively. The Temne in particular felt antithetical to the fact "that strangers should look down on them [which was] a particular blow

---

[1] Interviews, Chief Adikalie Gbonko, Pa Alimamy Yenki Kamara, and Sukainatu Bangura, Freetown, November 3–4, 2003. All interviewees were interviewed separately.

[2] Mandingo is used here to refer to those recorded as such in the literature, including those who described themselves as Mandingo.

[3] Aku is also used here to refer to those recorded as Aku in the literature and those members who identified themselves as Aku.

[4] Michael Banton, *West African City: A Study of Tribal Life in Freetown* (London: Oxford University Press, 1957), p.164.

to Temne pride, for the land on which Freetown now stands was once Temne territory. They still regard it as theirs and claim for themselves the privileged status of those who own the land."[5]

Against this background, the Temne formed the *Alimania* and *Ambas Geda*.[6] Though the emergence of the *Alimania* and *Ambas Geda* can be traced to the exigency of uplifting Temne pride lost to Mandingo and Aku communities, as Banton argues, the data suggest that the formation of Temne associations in general can be traced to a continuation of the trend of the rise of Temne institutions. This is evident in the fact that the Temne formed more associations than did other ethnic groups. In addition, while the TTA and various activists established numerous associations to burnish Temne image and prestige, Temne leaders and non-Temne leaders politically manipulated the associations. Clearly, the TTA and cultural elites practically collaborated to make Temne identity alluring to others, through the *Alimania*, *Ambas Geda*, Endeavor, *Ariah*, TPU, and Boys London. The makers of Temne identity adopted a two-pronged approach to achieve their objective: First, they set out to bring back to the community young Temne men and women who fled to the Mandingo and Aku communities. Second, they mapped out a strategy to engrave Temneness with social glamor by portraying the tangible benefits of membership in the associations.

The section below analyzes the social activities, structure, and underlying political ramifications of the Temne associations. The founders described them as Temne associations to distinguish them from other associations, and to shore up Temne hegemony in this ethnic *olio*.

Hegemony and Contested Identities: An Analysis of Temne Popular Culture

To fully appreciate the contributions of Temne associations in making Temne identity and uplifting Temne status, an analysis of the rise and range of the activities of the following associations are in order: *Alimania, Ambas Geda*, Endeavor, Temne Progressive Union (TPU), Boys London, *Nuru Jinati*, and *Ariah*.[7]

Temne cultural associations became vessels through which the Temne community asserted its popular culture in the colony. The Temne community also methodically used the associations to shore up its population for demographic advantage over Freetonians and other ethnic groups.

---

[5] Banton, *West African City*, p. 164.
[6] Banton, *West African City*, pp. 164–165.
[7] Founders and founding members described these as Temne associations.

Relying on its special relationship with Britain, the Freetonian establishment believed that, as the first Western-educated elites, including medical doctors, engineers, and civil servants, its accomplishments qualified it to inherit the mantle of leadership from the colonial authorities. On the other hand, many in the Temne community lacked Western education or specialized training in numerous fields, which potentially disqualified them from succeeding the colonial authorities. In recognition of this fact, the TTA and various Temne activists used variables other than Western education to proclaim Temne relevance and significance. As the dominant indigenous ethnic group, the Temne used cultural associations to expand their population and entrench their perceived ascendant status. The leadership of the associations embarked on a systematic process of constructing a polished image of Temne values and traditions. Each association offered unique but highly complementary services to the Temne community and its associates.

Alimania, which meant, "a group of humble people full of patience," became one of the first associations to assert Temne popular culture in the colony in the 1940s.[8] Established as a dance and religious association designed to promote the teachings of Islam, *Alimania* endeavored to "promote and foster more interest in social, educational and religious standards and so help enhance the progress of the African so as to take [his or her] place honourably in the affairs of the Democratic world in the near future."[9] It sought to foster solidarity among Temne Muslim men and women.[10] Apart from the *Alimania*, the TTA also supported Kande Bureh in founding a much more secular association, the *Ambas Geda*, in 1945.

Some founding members of this association reveal that Bureh formed the association after he fell out of favor with Gibril Sesay, leader of the *Alimania*, on the issue of religious syncretism. They claim that Sesay wanted the principles of the *Alimania* to be based on Islamic law while Bureh preferred a secular association, based on shoring up Temne popular culture. Both leaders failed to reconcile their differences, forcing Bureh to withdraw from the *Alimania*; he later founded the *Ambas Geda*, meaning, "we have gathered." Despite their differences, both associations worked toward achieving the same objective – to restore pride, prestige, respect and cohesion in the Temne community. Between 1942 and

---

[8] Interview, Hajj Hassan Bangurah, Freetown, November 1, 2003. He claimed to have been a member of this association.

[9] *SLWM*, May 14, 1949.

[10] Interview, Hajj Hassan Bangurah, Freetown, November 5, 2003.

1943, the *Alimania* started "elementary classes for children and adults in Arabic and vocational training."[11] The administrator in charge of organizing classes restricted the opportunity to members of the Temne community. In 1945, due to increased enrollment, the association funded the building of a school later known as the Temne School, or *Madrasa Immaniyia*.[12] The school became the main Islamic educational institution for the Temne in the post–World War II period.[13] Aside from this, in the 1950s, the *Alimania* contributed to the completion of the *Jam ul-Jaleel*, also known as the Temne Mosque.[14] The association also funded wedding ceremonies for indigent members, and financially assisted bereaved subjects. Further, association meetings served as venues of interaction for potential couples; such meetings fostered and facilitated marriage relationships, organized orientation programs for new immigrants, taught young men and women the value of communalism and business management skills.[15]

To strengthen the culture of marriage among its members, especially young members, the *Alimania* provided counselling services to couples, and regularly counselled them on the values of marital commitments and mores.[16] Simply stated, the *Alimania* provided a social space where new immigrants interacted "freely with their peers, expressed themselves on a wide range of issues" and learned the arts of leadership and management in the Temne community. The *Sierra Leone Weekly News* observes that in 1951, "Alpha Abu Bakar, the Spiritual Leader of the Alimania Association has been asked in the name of Allah ... to resume his good work as Imam of the Central Temne Mosque at Oldfield Street."[17] As spiritual leader, Bakar became one of the "most recognized Temne Muslim preachers" and served as a member of the Sierra Leone Muslim Congress and the Muslim Brotherhood discussed in Chapter 6.[18]

Over and above this, the *Alimania* contributed to the British war effort; it raised funds to help the British authorities and their allies in World War II. The Mayor praised the gesture when he stated:

During World War II realising that might is not right and that aggression will never bring peace on earth, and realising also that King Niambana's [Temne

[11] *SLWN*, Freetown, May 14, 1949.
[12] *SLWN*, Freetown, May 14, 1949.
[13] Interview, Hajj Hassan Bangurah.
[14] Interview, Hajj Hassan Bangurah.
[15] Interview, Hajj Hassan Bangurah.
[16] Interview, Hajj Hassan Bangurah.
[17] *SLWN*, Freetown, January 24, 1951.
[18] *SLWN*, Freetown, July 7, 1951.

chief] – the British people, were fighting for our rights and privileges so that peace may reign supreme on earth forever, the Alimania Association thereupon staged a Grand Native Dance at the Wilberforce Memorial Hall, the net proceeds of which amounted to twenty-five pounds was landed to Government.[19]

Akin to the above, the secular *Ambas Geda* proved effective in uplifting Temne culture and prestige. It helped new immigrants adjust to urban life by providing them with relevant information and education on multiple issues. For example, with a surge in immigration after the 1920s, it became imperative to provide basic services to new immigrants flocking to the colony. Some immigrants arrived in the colony psychologically broken, due to adverse conditions created by district commissioners, the Frontier Police Force, and the institution of slavery, which they had escaped.[20] It should be noted that, in spite of the abolition of slavery in the British Empire in 1807, the practice continued in parts of the protectorate. Due to the harshness of some of the living conditions, many slaves, also called "domestics," escaped from slavers and immigrated to the colony.[21] Their departure created worrisome economic gaps for chiefs, "who saw a mass exodus of their labourers to the coast and caused consternation to the Sierra Leone government, which found itself with stagnant production in the protectorate and a swollen city in Freetown."[22] The *Alimania* and *Ambas Geda* helped with the migrants' general orientation, particularly when most of these migrants felt disoriented by urban life.

The migration of Temne immigrants from the protectorate to colonial Freetown meant a departure from the traditional ways of life they had led in a tightly organized society. In the case of young female immigrants in particular, the Mammy Queens of the *Alimania* and *Ambas Geda* helped them "adjust to the culture shock in colonial Freetown."[23] Kenneth Little captures this sentiment, emphasizing,

The association helped the migrant adapt to the new life by providing him [or her] with new information about the town ... The association also reduces the migrant's isolation by acting as a "civilizing" agency on his behalf. It inculcates

[19] *SLWN*, Freetown, May 14, 1949.
[20] *West Africa Mail and Trade Gazette*, January 9, 1926.
[21] *West Africa Mail and Trade Gazette*, January 9, 1926. See also Allen Howard, "Pawning in Coastal Northwest Sierra Leone, 1870–1910" in Toyin Falola and Paul E. Lovejoy, eds., *Pawnship in Africa: Debt Bondage in Historical Perspective* (Boulder, Colorado: Westview Press, 1994), p. 276.
[22] Anne Phillips, *The Enigma of Colonialism: An Interpretation of British Policy in West Africa* (Bloomington: Indiana University Press, 1989), p. 34.
[23] Interview, Sukainatu Bangura; corroborated by Hajj Bangurah, who was an executive member of the Alimania in 1955. See also Kenneth Little, *African Women in Towns: An Aspect of Africa's Social Revolution* (London: Cambridge University Press, 1973), p. 50.

new standard of dress, social behaviour and personal hygiene; the advantage from the migrant's point of view is that he felt at home with his neighbours.[24]

Little states that migrants usually turned to the head of an association, rather than to his or her, family for advice when confronted with overwhelming circumstances in the colony. It is clear that the presence of these migrants affected the demographic makeup of the colony. As immigration heightened, many Temne and Mende immigrants took on menial jobs that were despised and ignored by residents in colonial Freetown, particularly Freetonians.[25] Historical sources show that immigrants felt relatively comfortable with their hosts, who guided them through their daily lives in a complex urban space. Oral data indicate that, when new immigrants faced legal trouble or financial difficulties, they felt comfortable reporting such matters to the cultural associations of their choice. The associations usually responded to these cases more promptly than did relatives.[26]

The *Alimania* and *Ambas Geda* also raised the standards of dress and cleanliness among their memberships.[27] Little states that cultural associations "prescribe a specific code of personal and moral conduct which is designed to regulate the public behaviour of members as well as their relations with each other."[28] The code of conduct of the *Alimania* and *Ambas Geda* outlined the penalty members of the associations would incur for indecorous behavior in private or in public. Both associations stressed the need for gender equality, as they instituted safeguards for women against abusive husbands. The discipline officers of both associations investigated claims of domestic abuse, or allegations of immorality. The Mammy Queen also sat on the panel that investigated allegations of abuse; she ensured victims received justice at all times. As chair or co-chair of the discipline committee, she helped determine the punishment for culprits. Usually, first offenders received a fine, while repeat offenders faced the possibility of expulsion from the association.[29]

The *Alimania* and *Ambas Geda* occasionally performed judicial functions, in addition to other social services. The chief whip handled interpersonal conflicts, and referred unresolved cases to the deputy chair in

[24] Kenneth Little, *West African Urbanization: A Study of Voluntary Associations in Social Change* (Cambridge: Cambridge University Press, 1970), p. 80.
[25] *SLWN*, Freetown, June 14, 1942.
[26] Interview, Chief Adikalie Gbonko.
[27] Interview, Chief Adikalie Gbonko.
[28] Little, *West African Urbanization*, p. 96.
[29] Interview, Sukainatu Bangura. As the first Mammy Queen of the Alimania, she informed me that she dealt with numerous cases of spousal abuse. She emphasized that, during her tenure, she reduced the number of such cases within the Alimania.

charge of personnel. On the other hand, the TTA handled cases dealing with divorce, conflicts over inheritance and property rights, and witch-craft. This means that colonial authorities allowed the TTA to handle cases that dealt with customary law. The judicial role played by the two associations saved the colonial administration resources and time, especially as English Law differed from customary law. This shows that colonial authorities recognized the role traditional elites played in maintaining law and order in an urban purlieu. On a broader level, it shows that colonial authorities did not make customary law, but rather "employed African customs as well as their own moral codes to seek to establish political, social and economic domination, while Africans – old and young, male and female – appealed variously to African, colo-nial, Muslim and Christian codes to defend their interests."[30] Added to this, the breadth of responsibilities assumed by the *Alimania* and *Ambas Geda* shows that the TTA supported both associations. Moreover, the associations' role in resolving disputes among members fostered the much-desired ethnic cohesion and unity that elders craved. Finally, the discipline enforced among members prepared them for potential challenges in other spheres.[31] The associations' emphasis on moral standards helped reduce crimes in the colony, not least in the Temne community.[32] The chief whip imposed fines for unpunctuality and rec-ommended suspension, or in some cases expulsion, for chronic tar-diness. In fact, the *Alimania*, like other cultural associations, taught immigrants economic discipline, as the treasurer enforced strict finan-cial rules involving the payment of loans and monthly subscriptions. The associations also practiced mutual benefit schemes for members, governed by strict regulatory concepts.[33] The limited credit scheme operated by the *Ambas Geda* provided microfinancing for members engaged in small-scale entrepreneurship. Late repayment of loans met with stiff penalties, which required the culprits to pay much higher interest rates. The executive of the TTA normally served as the guaran-tor of loans for some members, especially new immigrants. Ansumana Koroma, a beneficiary of such a microfinance scheme, recollected that the loan he and his business partner received proved helpful to his small

---

[30] Spear, "Neo-Traditionalism," *International Journal of Historical Studies*, p. 16.
[31] Interviews, Chief Gbonko, Pa Yamba Kalie and Sukainatu Bangura. All gave their views in separate interviews.
[32] Michael Banton, "Adaptation and Integration in the Social System of Temne Immigrants in Freetown." *Africa* 26, no. 4 (October 1956), p. 335.
[33] Little, *West African Urbanization*, p. 89–90.

scale enterprise.[34] He noted that the credit scheme contributed to the colony's informal economy.

Some informants for this study stated that, though men dominated the leadership of both associations, women contributed to their success as well. The first Mammy Queen of the *Alimania*, Sukainatu Bangura, a renowned and established leader among market women in the King Jimmy and Bombay Street Markets, recalled that she was the first to be consulted when Gibril Sesay nursed the idea of forming the *Alimania*. She persuaded her close business associates, like Yankaday Kargbo, Mbalu Conteh, Haja Nancy, Gbessay Sesay, Yebu Sesay, and Adama Kamara (her sister in-law), to attend the maiden meeting Sesay convened. At the meeting, the members present elected both Gibril Sesay as President and Bangura, also known as Kai Bangura, as Mammy Queen.[35] As Mammy Queen, she maintained discipline among female members, and ensured that the chief whip enforced dress codes during the association's public performances. The Mammy Queen headed the association's choir, and offered tutorials to young male and female performers. During public and private performances, the associations' bands sang songs in *Theimne*. Furthermore, the Mammy Queen co-chaired marriage ceremonies for young members, sponsored by the association. In short, the activities of the Mammy Queen and other female officials enhanced the cultural worth of the associations. This speaks to Geiger's argument about the important role of female activists in mass movements and nationalist struggles in colonial Africa.

In Tanganyika, Geiger argues, female lead singers, such as Bibi Titi Mohamed, played a significant role in amassing support for the Tanganyika African National Union (TANU). Bibi Titi's commitment to TANU helped broaden the appeal of the association beyond its traditional base of male supporters.[36] While Julius Nyerere, the widely acclaimed hero of Tanzanian independence, gave scripted speeches in English, and sometimes Swahili, and mobilized men, Bibi Titi recruited women, urging them through speeches and songs to join TANU in order to secure Tanganyikan independence. Through her courage and determination to give women agency in Tanganyikan nationalism, Bibi Titi increased the

---

[34] Interview, Ansumana Koroma, Freetown, September 5, 2003. Koroma served as one of the lead drummers. Born in Freetown, where he has since lived, he could not recall his date of birth. However, he claimed to be 78 years old.

[35] Interview, Sukainatu Bangura. The informant is not related to the author.

[36] Susan Geiger, "Tanganyikan Nationalism as 'Women's Work': Life Histories, Collective Biography and Changing Historiography" *The Journal of African History* 37, no. 3 (1996), pp. 467–468.

participation of women in TANU. Though an illiterate woman, she commanded great influence in TANU, and proved to be a leader of consequence. During heated confrontations between the nationalists and the colonial authorities that forced the men, especially Nyerere, to go into hiding, she fearlessly rallied the troops.[37] Bibi Titi's important role in TANU, as trumpeted by Geiger, attaches new meaning to the role of female activists in male-dominated associations in colonial Africa. Over and above this, Fatou Diarra and her colleagues used songs to convey their views on sociopolitical events in colonial Guinea: "[W]omen went to the markets every day ... if there was a new song all the women learned it and sang it in the taxis, teaching one another. When there was an event, the leader went to the market with the song to teach it to other women. After the 1954 elections, women sang at the markets that the colonial government had rigged the elections."[38]

In the same vein, since the 1940s, Sukainatu Bangura and others used songs to carve out a niche for themselves in the *Alimania*. For example, they used songs to laud and spread the principles of Islam, taunted perceived male cowards, and encouraged non-members to join the *Alimania*. Such contributions by groups of women in the historical development of African societies deserve more than a passing reference in African historiography.[39] This lacuna is especially profound in Sierra Leone historiography, which pays scant or no recognition to the role of women in the social formation of the colony.[40]

The influence of the *Alimania* and *Ambas Geda* went beyond the Temne community in the colony. In the 1950s, both cultural groups established auxiliary associations in the protectorate, especially in Temne- and Limba-speaking strongholds, such as Mateboi, Makeni, Kambia and Magburaka, and also in Mende-speaking regions.[41] Like the *Tarancis and Yankadee*, the quaint but unique public performances of the *Ambas Geda* and *Alimania* made them captivating to onlookers and nonmembers. Some public performances included drumming, dancing and

[37] Susan Geiger, *TANU Women: Gender and Culture in the Making of Tanganyikan Nationalism,1955–1965* (Portsmouth: Heinemann, 1997), pp. 58–61.
[38] Elizabeth Schmidt, "'Emancipate Your Husbands!': Women and Nationalism in Guinea, 1953–1958" in Jean Allman, Susan Geiger and Nakanyike Musisi, eds., *Women in African Colonial Histories* (Bloomington: Indiana University Press, 2002), p. 288.
[39] LaRay Denzer, "Yoruba Women: A Historiographical Study." *International Journal of African Historical Studies* XXVII (1994), pp. 1–12.
[40] See Joseph J. Bangura, "Gender and Ethnic Relations in the Sierra Leone Colony: Temne Women in Colonial Freetown." *History in Africa* 39 (2012), pp. 267–292.
[41] Interview, Chief Adikalie Gbonko. These are Temne strongholds; my dad hails from Magburaka. He recalled watching *Ambas Geda* functions as an onlooker when he was a high school student.

singing *Theimne* songs in groups of four, with each group wearing unique costumes. In spite of the attractiveness of the performances, critics strongly opposed some aspects of the social activities of the associations, especially the theatrical public performances which they characterized as "drunken women, the Temnes ... using their unbridled tongues" in the evening on the streets of the colony.[42]

Undeterred by such criticisms, the TTA and Temne cultural elites established other associations – such as Endeavor, Temne Progressive Union (TPU), Boys London, *Ariah*, and *Nuru Jinati* – that many perceived as offshoots of the *Alimania* and *Ambas Geda*. Though they differed in scope and genre, the Temne associations as a whole embarked on the overarching project of constructing a distinct Temne image, to achieve cultural and political hegemony. However, unlike the *Alimania*, some associations proved much more androcentric in their composition.

Pa Alimamy Yenkin Kamara, a local intellectual and tailor by profession, claimed he had founded both Endeavor and the Temne Progressive Union in 1938, and 1958, respectively. He recalled that he formed the associations because as "owners of Freetown [the Temne] needed associations outside the 'chief house' to discuss political and non-political matters."[43] He established Endeavor as a vocational institute to train young men in tailoring.[44] Born in the colony to Temne parents in 1918, Kamara became a tailor at an early age – upon graduation from elementary school. After he established Endeavor, he secured financial assistance from the TTA to buy sewing machines for his students.[45] With increased enrollment at Endeavor, the TTA partly sponsored the expansion of the facilities at the school. Additionally, the school expanded its curriculum to include carpentry and woodwork. On the recreational front, Endeavor helped to organize the annual lantern parades held during *Eid-ul-fitr* celebrations, which marked the end of the Muslim month of fasting; the lantern parades "attracted people from diverse ethnic backgrounds."[46] Between 1949 and 1952, the association promoted intercommunity soccer competitions with teams from all ethnic backgrounds competing in a four-day tournament. The tournament gave participating youths the opportunity to showcase their individual skills and talents. The tournament became an annual event, and served several purposes. First, it provided an avenue for youths to showcase and optimize their talents,

---

[42] *SLWN*, September 9, 1943.
[43] Interview, Pa Alimamy Yenkin Kamara, Freetown, November 2–3, 2003.
[44] Interview, Pa Alimamy Yenkin Kamara.
[45] Interview, Pa Alimamy Yenkin Kamara.
[46] Interview, Pa Alimamy Yenki Kamara.

and, second, it provided financial help for some participating teams; i.e. they received financial compensation from the income generated during the tournament. Third, the soccer tournament fostered good intercommunity and intra-community relations. Kamara states that "Endeavor was the only association which organized soccer tournaments involving teams from other ethnic communities."[47]

As a Temne association, members used *Theimne* as the official medium of communication during meetings and official transactions. However, though described as a Temne cultural association, Endeavor admitted Freetonians, Aku- and Mandingo-speaking candidates who learned and spoke eloquent *Theimne*.[48] In 1949, Messrs. Williams and Samu Johnson, both Freetonian young men, became "the first non-Temne members of the association; they both spoke Theimne well."[49] It is not clear how Kamara determined the identity of Messrs. Williams and Samu Johnson as Freetonians. In fact, Williams later rose to the rank of secretary-general of the association. It is unclear if Freetonian members abandoned their primordial identities, or carried multiple identities after they joined the association.

Two decades after Kamara formed Endeavor, he established a political association – the TPU. A former key member of the association recalled that "The TPU was founded by a group of dynamic Temne young men in the east of the colony led by a very prominent tailor, Borboh Yenkin Kamara with the objective of educating our less fortunate brother[s], unite the entire Temne youths in Freetown ... "[50] The TPU also supported the activities of the Temne Islamic School and the *Jam ul-Jaleel* (Temne mosque). Like Endeavor, TPU became a male-dominated organization. The association also passionately engaged in political activities and supported Temne candidates in national elections.[51] Based on this, it

---

[47] Interview, Pa Alimamy Yenki Kamara.

[48] Interview, Pa Alimamy Yenki Kamara.

[49] Interview, Pa Alimamy Yenki Kamara.

[50] Notes from Ambassador Sorsoh Conteh, Freetown. After many interview sessions with the former ambassador, he decided to do a short piece on the contributions of Temne institutions in the Colony. The notes are based on his personal experience. The author corroborated some of his accounts on the TPU with Pa Alimamy Yenkin Kamara himself. However, while Kamara corroborated much of what Ambassador Sorsoh Conteh wrote in his piece, the two men differed on the date the association was founded. Kamara stated that he founded the association in 1955, while Conteh indicated 1958 as the founding date. When the author asked about the discrepancy in the two dates, Kamara noted that he conceived the idea of forming the association in 1955 and then discussed the idea with friends who encouraged him to proceed with his initiative. But the first official meeting and launching of the association took place in 1958. Borboh was his childhood name.

[51] Interview, Ambassador Sorsoh Conteh.

is plausible to argue that the TPU mirrored the NCSL in tone and character – both groups became ethnic and political associations.

The TPU became prominent in 1960, when talks convened by the British government in Lancashire, United Kingdom, on the issue of independence for Sierra Leone, partially broke down. One prominent delegate at the independence conference, Siaka Stevens, opposed some aspects of the agreement, while other delegates accepted the agreement in its entirety. To protest the terms of the independence agreement, Stevens returned home and formed a political party. He converted a previous movement he had founded, the Elections Before Independence Movement (EBIM), into a political party, "the All Peoples Congress, with the sun as emblem."[52] Kamara recalled that Stevens, already suspicious of the ambition of the SLPP-led delegation, tapped into the TPU for political support. The TPU membership gave the new party unflinching support, and some TPU members, such as Sorie Ibrahim Koroma, played a very active role in its affairs. Koroma eventually rose to the post of First [Vice] President of Sierra Leone and secretary-general of the ruling All Peoples Congress (APC).[53] Though the TPU firmly supported the APC because of its staunch anti-Freetonian and anti-Mende agenda, Kamara acknowledged that some members of the TPU surreptitiously supported the SLPP.[54] One of his famous members, Kandeh Bureh, for example, maintained dual membership in the TPU and the SLPP. Informants for this study state that support of TPU members for the APC proved crucial, as the party became the dominant force in northwestern Sierra Leone. The APC eventually became the longest-ruling political party in Sierra Leone.

In 1951, another self-styled Temne activist, Pa Wusu, established a famous association, *Nuru Jinati*, which means "Heavenly Aspirations," based in Magazine Cut in the eastern part of the colony.[55] The association promoted Temne culture and communal values, such as respect for

[52] *West Africa*, September 24, 1960.
[53] Notes from Ambassador Sorsoh Conteh. The ambassador claimed to be a founding member of the APC; he states that his role in founding the party won him at least four ambassadorial appointments in Europe, Africa and Asia.
[54] *Daily Mail*, May 23, 1952.
[55] Interview with the author, Chief Gbonko. During field work for this study in Freetown, the author did not talk to old members of this association, as many are deceased. Chief Gbonko, who claimed to be a former colleague and friend of Pa Wusu, provided much of the information I use here. He claimed to have been an associate member of the association because of his close personal relationship with the founder. Since I could not access any other piece of information on this association, I relied on the accounts he provided. I should also point out that Magazine Cut was a community heavily dominated by Aku. Aku residents here were referred to as "Foulah Town," distinguishing them from Aku residing in the Fourah Bay area. Lots of Mandingos and Fulas also resided here.

the institution of marriage, sacred treatment of the dead, and the need to imbibe and spread the principles of Islam. It provided financial and manpower contributions to the construction of the *Jam ul-Tawid* (Temne mosque in Magazine Cut) project. On completion of the project, the *Jam ul-Tawid* became the second-oldest Temne mosque in the colony. Chief Gbonko recollected that public performances, such as dancing and singing on special occasions, became the association's main source of income.[56] The leadership of the association admitted people who claimed to be Temne either by birth or ancestry, or by the public flaunting of Temne identity, including demonstration of fluency in *Theimne*. The association emphasized strict adherence to the teachings of Islam, punctuality, punctiliousness, and regular attendance at meetings. Members found guilty of fetishism, sorcery, fornication, adultery, or superstitious activities deemed antithetical to orthodox Islam faced expulsion.[57] The participation of *Nuru Jinati* in the completion of the *Jam ul-Tawid* reveals its knack for community development. Though principally controlled by Temne Muslims in Magazine Cut, the mosque served Muslims of all stripes, especially non-Aku Muslims in Magazine Cut and neighboring communities, such as Bambara, and Foulah towns. The chief imam of the mosque, Alhaji Sillah, maintained that the mosque held all proceedings, such as the translation of sermons, official announcements, and correspondence, in *Theimne* and Arabic. Notwithstanding, Mandingo-, Mende-, Fula-, and Limba-speakers regularly attended prayer meetings at the mosque. It is fair to state that many non-Temne Muslims prayed at the mosque, because of its strategic location in the east-central part of the colony. It can also be assumed that some prayed at the mosque because their own ethnic communities lacked such facilities. On few occasions, officials of the mosque translated *Theimne* expositions into Krio, a Lingua Franca spoken in the colony.[58] Informants for this study did not clarify the process used to distinguish Temne and non-Temne worshipers in the mosque. In justifying his description of the *Jam ul-Tawid* as a Temne mosque, Imam Sillah accentuated the point that

---

[56] Interview, Chief Gbonko. To verify some of the claims made by Chief Gbonko, who emphasized his close personal relationship with the founder of this association, the author spoke with the current Imam of the *Jam ul-Tawid* mosque, Alhaji Usman Sillah. Alhaji Sillah, who was not a member of *Nuru Jinati*, confirmed that the mosque was indeed built largely out of funds received on behalf of the association and to some extent from personal donations/contributions by individual Temne members. Sillah was not born in the colony; he was born to Temne parents in Northern Sierra Leone. His parents migrated to the colony in 1920, when he was 10 years old. In 1942, he moved to Magazine Cut, his last known location at the time of the interview, in 2003.

[57] Interview, Chief Adikalie Gbonko.

[58] Interview, Alhaji Usman Sillah, Freetown, November 10, 2003.

Temne adherents constituted the overwhelming majority of worshippers in the mosque. Added to this, the chief imam and other executive members of the mosque claimed to be Temne.[59]

In 1952, Chief Adikalie Gbonko founded another prominent Temne cultural association, Boys London, designed exclusively to provide entertainment and promote Temne culture.[60] The anglicized name of the association implies that the founding members had some degree of Western orientation. As with other Temne associations, the leadership initially restricted membership to young Temne men. As chairman, Gbonko presided over general meetings, and closely supervised the activities of the executive. The association comprised a dancing troupe supervised by a manager during official ceremonies. During public performances, artists wore special costumes, such as *ronkoes* (dark brown country cloth) lined with red and gold stripes.[61] The composition of the troupes reveals that the association did not admit female singers, in contrast to the *Ambas Geda* and *Alimania* which admitted female applicants. It is surprising that the association excluded women from its ranks, even though it claimed to be an association designed to promote unity within the Temne community. It regulated the social mores and moral conduct of its members in the domestic and public spheres. Indecorous behavior in public, and proven domestic abuse cases, met with immediate expulsion. While the TTA helped establish law and order, Boys London played a relatively significant role in maintaining discipline within its membership.[62] Three years after its formation, Boys London became one of the most famous Temne cultural associations, at least in Bambara Town. In light of this, Chief Gbonko stated that he received numerous applications from young Mende, Limba, Loko, Fulah and Mandingo men and women seeking to join the association. The pressure to open the association to other ethnic community members forced the executive to accept applications from non-Temne candidates. However, the leadership insisted that non-Temne-speaking applicants had to learn *Theimne* and publicly "become" Temne as a prerequisite to join the association. Pa Buya recalled that the requirement stipulated by the executive forced enthusiastic applicants to learn *Theimne* using a variety of methods, including interactive learning and attendance at tutorial sessions organized by the leadership. The organizing officer of the association also scheduled special classes for non-Temne applicants, where he taught them songs in *Theimne*.[63] It remains

---

[59] Interview, Chief Adikalie Gbonko.
[60] Interview, Chief Adikalie Gbonko.
[61] Interview, Chief Adikalie Gbonko.
[62] Interview, Pa Buya, Freetown, November 5, 2003.
[63] Interviews, Chief Gbonko and Pa Buya. Both were interviewed separately.

unclear if these methods proved effective in attracting non-Temne members to the association. In spite of this, it is evident that the association forced non-Temne-speaking candidates to absorb Temne values and learn and speak *Theimne*. It is unclear if the leadership of the association treated bona fide Temne differently from those who merely passed themselves off as Temne. It also remains unclear if tension existed between new members who publicly became Temne, and primordial Temne. Finally, it is not clear if new members of Boys London who became Temne completely jettisoned their primordial identity, or if they carried dual identities.

The proliferation of Temne cultural associations continued with the formation of another exclusive Temne association, *Ariah*, founded in 1953 by Pa Wusu. *Ariah*, meaning "to adorn or beautify," sought to foster unity and cooperation among Temne residents in Magazine Cut and its environs. It primarily promoted intra-community relations and inter-community visits on Fridays after prayers.[64] Pa Wusu posits that inter-community interactions encouraged understanding, tolerance, peace, and harmony within the Temne community in Magazine Cut, Bambara Town and Fula Town.[65] The association contributed significantly to the completion of the *Jam ul-Tawid*. By encouraging inter-Temne community visitations, and promoting understanding among members of these Temne communities, it became easy to mobilize them to participate in national politics. Pa Dumbuya states that during the municipal elections of 1957, "all Temnes voted for Temne candidates because the Freetonians hated us and some Mende[s] could not be trusted in politics."[66] Pa Buya also maintained that the association devised a credit scheme used only during financial emergencies.[67] Because of the economic benefits it offered members, the association attracted residents from diverse backgrounds.[68]

All in all, cultural associations became symbols of Temne identity, conveyors of Temne values, and recruitment institutions. The *Alimania*, *Ambas Geda* and others became popular associations that played a major role in stopping the slide in Temne prestige and status. The stipulation

---

[64] Interview, Pa Dumbuya, Freetown, November 1–3, 2003. He was the secretary-general and a founding member of the association. Born in 1923 to Temne parents, a trader and Temne activist, he engaged in activities that promoted Temne cultural beliefs among young men and women. He is the only surviving member I had the opportunity to interview.
[65] Interview, Pa Dumbuya.
[66] Interview, Pa Dumbuya.
[67] Interview, Pa Buya.
[68] Interview, Pa Buya.

that non-Temne candidates must publicly assume Temne identity before joining many of the associations expanded the demographic makeup of the Temne community.

Historicizing the Politics of Exclusion: "Becoming" Temne

African historiography is clear on the role instrumentalist forces such as African elites, indigenous intellectuals, culture brokers, and the colonial establishment played in constructing ethnic identities in Africa. Glassman calls attention to the fact that instrumentalist literature downplays the role of "African intellectuals in the generation of tribal thought."[69] Similarly, J. D. Y. Peel highlights that human action contributed to the construction of Yoruba identity in the nineteenth century: "Yoruba in its modern connotation, was the product of missionary 'invention.'"[70] This means, Yoruba identity did not exist as a bound and homogenous entity before the nineteenth century. In the Sierra Leone Colony, Temne identity proved fluid and malleable. The various cultural associations became efficient means of transmitting Temne culture to agnostic members of the Temne and non-Temne communities. Alternatively stated, becoming Temne depended on the ability to learn and speak *Theimne* and to act Temne, not least in public. This means that, from the 1920s to the end of colonial rule, Temne identity became a negotiable and dialogic entity, and its composition proved permutable and expansive over a protracted period of time. This speaks to Bill Bravman's point about the instrumentality of Taita identity in Kenya. He states that "Taita identity began to be invoked in settings from officials' utterances, to elders' gatherings, to household struggles over resources and behaviors."[71] Taita identity, which appeared primordial in the nineteenth century, became mutable as colonial rule and/or policies, Christian missionaries, and immigrants challenged proper "Taitaness." Taitaness became disputable as well as negotiable.

In the Sierra Leone Colony, the leadership of the TTA and cultural associations stipulated the process of becoming Temne. A former member of the Mandingo *Tarancis*, Ibrahim Fadika, noted that though many Mandingo-speakers maintained their connection to the *Tarancis*

[69] Jonathon Glassman, *War of Words, War of Stones, Racial Thought and Violence in Zanzibar* (Bloomington: Indiana University Press, 2011), pp. 16–17.
[70] Peel, *Religious Encounter*, p. 278. See also T. C. McCaskie, *History and Modernity in an African Village, 1850–1950* (Athens, Ohio: Ohio University Press, 2001).
[71] Bill Bravman, *Making Ethnic Ways: Communities and Their Transformations in Taita, Kenya, 1800–1950* (Portsmouth, New Hampshire: Heinemann, 1998), p. 139.

and *Yankadee* societies, they "learned *Theimne* so they may become members of the *Alimania*."[72] Fadika recalled that many Mandingo-speakers joined the *Alimania* because it served the dual purpose of promoting Islam, and offering financial assistance to indigent members. The association also performed at the wedding and funeral ceremonies of its members free of charge.[73] Another informant, Salieu Jalloh, a Fula-speaking headman, reminisced that he admired the activities of the *Alimania* because it looked after the welfare of Muslims in the colony. He makes the point that "its leader, Alhaji Gibril Sesay ensured that Temne Muslims and non-Temne Muslims served the interest of Islam well."[74] In 1957, when the Fula-speaking community bickered over leadership positions, the *Alimania* intervened and negotiated a compromise. Jalloh recollected that many young men and women from Fula-, Susu-, and Mandingo-speaking communities publicly claimed Temne identity to be "part of the Alimania organization."[75] It is unclear how many non-Temne members flocked to the Temne associations to accrue benefits from such associations. Oral data indicate that speaking *Theimne* became a principal requirement for admission in all Temne cultural associations. The leaders of the associations stressed the language requirement to avoid the possibility of using "several languages including the Lingua Franca, Krio in any of the associations to avoid undermining core Temne values."[76] Therefore, all official discussions, and conversations, including the singing of songs at public performances, were conducted in *Theimne* and/or Arabic, in the case of the *Alimania*. Part of the attraction of the associations revolved around their theatrical displays, the meaning of their songs in *Theimne*, and their titivating mien. During public performances, songs sung by members of the associations addressed intercommunity and intra-community matters. In some cases, the artists used songs in *Theimne* to convey subtle political messages directed at rivals and perceived enemies.[77] They also sang songs that heaped unparalleled encomiums on Temne prestige and the stature of their leaders in society.

---

[72] Interview, Ibrahim Fadika, Freetown, November 4, 2003. Fadika described himself as Mandingo. Born in Freetown in 1922, he attended the Islamia School in Foulah Town in 1941.

[73] Interview, Ibrahim Fadika.

[74] Interview, Salieu Jalloh, Freetown, November 1, 2003. Born in 1932, Jalloh is one of the Alimamies in Freetown. His parents migrated from Futa Jallon in the nineteenth century, his place of birth.

[75] Interview, Salieu Jalloh.

[76] Interview, Alhaji Gibril Kamara, Freetown, November 4–5, 2003. Kamara is currently the Secretary-General of the Temne Central Mosque.

[77] Interview, Alhaji Gibril Kamara, Freetown, November 4–5, 2003.

For instance, in one of the songs by the *Alimania*, the members trilled the following:

Alhaji Sesay has done well for us, God bless him! Oh, good friendship is a precious thing. Alhaji Sesay of the Temne tribe, when no one knew the Temne would progress; Alhaji Sesay did well for us, God bless him![78]

Another marker of Temne identity in the colony centered on the requirement that all Temne cultural associations wore specially designed costumes for all public performances; the costumes embodied the associations' values and traditions. Informants for the study highlighted that, though many non-Temne members of the *Alimania* imbibed Temne culture and passed themselves off as Temne, some of these members did not speak *Theimne* eloquently. The informants could not verify if all perceived, bona fide Temne demonstrated eloquence and mastery of *Theimne*.

Pa Sorie Dumbuya, a section chief of the Limba community based in the east of the colony, recollected that many members of his household joined the *Ambas Geda* in 1954. He avers that young Limba-speaking men and women, impressed by the extravagant theatricality of the *Ambas Geda*, "publicly passed off as Temne" so they could join the association.[79] Dumbuya "knew many of the Limba young men and women who passed off as Temnes and who sang songs in *Theimne* and wore heraldic emblems of the *Ambas Geda*."[80] He did not comment on the number of young Limba-speaking men and women who fled to some of the Temne associations. He also believed that many Limba-speakers joined some of the associations because their communities lacked social or cultural associations with similar illustrious gravitas.[81] Apart from the reasons adduced by Pa Dumbuya, Chief Gbonko advanced other reasons why Limba-speakers publicly embraced Temne identity in the colony. First, both languages appeared exoteric and to some extent mutually intelligible. Second, many young Limba men and women flocked to Temne associations because of a perceived inferiority complex, born out of their knack for lancing wine from palm trees and vending the same to vendees in rural locales. The community's culture of commercializing palm wine, a natural beverage extracted from palm trees, drew scorn and disrespect from the wider public.[82] Third, some Limba-speakers learned *Theimne*

---

[78] Banton, *West African City*, p. 174.
[79] Interview, Pa Sorie Dumbuya, Freetown, November 10, 2003. He was born in 1930 in Kambia District before his parents migrated to Freetown with him at age 10, where he has since lived. He has been section chief of Kissy Village since 1971.
[80] Interview, Pa Sorie Dumbuya.
[81] Interview, Pa Sorie Dumbuya.
[82] Interview, Chief Gbonko.

through interaction with Temne members either in the colony or the protectorate, especially in Makeni and Kambia, where the two ethnic communities constituted the preponderant population. Chief Gbonko stated that many Limba young men and women admired the public rituals of the *Ambas Geda*. Similarly, Brima Sesay, the headman of Loko-speakers in Wellington, related that some Loko-speakers abandoned their Loko identity and embraced Temne identity so they could join the *Ambas Geda*. Chief Sesay pointed out that, in the 1950s, some of his subjects, particularly young men and women, "admired the melodrama of the *Ambas Geda*; they proudly and enthusiastically learned *Theimne* and publicly 'acted' Temne."[83] Similarly, young Mende men and women became attracted to the *Ambas Geda* and *Alimania* for a variety of reasons. Chief George Caulker, a section chief of the Mende community [based in the Kingtom neighborhood], highlighted that some Mende-speakers passed themselves off as Temne in the late 1940s and early 1950s for artificial reasons. Others passed themselves off as Freetonians for social and political advantage. In the case of those who passed themselves off as Freetonians, many did so to gain membership into the Freetonian-controlled freemasonry. On the other hand, Mende-speakers who joined the *Alimania* and *Ambas Geda* did so to enjoy all the benefits associated with Temneness.[84] Little reinforces this point when he states that, in the protectorate, many successful associations in Mende-speaking locales had Temne leadership.[85]

The oral data and historical documents suggest that the increase in the Temne population in the 1940s and 1950s may be attributed to the recruitment of non-Temne by gatekeepers of Temne identity. Affluent members of non-Temne communities hired the *Ambas Geda* to perform during weddings or on special occasions. Pa Mohammed Kallay, a Mandingo business man, stated that he hired the *Ambas Geda* for the wedding of his daughter in 1955; the association graced the occasion "with exemplary performance accompanied by melodious songs in *Theimne*. Though I am Mandingo, my family had a fondness for the *Ambas Geda* stagecraft."[86] The popularity of the Temne associations turned the tide on the portrayal of Temne identity, particularly by

---

[83] Interview, Brima Sesay, Freetown, November 10, 2003. Chief Sesay lives in Grafton, but his jurisdiction covers Wellington. He was born in 1937 and elected section chief in 1969; he was not a member of the *Ambas Geda*.

[84] Interview, George Caulker, Freetown, November 4–5, 2003.

[85] Kenneth Little, "Structural Change in the Sierra Leone Protectorate." *Africa* 25 (1955), pp. 222–223.

[86] Interview, Mohammed Kallay, Freetown, November 2, 2003. Kallay is a prominent Mandingo businessman in central Freetown.

young men and women who hitherto became attracted to the *Tarancis* and *Ogoogoo*.

Conclusion

It is clear that Temne identity was continuously shaped and reshaped over a period of time. The TTA, cultural elites, and ethnic entrepreneurs used specific symbols to create a sense of being Temne. Temneness became instrumental, and therefore socioeconomically and politically beneficial. The relative success and allure of the associations resulted in the establishment of auxiliary associations in different sections of the colony and protectorate.[87] Because of this, it can be argued that the influence of Temneness became widespread, both in the colony and the protectorate.

In the mid-1950s, ethnic entrepreneurs invoked pan-Temne unity for political and personal gain. Bureh used his status as leader of the *Ambas Geda* to solicit support in his bid to win the headship of the TTA. He also appealed to Temne solidarity to garner support for the SLPP, and in running for national office. Analogously, Gibril Sesay used his position as chief imam of the Temne mosque to gain national recognition. In the 1960s, Sesay served as Sierra Leone's ambassador to Egypt. In his capacity as head of the Temne Central Mosque, Sesay also served on the municipal council and the education board as a nominated member. His position as chief imam of the largest non-Aku mosque in the colony made him chair numerous panel discussions on topics related to Islam on national radio. In short, pan-Temne solidarity meant leaders of the community invoked and manipulated Temne identity for instrumental reasons. This is similar to the approach adopted by elders in the Taita community in Kenya, who continuously elicited reverence from young men and women as "a matter of Taita ways."[88] In the politically charged atmosphere of the 1950s, "proper" Temne ways became synonymous with public assertion of "affective belonging," and acceding to the demands of the political leadership.[89] The available evidence shows that in the 1950s and 1960s, Temneness carried primary and secondary meanings: the former emphasized birth rights, descent, and shared historical experience, while the latter underlined good comportment, as qualifications of belonging. The secondary meaning of "being" Temne promoted by gatekeepers of the Temne associations emphasized the

---

[87] Interviews, Chief Adikalie Gbonko, Pa Alimamy Yenki Kamara, and Sukainatu Bangura, Freetown, November 3–4, 2003. I interviewed all three separately.

[88] Bravman, *Making Ethnic Ways*, p. 252.

[89] See Bravman, *Making Ethnic Ways*.

assimilation of culture and acceptance of Temne values; this means they focused less on other attributes, such as shared historical experience and primordiality, among others. Thus, the various leaders of the associations became effective wardens of Temne identity; they determined and defined "Temne ways" or "proper" Temneness.

The next chapter examines the Temne community's creation of Islamic institutions, and the social impact of these institutions in the colony. As Temneness evolved and suffused, its outreach broadened and deepened. Put differently, Temneness proved to be an asset rather than a liability after the 1930s.

6 Islamic Triumphalism in a Christian Colony: Temne Agency in the Spread and Sierra Leonization of Islam

This chapter argues that the successful entrenchment and propagation of Islam and Muslim practices in a colony proclaimed as Christian in its root and orientation was a multiethnic effort, contrary to the assertion of the dominant literature. The collective efforts of Muslim clerics, agents, and missionary activists from diverse ethnic communities contributed greatly to the acceptance of Islam as a major force in the colony by "Christian Creoles" and the colonial administration. The prevailing Temne Islamic Community (TIC) and the numerous Islamic institutions it established undergirded this multiethnic enterprise. On this basis, this chapter shows the growing influence of the Temne community in the social formation of the colony. It also argues that the Temne Islamic Community, including those who identified themselves as Temne Islamic missionaries and elites, played a much bigger role in the propagation, popularization and/or Sierra Leonization of Islam than acknowledged in the historical literature. Like the TTA and cultural associations, Islam also became a symbol of pan-Temne unity.

As a matter of fact, the Temne became one of the earliest groups to convert to Islam before and after the establishment of the Sierra Leone settlement in the eighteenth century. They established several Islamic institutions, such as mosques, cultural associations such as the *Alimania, Ariah, and Nuru Jinati*, the Temne Qur'anic School, or the madrasah, *Immaniyia*. The activities of these institutions, combined with the activities of Islamic impresarios such as imams and sheiks, helped entrench the principles of the Islamic faith in the TIC, in the colony, and in the interior of Sierra Leone as a whole. Moreover, these institutions served as venues for worship, and an outlet for the preaching of the principles of the faith. Thus, by the end of the nineteenth century, Islam spread rapidly among the Temne; they became one of the largest and passionate adherents of that religion in the colony. Though Temne Muslims became some of the major, and most luminous, propagators of Islam, it is also clear that the Islamic religion indurated Temne identity in the wider

Islamic community. Expressed another way, the spread of Islam among the Temne increased the profiles both of the religion and of Temne identity; that is, Islam and Temneness became dominant and highly influential in a predominantly Christian environment. In addition to this, the TIC also generated a new form of Islamic practice in the colony; Temne Muslims helped shape the Islamic religion, which resulted in the Sierra Leonization of Islam.

The Spread of Islam in the Colony: A Capsule History

This section traces the history of Islam and the roles key contributors played in spreading Islam in the colony. Clearly, Christianity formed part of the colony's historical trajectory and social fabric. In fact, many of the early settlers – the Black Poor, Nova Scotians, and Maroons – practiced Christian principles and traditions in their daily lives.[1] However, starting in the nineteenth century, Islam played an influential role in the religious development of the colony, particularly among indigenous groups and those described as Muslim Creoles.[2]

As stated by J. S. Trimingham and others, numerous factors contributed to the Islamization of Africa, west of the Sudan: trade, politics, and revolution. Colonial officers, in rationalizing the easy spread of Islam in many African societies, point out that Islam "was closer to supposedly simple African religious traditions than sophisticated Christianity," particularly the religion's embrace of practices such as polygyny and "spirit possession cults."[3] In the Sierra Leone Colony, itinerant Mandingo and Fula merchants became the first residents to interact with Islamic merchants and "Arabic holy men."[4] These merchants became the first to propagate the principles of Islam in Sierra Leone, and in the colony

---

[1] J. J. Crooks, *A History of the Colony of Sierra Leone: Western Africa* (London: Browne and Nolan, Ltd., 1903), pp. 108–115.

[2] Crooks, *History of the Colony*, pp. 108–115. Muslim Creoles referred to Aku Muslims; i.e., the segment of Freetonian society that stuck to its Islamic tradition. On the other hand, by indigenous communities, I mean those communities who occupied Freetown and its surrounding areas before it became a settlement for freed slaves. These groups primarily include the Temne, the original owners of the land, and Mende-, Limba-, and Loko-speakers, although an argument can be made to include Fula- and Mandingo-speakers as well.

[3] Roman Loimeier, *Muslim Societies in Africa: A Historical Anthropology* (Bloomington: Indiana University Press), p. 27.

[4] Timothy Insoll, *The Archaeology of Islam in Sub-Saharan Africa* (Cambridge: Cambridge University Press, 2003), p. 324; see also Pade Badru and Brigid Maa Sackey, eds., *Islam in Africa South of the Sahara: Essays in Gender Relations and Political Reform* (Lanham, Maryland: The Scarecrow Press, 2013).

in particular.[5] In underscoring the point, Christopher Fyfe states that "Muslim penetration linked a wide area behind the colony to North Africa."[6] As Islam spread to the colony from various places, including the hinterland, Temne-, Limba-, Mende-, and Loko-speaking communities embraced it; they simply appreciated its basic teachings and principles. Barbara Harrell-Bond and others state that many Islamic institutions "fulfilled an integrative function for many of the Native migrants to the colony. There was also a considerable amount of syncretism between Islamic and local beliefs and practices. Many aspects of social and family life, however, were partially affected by Islam."[7] The scholars contend that Islam provided for and, to some extent, reinforced communal values and norms of behavior among non-Freetonian groups.

As a majority religion with minority status in a predominantly Christian environment, Islam encountered encumbrances and paranoia from a wide variety of detractors, not least colonial authorities and Christian adherents. In 1843, due to persistent objections by the Christian community, colonial authorities destroyed a mosque which Islamic adherents used not only as a prayer house, but also as a meeting place. Such persecutory attacks united Muslims of all ethnic backgrounds in conformity with the Islamic doctrine of brotherhood. It must be pointed out that the negative attitude of colonial authorities towards Islam represented a general trend in European colonial policy, and efforts to "weaken Islamic power in the name of Christianity and to establish imperial preserves in glorification of their newly fashioned nationalisms."[8] British and French colonialists in particular viewed Islamic activists in colonial Africa with suspicion, especially followers of the Sufi sects, such as Wahhabists, the Tijaniyya, the Mouride, and the Muslim Brotherhood. Such paranoia forced European colonizers to suffocate Islamic activities in their territories. As Pade Badru states, "the British strategy of containment of Islam in West Africa was a combination of accommodation and forceful pacification."[9]

---

[5] Alusine Jalloh, *African Entrepreneurship: Muslim Fula Merchants in Sierra Leone* (Athens, Ohio: Ohio University Center for International Studies, 1999), p. 153.

[6] Christopher Fyfe, *A History of Sierra Leone* (London: Oxford University Press, 1962), p. 66.

[7] Barbra Harrell-Bond, Allen M. Howard and David E. Skinner, *Community Leadership and the Transformation of Freetown (1801–1976)* (The Hague: Mouton Publishers, 1978), p. 8.

[8] Sulayman S. Nyang, "Islam and the African World," in Pade Badru and Brigid Maa Sackey, eds. *Islam in Africa South of the Sahara: Essays in Gender Relations and Political Reform* (Lanham, Maryland: The Scarecrow Press, 2013), p. 21.

[9] Pade Badru and Brigid Maa Sackey, eds. *Islam in Africa South of the Sahara: Essays in Gender Relations and Political Reform* (Lanham: Scarecrow Press, 2013), p. 38.

In spite of the negativity directed at Muslims, Islam steadily flourished, especially in the eastern part of the colony – an area heavily populated by Temne-, Aku-, Mende-, Loko-, Fula-, and Limba-speaking communities. Historical sources indicate that, between 1893 and 1894, the number of Muslim adherents, also known as "interior Mohammedans," surged.[10] This development rattled critics, who charged that the "alien faith" practiced by the interior Mohammedans in a "Christian city" must be stopped.[11] However, some sections of the public sympathized with the plight of Muslims, and used the media to appeal for religious tolerance and mutual respect. One such appeal effusively states:

Sierra Leone people [Freetonians] should note that there are more English educated Christians than there are Muslims in this colony. They should know that it is their patriotic duty to help their backward Muslim brethren (born in the same country) as much as themselves. They should remember that the susceptibilities of loyal subjects like the Muslims should not be injured.[12]

It is unclear why the author referred to Muslims as backward. It can be assumed that the author made this charge because many Muslims had little or no Western education, then viewed as a hallmark of civilization, high status, and prestige. Nonetheless, Islam remained visible, and it survived throughout the colonial period; it impacted and continuously influenced the lives of Islamic aficionados in multiple ways.

In the early twentieth century, the Islamic community experienced intra-community challenges, as dissention and ideological conflicts undermined the unity it once enjoyed. In particular, disharmony and accusations of a superiority-complex characterized the relationship between Creole Mohammedans and other ethnic Muslims.[13] Mandingo, Fula, Temne, Mende and other Muslims accused Creole Mohammedans of promoting group exclusivity. As a result, in 1917, these groups deserted the places of worship controlled by Aku Muslims; they flocked to the Mandingo-led *Jam ul-Qudus* (Mandingo mosque), which became their central place of worship. In addition to the conflict between Creole Mohammedans, on the one hand, and non-Creole Mohammedans, on the other, conflict also occurred between Temne and Mandingo Muslims. Thereupon, Temne Muslim worshippers abandoned the *Jam ul-Qudus* and embarked on the construction of their own place of worship, eventually known as the Temne Central Mosque.

---

[10] *SLWN*, Freetown, April 22, 1893, and *SLWN* December 16, 1895. Interior Mohammedans referred to Muslims living in the interior of Sierra Leone.
[11] *SLWN*, Freetown, April–June 1893, and *SLWN*, March 15, 1894.
[12] *West African Mail and Trade Gazette*, April 10, 1926.
[13] *SLWN*, Freetown, April 20, 1892. "Creole Mohammedans" referred to Aku Muslims.

The construction of the Temne Central Mosque enabled the Temne Islamic Community to practice and integrate Islam into local contexts, which enhanced Temne cultural values. Though intra-Temne conflict also engulfed the Temne Central Mosque in the mid-twentieth century, many Temne Muslims gravitated toward the Mosque and the mainstream Temne Islamic Community.

Gateway to Islamization: The Influence of Madrasahs or Qur'anic Schools in the Spread of Islam

Muslim landlords, Islamic schools, mosques, missionaries, imams, *sheiks*, and merchants contributed greatly to the spread of Islam in the colony. While Christian Creoles and colonial officials stressed the attainment of Western education as a status symbol and the "royal road to success," Muslims lauded Islamic education as the gateway to success and eventual salvation "from worldly sins encountered on a daily basis."[14] Many Muslim communities constructed madrasahs to train young Muslims in the value of Islamic education, leadership skills, and missionary work. The curricula in these Qur'anic schools offered courses in Arabic and Islamic theology.[15]

The Temne Islamic Community, as one of the largest Islamic communities, built on the above Islamic tradition and foundation by generating new dimensions of Muslim practice in the colony: it achieved this in several ways. First, like the Mandingo-speaking community, the TIC established a madrasah primarily devoted to the teaching of Islamic doctrine. Second, it hired knowledgeable *Alfas* and *sheiks* to offer specific classes on theology at the school. Third, the TIC constructed the highest number of mosques or Islamic centers of worship – a phenomenon attributed to the passion and influence of Temneness by informants of this study. Moreover, Temne religious entrepreneurs became highly respected disseminators of the principles of the Islamic religion in Sierra Leone as a whole. Finally, Temne Muslims infused cultural values into the practice of Islam, which made it easier for Temne Muslims illiterate in Arabic to appreciate the religion – this process, described as the Sierra Leonization of Islam in this study, played a key role in converting numerous scoffers and banterers to Islam. On account of this, cultural elites and local intellectuals used Islam to reinforce Temne hegemony and clout in a

---

[14] Pade Badru, "Basic Doctrines of Islam and Colonialism in Africa" in Badru and Sackey, eds., *Islam in Africa South of the Sahara*, p. 28.
[15] David Skinner, "Islam and Education in the Colony and Hinterland of Sierra Leone (1750–1914)." *Canadian Journal of African Studies* 3 (1976), p. 503.

competitive urban space. By the mid-twentieth century, Temne Islamic institutions, through their graduates, became effective proselytizers and popularizers of Islam.

The growing strength of Islamic institutions influenced a change in colonial policy toward Islam. Recognizing the significant influence of the religion on many adherents, especially Temne-, Mende-, Limba-, Fula-, and Mandingo-speaking Muslims, the colonial administration adopted a tolerant but cautious policy toward the Islamic community. It permitted ethnic communities to establish privately-owned and privately-run madrasahs. In 1901, colonial authorities enacted legislation regulating Islamic education, and appointed Dr. Edward Blyden III as the first Director of Mohammedan Education.[16] Subsequently, a distinct pattern emerged: various ethnic communities established madrasahs that promoted their cultural values and agendas. Historical records show that, between 1901 and 1943, the Aku community established and ran the madrasahs *Sulaimania, Harunia,* and *Amaraia,* while Mandingo and Fula Muslims created madrasahs *Islamia* and *Umaria,* respectively.[17] On the other hand, the Temne Islamic Community established and administered the madrasah *Immaniyia,* also known as the Temne School. The names of the schools reflect their ethnic and cultural identities, and geographic locations. Hence, madrasah *Islamia,* based in Magazine Cut, principally served Mandingo Muslims and their associates, while madrasahs *Sulaimania* and *Harunia,* established at Fourah Bay and Fula Town, served Aku and Foulah Town Muslims, or those referred to as Creole Mohammedans. Akin to this, madrasah *Immaniyia,* established in the eastern section of the colony, an area with dense Temne population, served the Temne Islamic Community. The criteria used by the administrations of different madrasahs in identifying the ethnic categories of their students are unclear. Oral data suggest that the Aku, Mandingo and Fula madrasahs allowed students from all ethnic background to enroll at their schools, as long as the students claimed to be Islamic adherents.[18]

In 1902, the colonial administration adopted an ordinance that provided funding for Islamic education. The ordinance informed proprietors that "all Mohammedan schools in the colony and the protectorate may receive from the public funds grants-in-aid under this ordinance."[19]

---

[16] C.S.O. *An Ordinance for the Development and Expression of Education on Western Lines Among the Mohammedans of the Colony of Sierra Leone and Protectorate* (Freetown: Government Printing Office, 1902), p. 1.

[17] C.S.O. *Report on Mohammedan Education, 1912* (Freetown: Government Printing Office, 1912), p. 15.

[18] Interview, Hajj Hassan Bangurah, Freetown, November 1–4, 2003.

[19] C.S.O. *An Ordinance for the Development and Expression of Education,* pp. 1–2.

It established formal rules governing their administration, including the appointment of teachers and school administrators. The colonial administration ensured that the madrasahs offered a variety of courses: arithmetic, English, geography and history.[20]

As Islam became prestigious and popular, Temne Muslim adherents sought Islamic education as an alternative path to social status in an urban environment dominated by Western culture and mores. This is evident in the increased enrollment of Temne students in the various madrasahs in the colony. In fact, by the end of the 1905 academic year, there were far more registered Temne students across the Islamic school system, relative to the number of students from other ethnic Muslim communities. In the same year, the report from the Director of Mohammedan Education indicated that, at the start of the first term in April, Aku students had an enrollment of 300, while enrollment for Mandingo-speaking students stood at 100. In the same vein, students described as Temne Muslims had a total enrollment of 60, while Fula- and Susu-speaking students stood at 29 and 45, respectively. The figure for registered Limba students remained at 33, while enrollment for other ethnic groups remained below 5. By the end of the first semester, the average attendance for Aku, Mandingo and Temne students remained the same, while enrollment for students from other communities fell. Alusine Jalloh states that Fula-speakers established many madrasahs in the colony, and thus became prolific propagators of the religion. Historical sources reveal that the number of registered Fula Muslim students across the Islamic school system fell far short of that of Temne Muslim students in 1905. That is, the number of registered Temne students remained unchanged throughout the academic year, while registered students from the Fula, Mandingo and Limba Muslim communities fell slightly, possibly for personal reasons. Figure 5 shows the number of registered students across the Madrasahs between 1905 and 1943 in the Colony.[21]

Figure 5 shows an overwhelming number of Temne students registered in the madrasah Immaniyia for the 1942/43 academic year. It is discernible that the gender composition of the madrasahs is nebulous.

There are no available records of registered students in the archives in Freetown or in London for other academic years. There are also

[20] C.S.O. *Report on Mohammedan Education, 1912*, p. 18, and C.S.O. *An Ordinance for the Development and Extension of Education*, pp. 1–2.
[21] C.S.O. *Returns of Mohammedan Schools*, pp. 14–15. In the Sierra Leone Public Archives located at Fourah Bay College, the only available records on the returns of Mohammedan education are those for 1905 and 1912. The author therefore used the statistics provided in these periods to analyze the enrollment of pupils in the various schools. Informants and/or interviewees also did not provide useful information on this subject.

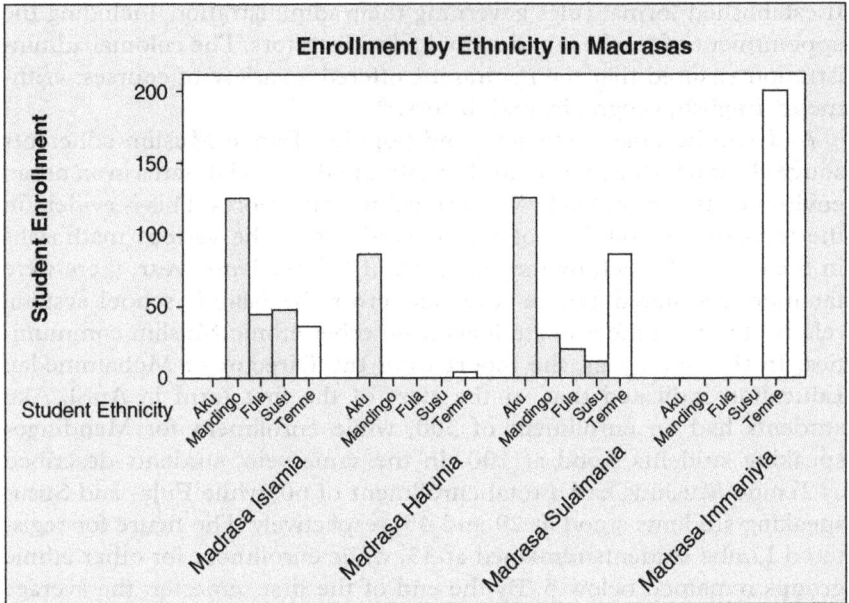

Figure 5 Enrollment of Muslim Students in the various Ethnic
Madrasahs in 1942/43.

no available records of registered students in the madrasahs *Amaria*
and *Umaria* for the same period. Nonetheless, Figure 5 indicates that
Temne students attended all the madrasahs, and had a particularly
compelling enrollment figure of 36 students in the madrasahs relative to enrollment figures of non-Temne students. As a matter of fact,
Temne Muslim students were the only non-Mandingo-speaking enrollees at the madrasah *Islamia*. By the end of the first semester in 1905,
enrollment for Mandingo-speaking students fell by ten per cent.[22] In
the madrasah *Harunia*, Temne students remained the only non-Aku
community enrollees in the school, with a total of 4 students. Fula
and Mandingo Muslim students did not record any enrollment at the
madrasah *Harunia*. Figure 5 also shows that 86 Temne students enrolled
in the madrasah *Sulaimania*; this means more Temne students enrolled
at the madrasah than did students from Mandingo-, Fula-, and Susu-
speaking communities. Furthermore, the number of Temne enrollees
in the madrasah *Sulaimania* exceeded the combined enrollment of the

[22] C.S.O. *Returns of Mohammedan Schools, 1905*, pp. 14–15.

three communities Fula-, Mandingo-, and Susu-speaking students. It is clear that, though the madrasahs carried ethnic designations, the composition of registered students in the schools remained multiethnic. It may be argued that the trans-ethnic nature of the student populations in the madrasahs speaks to the putative unity of Muslims in the colony.

Despite the tension that engulfed the Islamic community in 1917, the early madrasahs, *Harunia, Sulaimania* and *Amaria,* pursued a policy of unity, which admitted students from other ethnic Islamic communities. This policy reinforced the proclaimed notion that Islam "catered for the needs of all Muslims regardless of their cultural and financial background."[23] The graduates of these institutions became effective promoters of Islamic doctrine and teachings, even after the madrasahs declined in importance and influence in the late 1930s and early 1940s. The colleagueship developed by students in the madrasahs influenced the organization of trans-ethnic Islamic networks, such the Sierra Leone Muslim Congress, and the Muslim Association, among others. Though dominated by Aku Muslims, the founders of the Muslim Congress established the organization to achieve pan-Islamic solidarity and "mutual understanding among the general Muslim communities of [the] colony," and "to discourage tribal discrimination."[24] In the late 1940s, the executive committee of the congress expanded its membership to include non-Aku Muslims, such as Temne Muslims. Notwithstanding the pan-Islamic effort of the association, incessant bickering over leadership rights between the two dominant groups – Aku and Temne – undermined the viability of the Congress.

The foregoing analysis shows that the spread and entrenchment of Islam and its principles in the colony, though fraught with rancorous antipathy, proved to be a multiethnic enterprise. Put differently, many ethnic communities contributed to the development and growth of Islamic education through the creation of numerous madrasahs. The enrollment of Temne Muslim students in all madrasahs in the colony highlights the importance of Islam in the Temne community. This is evident in the activities of Temne Muslim clerics and missionaries, such as Abu Bakar Moyi-Dean Kamara, and Alhai Gibril Sesay. Kamara and Sesay contributed immensely to the organization and development of Temne Islamic institutions, including the proliferation of mosques,

[23] Pade Badru, "Basic Doctrines of Islam and Colonialism in Africa," *Islam in Africa South of the Sahara*, p. 29.
[24] Leslie Proudfoot, "Towards Muslim Solidarity in Freetown," *Africa* 29 (1961), p. 148.

and offering tutorial classes to illiterate men and women in Arabic and Islamic theology, as chronicled in the next section.[25]

Temne Islamic Institutions and the Propagation of Islam

This section examines the role played by the ascendant Temne Islamic Community and its institutions in spreading and entrenching the principles and obligations of the Islamic religion. Fyfe, Porter, and others argue that Western education became the royal road to success, and that many residents in the colony emulated Freetonian culture because of its superiority and aristocratic panache. A careful examination of the historical documents reveals that power and culture brokers, the elite media, Western and non-Western educated elites measured success and prestige differently. While Western-educated elites and culture brokers emphasized the attainment of Western education as a marker of success and accomplishment, local intellectuals of the Temne community used disparate variables, including Islam, to measure success, prestige, and high status. Like Muslims in the western Sudan in the nineteenth century, Temne Muslims perceived and practiced Islam as "constitutive of personal and collective identity"; that is, "being Muslim facilitated the emergence of a new distinct domain of spiritual power and social organization."[26] For many in the Temne Islamic Community, Islam became an ultra-religious phenomenon laden with meaning and vested power; it provided an authoritative counterweight to the British institutions dominated by Western-educated Freetonians. Simply put, many in the Temne community found Islam attractive because its core doctrinal teachings and principles dovetailed with traditional Temne values: the belief in a transcendent God, social and economic justice, polygynous marriages, and a symmetrical pattern of funeral rites. In the post–World War II period, Temneness and its institutions, including the madrasah *Immaniyia* and the various Temne mosques, grew in influence.

In the mid-1940s, the madrasah *Immaniyia* turned out to be the only surviving Qur'anic school as the other madrasahs – *Islamia, Harunia,* and *Sulaimnia* – disintegrated, some becoming affected by decrepitude. The reasons for the survival of the madrasah *Immaniyia* in the midst of the turmoil that engulfed other madrasahs are threefold: first, the madrasah

---

[25] "Pen Portrait of Muslims in Sierra Leone" (Freetown: Unpublished Pamphlet, n.d.), pp. 4–5.
[26] Sean Hanretta, *Islam and Social Change in French West Africa: History of an Emancipatory Community* (New York: Cambridge University Press, 2009), p. 32.

Immaniyia pursued exclusive policies that barred non-Temne Muslim students from enrolling at the school; the school only admitted Temne Muslim
students.[27] Second, officers of the Temne Central Mosque persistently
urged congregants during prayer sessions to sign up for classes at the school
for free. Added to the above, it is also likely that the fear of non-Temne
students dominating the school influenced the leadership of the school to
adopt such exclusionary policies. Given the fluidity and mutational feature
of Temne identity, as indicated in the pattern of institutional recruitment
employed by Temne cultural associations to bolster Temne prestige and
status, it is plausible to assume that some Temne Muslim students may
have claimed to be Temne to gain admission at the madrasah *Immaniyia*, as
other Qur'anic schools collapsed. The key courses offered at the madrasah
included Arabic, arithmetic, English and Islamic theology, which involved
learning the basic institutions and obligations of Islam. As a private enterprise, the colonial government did not provide financial support, nor did
it superintend the operations of the school. Funds for the *Immaniyia* came
from a number of sources, not least from monthly subscriptions and contributions, and private donations from Temne cultural associations.[28]

To improve the quality of instruction at the school, the administration recruited a *sheik* from abroad, Sheik Al Hassan Dubai, to help with
curriculum development and staff training. Sheik Dubai taught Arabic
and the History of Islam, while the proprietor of the school and imam
of the Temne Central Mosque, Alhaji Gibril Sesay, taught Arabic and
Islamic theology.[29] Graduates of the school served in various capaci-
ties: *Alimamies* (section chiefs), *Sheiks* (scholars or teachers), *Alikalies*
(community heads or sub chiefs) and imams. In short, the madrasah
Immaniyia became an alternative institution to Christian schools for
Temne Muslims.

Parallel to the role of the Temne School in propagating Islam, the TIC,
in collaboration with the TTA, facilitated, funded, and constructed a
total of seven mosques in different communities, the bulk of them built
in the eastern section of the colony. As already mentioned, incessant
bickering and sniping forced Temne Muslims to break away from the
Jam ul-Qudus. This means that, in the early twentieth century, the majority of Temne Islamic adherents worshiped at a makeshift mosque. Over
time, the makeshift mosque became drearily incommodious; this caused

[27] Hassan Bangurah interviewed by Joseph J. Bangura, Freetown, November 5, 2003.
[28] Sesay Private Papers "Notes on Islamic teachings" (Freetown: 1951). These are private
papers of the founder and proprietor of the school, Alhaji Gibril Sesay hereafter abbreviated as S.P.P.
[29] S.P.P. "Notes on Islamic Teachings," pp. 19–20.

a tentative dislocation among the community's votarists. The number of Temne Muslim adherents and abecedarians triggered the need for the construction of a mosque within a particular locale.

Thus, in 1937, the TTA and some community leaders constituted a committee charged with the responsibility to construct a capacious mosque that "will serve as the central mosque for Temne Muslims all over the colony."[30]

In 1944, the committee secured land at Oldfield Street, and completed the first phase of the project; it partially constructed the mosque and named it *Jam ul-Jaleel*, or Temne Central Mosque.[31] The building of the mosque in the east proved important, because many Temne Muslims lived in this section of the colony. A few years later, the committee launched a second fundraising campaign, and solicited donations from prominent clan or family members and from Islamic-based Temne cultural associations to complete the final phase of the project. Informants for this study recalled that the second phase of the project was completed ahead of schedule, because prominent families like the Banguras, Kamaras, Koromas, Sankohs, Kargbos, and Contehs made large donations; the mosque became the largest place of worship for Temne Muslims in the colony. The mosque served a multifunctional purpose: it became a place of worship, a rendezvous for political and business meetings, and an avenue for the weddings of key family members. Additionally, the Temne Mosque proved to be a thoroughfare where Temne Muslims and non-Temne Muslims worshiped and interacted. As the quintessential place of worship for members of the TIC, *Theimne* became the official medium of communication during expositions, meetings, and other business transactions. While imams prayed in Arabic, the use of *Theimne* in expositions enhanced the understanding of the basic principles and obligations of the religion. To cater to non-Temne Muslims who worshiped at the mosque, a translator occasionally translated the imam's expositions into Krio.

In the 1950s, a good number of Temne Muslims in other sections of the colony, such as the Bambara Town, Magazine Cut, and Frederick Street neighborhoods, commuted to and from the Temne Central Mosque weekly to attend Friday prayers, meetings, and weddings. Others commuted on a daily basis to attend evening prayers at the mosque. Analogously, those unable to make the daily commute worshiped at the Foulah Town mosque, largely administered by the Aku. Oral data suggests that non-Aku Muslims, such as Temne-, Loko-, and Limba-speakers, who visited the mosque for *juma*, or Friday prayers encountered difficulties

[30] S.P.P. "The Temne Mosque Project," p. 15.
[31] Hassan Bangura, interviewed by Joseph J. Bangura, November 1, 2003.

comprehending expositions heavily influenced by Yoruba dictions and Aku "traditional values."[32] As the number of Temne Muslims in these neighborhoods grew, the clamant need to construct a mosque to serve the community proved unbearable. A task force of *Alimamies and Alikalies*, representing the TTA and community elders, embarked on a fundraising drive to construct a Temne mosque in the Magazine Cut neighborhood. The task force for the project solicited donations from a variety of constituents all over the colony – Temne cultural associations, young Temne men and women (for free labor), Temne market women traders (for free labor), Temne business entrepreneurs, and prominent Temne politicians, to help fund the Construction of the mosque. Informants for this study state that some members of the TIC who could not make cash donations, such as Boys London and *Ariah*, offered free labor. In 1952, the project was completed, and the *Jam ul-Tawid* and the TIC officially inaugurated the mosque. Strategically located in Bambara Town, the mosque became the second largest Temne mosque – it served Muslims in the central and western sections of the colony. As at the *Jam ul-Jaleel*, officials conducted all proceedings and Islamic expositions in *Theimne*. One of the first imams of the mosque, Usman Sillah, recalled that over time, the number of worshipers at the mosque increased, making it the second important meeting place for Temne Muslims in the colony.[33]

Temne Muslims living in other parts of the colony experienced logistical and social challenges similar to those faced by their compatriots in the Bambara Town, Frederick Street, and Magazine Cut neighborhoods. Between 1950 and 1953, Temne Muslims in the Brook Street community, through the support of the TTA, cultural associations, and the Temne Central Mosque, constructed the *Jam ul-Hamdallah*, the third Temne mosque in the northwestern section of the colony.[34] The construction and official opening of the *Jam ul-Hamdallah* provided much needed relief for Temne and non-Temne Muslims in the Brook Street community. Prior to the construction of the mosque, Temne Muslims in this community commuted to the *Jam ul-Jaleel* or *Jam ul-Tawid* for *juma* prayers on Fridays, community meetings, conflict resolution and wedding ceremonies, among others. As a matter of fact, Islamic doctrine considers prayers on Fridays to be part of the five pillars of Islam and a "particularly important event in the weekly calendar

---

[32] Interview, Alhaji Usman Sillah, Freetown, November 10, 2003. Aku here means a bridge language with extensive Yoruba words and expressions. It serves as a noun and an adjective.
[33] Interview, Alhaji Usman Sillha, Freetown.
[34] Interview, Sheik Gibril Kamara.

of a Muslim."[35] Pade Badru states that Friday prayers are considered "a communal act to be performed in a mosque with an imam leading the prayer."[36]

With the successful construction of the *Jam ul-Hamdallah* in the Brook Street neighborhood, Temne Muslims residing in other sections of the colony without commodious centers of worship launched fundraising campaigns for the construction of mosques in their neighborhoods: Kissy, Race Course, Kanikay, Cline Town, and Wellington. After several fund-raising campaigns passionately undertaken by community leaders, section chiefs, local intellectuals, and sheiks, Muslim acolytes in the affected communities built the *Jam ul-Huda* and *Jam ul-Masjid*, respectively.[37] Informants for this study reminisced that, between 1955 and 1960, the number of Temne loyal adherents of Islam steadily increased, as evident in the cluster of mosques constructed in different parts of the colony. There are no available statistical data on the Temne Muslim population in the various parts of the colony, or the number of Temne Islamic devotees per neighborhood. However, several informants state that a "substantial number of Temne Muslims resided in east and central parts of the colony which triggered the need to provide respectable places of worship for them."[38] Moreover, Hajj Bangurah, an ex-officiant of the *Jam ul-Jaleel*, recollected that the number of attendees "at Friday prayers, surged over time and continued to do so in the late 1950s and 1960s."[39] Corollary to this, Proudfoot acknowledged that in 1944, "the Temne [had] the single largest tribal group" and the largest mosque "in the city."[40]

The Islamic institutions discussed above formed part of the growing sociopolitical and religious influence of Temneness in the post–World War II period. While the Aku constructed a total of five mosques in different parts of the colony, non-Aku Muslims, such as Limba, Loko and Mende Muslims, built a total of three mosques – one mosque per community (*jammat*).[41] A number of conclusions can be drawn from the

[35] Abdulkader Tayob, *Islam in South Africa: Mosques, Imams and Sermons* (Gainesville, Florida: University Press of Florida, 1999), p. vii.
[36] Pade Bardu, "Basic Doctrines of Islam and Colonialism in Africa" in Badru and Sackey, eds. *Islam in Africa South of the Sahara*, p. 28.
[37] Interview, Sheik Gibril Kamara. The author briefly worshiped at the *Jam ul-Masjid* mosque as a high school student.
[38] Alhaji Usman Sillah, interviewed by Joseph J. Bangura, Freetown, November 4, 2003.
[39] Interview, Hajj Hassan Bangurah.
[40] L. Proudfoot, "Mosque Building and Tribal Separatism in Freetown East," *Africa* 29 (1959), p. 406.
[41] Barbara Harrell-Bond, Allen M. Howard and David E. Skinner, *Community Leadership and the Transformation of Freetown (1801–1976)* (The Hague: Mouton Publishers, 1978), p. 47.

proliferation of Temne mosques in the colony. First, the construction of the *Jam ul-Jaleel* speaks to the religious independence of the TIC. It shows that Temne Muslims used the clout of their Islamic institutions to disseminate the doctrine of the religion. Second, as one of the largest agglomerations of Islamic adherents, Temne Muslims gave Islam a demographic advantage and strength in a Christian-dominated colony. This also speaks to the influence of the Temne, and their obtrusive clout in the colony's Islamic community. In other words, the cluster of Temne mosques in response to the needs of community members shows the dedication of the Temne Islamic Community to the propagation of Islam.

Summing up, then, Temne Islamic institutions played a central role in the propagation and entrenchment of Islam in the colony. The *Immaniyia, Nuru Jinati, Alimania*, and the numerous Temne *jammats* in particular played a cardinal role in the popularization of the religion in the mid-twentieth century. The *Immaniyia* became one of the key institutions of Islamic education for Temne students. It taught Muslim students the need to cultivate Islamic values, cultural norms, and moral uprightness. Many graduates of the school went on to serve various Muslim communities as sheiks, *Alfas*, imams, Islamic missionaries and religious leaders in the colony and protectorate. In addition to the role of the Immaniyia in spreading the values of Islam, the array of Temne mosques also greatly contributed to the spread and entrenchment of the Islamic faith in a number of ways. The mosques served as meeting places where Muslim business partners brokered deals and/or explored new commercial networks; participants in these negotiations considered the deals usually discussed after final prayers morally binding. Not only that, the mosques served as venues where politicians discussed community politics, and sometimes rallied members around specific issues. Third, imams and other subordinate officiants regularly officiated weddings of members at the various Temne mosques. Informants for the study stated that many Temne Muslim adherents privileged Islamic weddings over traditional weddings because of the prestige associated with such Islamic weddings. Hajj Bangurah recalled that because of the prestige associated with Islamic weddings, he married his wife at the *Jam ul-Jaleel* in 1955, over the objection of some family members who preferred a civic wedding officiated by the government registrar. Given his status and position as a member of the mosque's hierarchy, Bangurah claimed that the executive of the *Jam ul-Jaleel* sponsored his wedding. Beyond this, in 1947, the celebrated head of the TTA, Kande Bureh, married his second wife at the *Jam ul-Jaleel*, shortly after he won reelection as Temne Tribal Headman.[42] Other functions performed by officials of the various Temne mosques included the management and resolution of inter- and intra-community conflicts, and adjudicating cases of domestic abuse, divorce, and adultery. In cases involving domestic abuse, divorce, and adultery, the chief imam or his deputy imposed a solution and levied a penalty on the guilty; the litigants accepted the imam's ruling as binding. The imam's interventionist role helped minimized tension and conflict in the Temne Muslim community. His intervention also reduced the burden on the TTA and/or colonial courts, as many disputants held the imam, or a sheik, in high esteem and always deferred to these officials in conflict situations. As a matter of fact, many litigants felt comfortable in reporting personal cases to their religious officials, rather than openly litigate such cases in "alien" courts presided over by non-Temne secular elites.[43]

Thus, the *Jam ul-Jaleel* became the main venue for conflict resolution, particularly conflicts that involved major figures in the TIC. In 1945, for example, the elders of the Temne community called on the chief imam of the mosque to resolve a political dispute between two major candidates, Kedi Kamara and Kande Bureh – each candidate wanted to head the TTA. The vacancy occurred with the passing of the incumbent head of the Temne Authority, Alimamy Koroma. Before and after the vote, both campaigns adopted vitriolic rhetoric, as supporters of both campaigns incessantly harangued each other. The electoral commissioner eventually declared Kande Bureh the winner of the vote, but Kamara and his supporters flatly rejected the results. As the situation degenerated into violence, the chief imam of *Jam ul-Jaleel* swiftly intervened, and summoned both parties to a meeting. At the end of the meeting, both candidates accepted a resolution to the conflict – Kamara pledged to accept the results and later congratulated Bureh on his victory.

On the political front, officials of the Temne mosques also used their clout to campaign for Temne Muslim candidates during national elections. In the municipal elections of 1957, Gibril Sesay and Kandeh Bureh urged Temne Muslims to vote for "Temne Muslim candidates."[44] In fact, Bureh, a Muslim secularist, called on all members of the *Ambas Geda* and Temne Muslims to support and vote for Temne Muslim candidates. As a prominent member of the Sierra Leone Peoples Party, Bureh entreated Temnes and Muslims to support the party, because of its protectorate roots and respect for Islam and Muslims. Bureh used

[42] Interview, Morlai Kamara, Freetown, November 10, 2003.
[43] Interview, Imam Sillah, and Morlai Kamara.
[44] *Shekpendeh*, Freetown, October 15, 1958.

his popularity in the Temne and non-Temne communities in the colony and protectorate to drum up support for the SLPP and Temne politicians. He used his eloquence in *Theimne* and Krio to denounce what he perceived as the provincial politics of colony-based parties like the NCSL. He mordantly bashed the exclusionary politics of the NCSL, and described it as a "Creole party."[45]

The Temne mosques also helped orient Temne Muslim immigrants in the Colony. When Temne immigrants relocated to the colony, many received help from the *jamaats* in the neighborhood they lived. Further, the *Jam ul-Jaleel* also served non-Temne Muslim communities. Sources show that between 1917 and 1952, many Limba-, Loko-, and Mende-speaking Muslims in the Kissy Road and Dove Cot neighborhoods prayed at *Jam ul-Jaleel* on Fridays for logistical reasons. Moreover, non-Temne Muslims residents in the Cline Town and Kanikay locales also prayed at the *Jam ul-Huda* and/or *Jam ul-Masjid*.[46] Withal, Loko and Limba Muslims occasionally worshipped at these mosques, until "the Limba mosque was partially completed in 1959."[47]

The Temne mosques also served as tutorial centers for community members deterred from attending the crucial *juma* prayers with their attendant rituals. Some of the tutorial classes targeted young men and women interested in deepening their knowledge of the Qur'an. The classes gave attendees the opportunity to interact and directly speak with their Islamic teachers.

The role of Temne Islamic institutions fits into the role of the Temne cultural associations. It is obvious that the institutions not only complemented each other's roles in spreading the principles of Islam, they served as alternatives to Christianity and Western culture. Because the Temne mosques organized weddings for their members, Temne Muslims disregarded the need to obtain marriage licenses from the office of the government registrar. During Islamic expositions at the central and community mosques, imams enjoined congregants and adherents to spread the Islamic faith among those considered infidels – non-Muslim members of their households, friends, colleagues, and business associates – with the aim to convert them to Islam. The imams encouraged worshipers to uphold the pillars of Islam – belief in a transcendent God, observance of the various types of prayers five times a day, fasting in the

---

[45] Interview, Mohamed Turay, December 4, 2003. *Shekpendeh* also made similar charges, but stopped short of mentioning mosques as an arena used to canvass support.
[46] Interview, Imam Sillah; see also Proudfoot, "Mosque Building," p. 415.
[47] Interview, Gibril Kamara. Hajj Bangurah and Morlai Kamara corroborated this information at separate interviews.

month of Ramadan, giving alms to impecunious seekers, and performing the hajj at least once in a lifetime (if affordable).

On the other hand, the proliferation of Temne mosques highlights dissonance in the Temne Islamic Community. Historical sources show that personal rivalries and factional politics to some extent influenced the proliferation of Temne mosques. Some Temne communities took pride in establishing their own mosque, led by an imam of their choice based in the community. Bickering over educational qualifications and the position of imams also engulfed some Temne Muslim communities. Closely related to this, the construction and ethnicization of the Aku, Mandingo, Loko, Fula mosques, including the numerous ones established by the TIC, showed disharmony in the Islamic community. In other words, the construction of numerous ethnic madrasahs and mosques illustrates a lack of coadunation in the wider Muslim community. The inability of the Aku-, Temne-, Fula-, Susu-, and Mandingo-speaking Muslims to agree on a central place of worship betrays the ethnic agendas of these groups. In the case of the Temne, their numerical strength and need to uphold the virtues of Temneness influenced their activities and interactions with other ethnic groups they perceived as strangers in their land.[48] On this basis, it is reasonable to argue that, though Temne Muslims became enthusiastic propagators and proselytizers of the Islamic religion, their inability to work with other Islamic communities exposed their ambition and determination in asserting cultural hegemony.

Withal, though the Temne Islamic Community played an important role in the spread of the religion, Islam also contributed to the influence of Temne identity in the colony. Temne Muslims "'felt gratified by the fact that they did not have to attend prayers at mosques other than their own and they did not have to be led in prayers by imams from other tribal communities."[49] Simply put, Temne imams regularly served as religious solicitors and counselors to married couples – a service largely restricted to members of the Temne Islamic Community. Such privileges helped promote the importance of being a Temne Muslim. They also encouraged visiting worshipers at the various Temne mosques to aspire to become full members of such mosques. The historical literature pays insufficient attention to the activities of these institutions.

The next section highlights the social biographies and roles of two of the most prominent Temne Islamic missionaries in the mid-twentieth century, in the colony and Sierra Leone as a whole. Albeit many perceived the two Islamic scholars as a national *beau ideal* in the Temne

48 Interview, Hassan Bangura, Freetown, November 4, 2003.
49 Interview, Hassan Bangura, Freetown, November 4, 2003.

community, a lot of Muslims and non-Muslims venerated both men as national icons.

Reconfiguration of Religious Authority: Temne Islamic Missionaries and the Spread of Islam

Moyi-Dean Kamara: A Social Biography

Moyi Deen Kamara, also known as Moyi Dean, became one of the highly revered Temne intellectuals and Islamic missionaries in the colony. His fans and supporters venerated him as a Pollyannaish Islamic intellectual, a knowledgeable and distinguished teacher. Born to Temne parents in the protectorate, he immigrated to the colony with his parents at the tender age of 10. In 1920, he travelled abroad, to Futa Toro (now part of Senegal) and Guinea, to study theology.[50] On his return to his country in 1922, Moyi-Dean eventually served as the first chief imam of *Jam ul-Jaleel*.[51]

Moyi-Dean played a key role in laying the foundation for the construction of the *Jam ul-Jaleel* in the eastern section of the colony. Upon completion of the first phase of the mosque, he initiated the idea of using the premises of the uncompleted mosque to conduct *juma* prayers and also offer tutorial classes in Arabic and theology. The tutorial classes benefited many students, especially future Islamic leaders like Gibril Sesay. In fact, Sesay succeeded Moyi-Dean as chief imam of the *Jam ul-Jaleel*.[52] Other beneficiaries of Moyi-Dean's intellectual and homiletic exercises included Sheik Gibril Kamara, former secretary of the Temne mosque and an informant for this study, and Brimah Kargbo, chief Imam of the Limba mosque in 1953.[53] In the 1950s, in his capacity as chief imam, Moyi-Dean served as guest imam at a number of community mosques, such as the Jam ul-Qudus, and other Aku community mosques, where he presented moralizing discourses on various topics and themes in Islam.

His supporters widely perceived him as a statesmanlike figure with impeccable credentials. Generally deemed as a national figure and hortative preacher per excellence, Moyi-Dean's piety was beyond reproach. A regular guest of honor, he delivered declamations to several Muslim communities in the protectorate over several years. In his didactic exhortations, he adjured his congregants to perpetuate Islam's core mission of

---

[50] *"Pen Portrait,"* p. 4.
[51] Interview, Hajj Hassan Bangurah. (Moyi Dean and Moyi-Dean refer to the same person. The variation in spelling reflects the recording of the name in various accounts.)
[52] Interview, Sheik Gibril Kamara, Freetown, November 6, 2003.
[53] Interview, Sheik Gibril Kamara.

abiding and living a life steeped in probity and integrity. This exposition dovetailed with the Islamic faith, which committed "followers to a life of moral rectitude, accountability and by God's rule of law. It stressed the Day of Judgment, Hell and Heaven."[54] In some of his preaching, Moyi-Dean used elocution and prophetic clairvoyance to capture the imagination of his audience. Hajj Bangurah stated that such homilies contained "words of wisdom and the benefit of incorporeal hereditament," and his perorations always offered solace, hope and inspiration to the downtrodden.[55] Congregants and listeners of his expositions perceived them as discursive symbols, because they carried deep meaning and significance. Though he largely stayed out of politics, his expositions addressed the connection between Islam and nation-building.

Oral data reveal that Moyi-Dean helped train some of the first crop of Limba-, Mende-, and Loko-speaking imams. Alusine Jalloh, in one of his major works, assigned major agency to Fula-speakers in spreading Islam in colonial Freetown. In fact, Jalloh extolled the contributions and the role of Fula Muslim merchants, such as Alhaji Allie, Alhaji Seray Bah, and Alhaji Misbaahu Bah, in "spreading Islam in Freetown."[56] The work overlooks the ostensible legacy of Moyi-Dean Kamara and his missionary work in the colony.

As a scholar and missionary, Moyi-Dean supported the notion of spreading Islam via what David Robinson calls "appropriation through space and time."[57] That is, he supported the idea of the construction of mosques in neighborhoods with an appreciable number of Temne adherents, to show devotion and entrench Islamic practices in these communities. He also believed that having mosques in different parts of the colony potentially minimized bickering and personal rivalries among the bourgeoning class of Temne Muslim clerics, sheiks, and *Alfas*. This hypothesis failed, because intra-community and intercommunity rivalry and contretemps continued to besiege Temne Muslim communities.

Overall, Temne Muslims and supporters revered Moyi-Dean as an ethnonationalist who uplifted the Temne image and prestige. They believed Moyi-Dean achieved national "popularity and stature because of his role as chief imam of *Jam ul-jaleel*."[58] This is because Muslims in the colony suffused Islam with identity politics; they perceived Islamic

[54] David Robinson, *Muslim Societies in African History* (New York: Cambridge University Press, 2004), p. 77.
[55] Interview, Sheik Gibril Kamara.
[56] Alusine Jalloh, *African Entrepreneurship: Muslim Fula Merchants in Sierra Leone* (Athens, Ohio: Ohio University Center for International Studies, 1999), p. 154.
[57] See David Robinson, *Muslim Societies*.
[58] Interview, Hajj Bangurah, Freetown, November 5, 2003.

icons through ethnic lenses. Though sources show that he passionately
believed in and contributed enormously to the spread of Islam, Moyi-
Dean did not receive any national awards. His sermons concentrated on
devotional literature and emphasized the good Muslim life. Informants
for this study portray him as a leader with an exquisite intellectual apti-
tude, accompanied by a charismatic posture and drive. Put another way,
Moyi-Dean's influence remained and lingered far beyond the confines of
Dar al-Islam.

Alhaji Gibril Sesay and the Spread of Islam: Islamic
Evangelist, Cleric and Ethnonationalist

A former student of Moyi-Dean Kamara, Alhaji Gibril Sesay was a missionary, ethnonationalist, politician, and religious entrepreneur. Historical
records depict Sesay as one of the most influential Islamic missionaries in
the colony, and in the protectorate of Sierra Leone. His numerous achievements climaxed when the government of Sierra Leone conferred on him a
national award for his range of activities and knack for proselytizing Islam,
both of which are underplayed in the dominant literature.

Born in 1909 to Temne Muslim parents in Port Loko, Sesay moved
to the colony in the 1920s, where he attended the Bethel Day Primary
School, and later the madrasah *Islamia* to study rudimentary theology.[59]
In the 1930s, he proceeded to the Gambia, and later Senegal, where he
studied Islamic theology and social science.[60] He returned from his study
abroad in 1942, and founded the madrasah *Immaniyia*, serving as its first
principal and teacher. A few years later, following his founding of the
Immaniyia, he helped found the *Alimania*, as already mentioned.[61] The
school had a total enrollment of 300 hundred students within the first
few years of its establishment, which triggered the need for its expansion.[62] In 1960, as a result of this need for expansion, Sesay borrowed an
interest-free loan of $150.00 from the colonial administration, through
the Freetown City Council, and both parties agreed on a payment plan.[63]

---

[59] Interview, Alhaji Gibril Sesay, cited in Skinner, *Islam in Sierra Leone*, p. 220.
[60] Harrell-Bond, et al., *Community Leadership*, p. 180.
[61] S.P.P. "The Alimania" (Freetown: 1951), p. 10. Hajj Bangurah repeated the information
to the author in one of our several interview sessions.
[62] Interview, Alhaji Gibril Sesay as quoted in Skinner, *Islam in Sierra Leone*, p. 221.
[63] S.P.P. *Sesay to Ministry of Trade and Industry 22 February 1960*, (Freetown: 1960). The
author couldn't see a copy of this letter from the library of the Ministry of Trade and
Industry in Freetown; the clerk at this Ministry noted that many of the records have been
lost due to changes of office location on a few occasions. However, he looked at some of
these documents to verify their content and accuracy. He acknowledged the accuracy of
Sesay's letter and also recognized the official letterhead used in the correspondence.

As principal of the *Immaniyia*, Sesay established and regularly chaired a Social and Literary Society to enhance the students' research and communication skills. The *Immaniyia* proved successful in carrying out its core function: educating future leaders of the Temne Islamic Community, and training aspiring Muslim community leaders and organizers. Graduates of the school became *Alfas, sheiks* and imams in various sections of the Muslim community. Some of the prominent graduates on record include Alhaji Ibrahim Kargbo, who later became one of the longest serving chief imams of Jam ul-Jaleel, and eventually rose to the rank of National Chief Imam.

Alhaji Sheik Gibril Sesay
Source: Sesay's Private Papers, Freetown. The author is enormously grateful to Macksood Sesay, son of Alhaji Gibril Sesay, for granting me unlimited access to his late father's photographs and papers.

Other prominent graduates of the Temne School include former chief imams of the Loko- and Limba-speaking mosques, Alhaji Sheik Abass Kamara, treasurer of the Jam ul-Jaleel, Sheik Abdul Latiff, and Sheik Foud.[64] Sesay also regularly served as adjunct teacher in Arabic in the madrasah *Islamia*, and in 1958, served as adjunct professor of Arabic and Islamic Religious Studies in the Department of Extramural Studies

[64] Interview, Sheik Gibril Kamara. Kamara states that these were prominent religious leaders in their communities.

at Fourah Bay College, University of Sierra Leone.[65] As a member of the department he helped organize well-attended national conferences at the Fourah Bay College campus, on various themes dealing with cultural studies.[66]

In the 1930s, continuing his national Islamic stewardship, Sesay became the first Temne Muslim to serve on the executive board of the *Sierra Leone Muslim Congress* (SLMC), hitherto dominated by Aku Muslims. He served as one of four secretaries and became Secretary General between 1953 and 1964.[67] The SLMC provided the "means of giving Muslims the concerted voice which would enable them speak with authority equal to that of established Christian society and to contribute to the educational organization of the country effectively whilst benefiting from it more fully."[68] It funded many Muslim students to study abroad, particularly at the famous Al-Azhar University in Cairo, where Sesay himself had studied.[69] He graduated with "degrees in law, theology and Arabic from this institution and returned to Sierra Leone in 1952."[70] This shows that in 1943, when Sesay taught Arabic and theology at the *Immaniyia*, he did so as a non-degree holder.

In his capacity as chief imam of the largest mosque in the colony, Sesay became active in promoting the spread and influence of Islam, particularly during his expositions at the *Jam ul-Jaleel*, or venues where he spoke either as guest imam or guest of honor. In many of his sermons, he implored adherents to spread the teachings of Islam beyond their immediate communities.[71] In 1957, he contributed to the founding of the multiethnic *Sierra Leone Muslim Pilgrims Association* (SLMPA), and served as its first Secretary-General. Other executive members of the association included Abdul Cole as Financial Secretary, Alhaji Mohamed Sillah, a Mandingo-speaking Muslim, as Organizing Secretary, and Abu Bakar Koroma (a Temne Muslim) as Publicity Secretary.[72] As a pilgrims' association with sixty active registered members in total, it became highly multiethnic and coordinated the annual pilgrimage to Mecca, a function previously undertaken by potential pilgrims themselves, or by

[65] S.P.P. *Proudfoot to Sesay, June 1, 1960*, (Freetown: 1960). Proudfoot was the Director of the Extramural Department at Fourah Bay College.
[66] S.P.P. *Proudfoot to Sesay*, September 9, 1958.
[67] Interview, Gibril Sesay, as quoted in Skinner, *Islam in Sierra Leone*, pp. 221–222.
[68] L. Proudfoot, "Towards Muslim Solidarity in Freetown." *Africa* XXIX (1961), p. 155.
[69] L. Proudfoot, "Muslim Solidarity," p. 150.
[70] Harrell-Bond, *Community Leadership*, p. 180
[71] S.P.P. *Sesay to the Temne Congregation, General Meeting, 11 May 1959*, Freetown.
[72] S.P.P. *Sesay to Members of the Sierra Leone Pilgrims Association, May 28, 1957*, Freetown. Hajj Bangurah corroborates this information; he was a member of this association.

private organizations.[73] The SLMPA became the national organization for would-be pilgrims; it promoted their general welfare and liaised between them and colonial authorities.[74] The SLMPA also organized the purchase of air tickets and negotiated low hotel rates for its pilgrims in Saudi Arabia.[75] In 1949, Sesay achieved "the enviable feat" of becoming the first Muslim to organize pilgrimages to Mecca on a grand scale; he led delegations of pilgrims from all ethnic backgrounds to Mecca during the annual pilgrimage.[76]

In the 1950s, Sesay founded the *Sierra Leone Muslim Reformation Society* (SLMRS).[77] The SLMRS strove to "fortify the faith of young Muslims who have been long in contact with Western ways. In this it has been largely successful."[78] At the launching ceremony, Sesay emphasized the religious and apolitical nature of the association, because it was established "to elevate Islam in Sierra Leone" with a distinct membership of "over 500 members both in the colony and the Provinces."[79] It is clear that the Reformation Society had a broad membership that comprised numerous members in the colony and protectorate. In one of his many letters, Sesay emotively appealed to the colonial administration to recognize and declare *Eid al-fitr* as a public holiday.[80] *Eid al-fitr* is

---

[73] *Shekpendeh*, Freetown, September 15, 1958. This information was referenced in separate but extensive interviews with SLPMA members, Haja Sukainatu Bangura, Abdul Bangura, and Hajj Bangurah. The author could not verify these figures in newspapers or archival documents. Abdul Bangura is the eldest surviving son of Sukainatu Bangura; he was 70 years old and lived in Freetown at the time of this interview. Hajj Bangurah and Sukainatu Bangura are not related. Both knew each other as young Temne activists in colonial Freetown. See Appendix 1 on the biography of Abdul Bangura.

[74] Interview, Hajj Bangurah, Freetown.

[75] Interview, Hajj Bangura; Abdul Bangura corroborates this information.

[76] Interview, Hajj Bangurah.

[77] Proudfoot, "Muslim Solidarity," p. 154.

[78] Proudfoot, "Muslim Solidarity," p. 154.

[79] S.P.P. *Sesay to the Mayor, Freetown City Council, August 19, 1958*, Freetown.

[80] S.P.P. *Sesay to His Excellency the Governor, Eid-ul-Fitri Celebrations in Sierra Leone, April 1958*, Freetown. The author took this document and others connected to the City Council and the Ministry of Internal Affairs for verification. First, the Ministry of Internal Affairs, now Local Government, have no letters by colonial governors, citing poor library facilities. They also noted that the Ministry, since its establishment, has undergone significant changes over the last forty years of independence and so all old documents were sent to the government archives located at Fourah Bay College. The staff at Fourah Bay College dispute this account. Nonetheless, many of Sesay's correspondences relating to the Ministry of Internal Affairs were carried on official letterhead, which the Permanent Secretary of this Ministry confirmed to be accurate. In the case of the City Council, the rebels burned down the main library of the council in 1999. All precious documentary data relating to the Council and its activities in the colonial era were permanently destroyed. But the Town Clerk confirmed the authenticity of the letterheads used by Sesay in his official correspondence, especially matters that pertained to the Council. Both the Permanent Secretary and Town Clerk did not dispute the information contained in this particular document, though they were not members

the end of *Sawm*, which is the end of "fasting for thirty-days beginning from dawn to dusk, during Ramadan. During this period, believers must refrain from food, drinking, idle talk, and worldly pleasures from sunrise to sunset."[81] Fasting is one of the five pillars of Islam, and its climax constitutes an important event in the Muslim calendar, usually marked by profuse celebrations by Muslims and non-Muslims in the Muslim world. Devoted Muslims look forward to this day, when many believe Allah forgives their sins and iniquities. Sesay states that colonial authorities accepted his appeal, and thus declared *Eid al-fitr* a national holiday recognized all over Sierra Leone. The declaration of *Eid al-fitr* as a national holiday championed by a Temne Muslim elite illustrates the growing influence of Islam in a Christian-dominated colony. In his acknowledgement of the authorities' magnanimous overture, he further requested that it would be appropriate for the government to extend the same recognition to *Eid al-adha*, being "the month of pilgrimage" and also the "calligraphic representation of the name of the Prophet Muhammad."[82] The appeal for the recognition of this event, widely believed to be the birthday of the Prophet Mohammed, as a national holiday received official imprimatur from the colonial administration in 1958.[83] In a press release marking this accomplishment, Sesay states, "through our instrumentality we have been able to get the birth day of the Holy Prophet Muhammad O. W. B. P. declared a public holiday throughout the length and breadth of Sierra Leone."[84] It should be pointed out that Sesay's push for the recognition by colonial authorities of these events in the Islamic calendar was influenced by the doctrine of Sufism, which he believed in and expounded in his many exegeses.

As president of the Reformation Society, an association dismissed by Lamin Sanneh and overlooked by others, Sesay enjoined Muslims of all ethnic backgrounds to celebrate the newly declared public holidays by processing on the streets in congregational bands and in colorful displays. He personally led these processions by sitting on a white horse while he addressed the various congregations assembled at the grounds

of Sesay's association and did not know much about the association. It is possible that some newspapers reported on these issues; the ones I read during this research did not.
[81] Pade Badru, "Basic Doctrines of Islam and Colonialism in Africa." *Islam In Africa South of the Sahara*, P.28.
[82] Roman Loimeier, *Muslim Societies in Africa*, p. 20.
[83] S.P.P. *Sesay to Imams in Freetown Moulid Nabi's Celebrations August 12, 1958*, Freetown. Hajj Bangurah corroborates this.
[84] S.P.P. *Sesay to Imams in Sierra Leone, July 1959*, Freetown. I could not independently verify this claim; i.e. the author found no evidence of this in the press in colonial Sierra Leone.

of the judiciary building.[85] It may be argued that, though Sesay personally sent letters of appeal for the recognition of *Eid al-fitr* and *Eid al-
adha*, colonial authorities may have recognized the two Islamic events
as national holidays because of the ascendance of Islam in the colony
and protectorate. Sesay used the Sierra Leone Reformation Society to
lobby colonial authorities for recognition of other events in the Islamic
calendar. He stated that the Reformation Society, which proved to be
"non-sectarian and non-political ... has contributed in its own little way
to make the government see the necessity of declaring *Moulid Nabi* as
a public holiday throughout Sierra Leone."[86] The declaration of *Moulid
Nabi* as a public holiday became another milestone in Sesay's contribution to the propagation of Islam and its teachings.

Sesay promoted another annual multiethnic religious event – the lantern parades – as part of the series of celebrations that marked the end
of Ramadan in the 1950s.[87] The cavalcade of congregations showed the
beauty of their handicrafts and handiworks in the form of aesthetic lanterns
in the major streets of the colony. A technical committee assessed the lanterns and presented awards to the group with the best aesthetic craft. In his
assessment of Muslim associations in Sierra Leone, Proudfoot portrays the
Reformation Society as an Aku-led and Aku-dominated society. However,
historical data, including oral accounts from ex-participants in these events,
contradict this claim. The sources reveal that the Reformation Society was
multiethnic and led by Sesay. Gibril Sesay also served as the secretary of the
National Board of Imams in the 1950s, and became the link between the
board and the prime minister's office.[88]

As a missionary, Sesay traveled the length and breadth of the colony
and protectorate giving Islamic homilies to Muslim communities. In
1959, he visited the *Gorahun Tunkia* chiefdom, a Mende Islamic community in the southern province, where he preached about the principles
and advantages of embracing the Islamic faith. In a follow-up visit, he
pithily observed that:

As my last visit was so much appreciated and the response so remarkable and
encouraging, I have thought it very expedient to visit you again for at most two
days ... I shall be much obliged if you will inform all prominent Muslims of your
district and you kindly convene a meeting against my arrival.[89]

---

[85] Interview, Gibril Kamara. He noted that Sesay paraded the streets of Freetown on a
white horse monitoring these processions.
[86] S.P.P. *Sesay to Imams: Moulid Nabi's Celebrations.*
[87] S.P.P. *Permanent Secretary to Sesay, Lantern Procession, 22 July 1959.*
[88] S.P.P. *Prime Minister to Sesay: Eid-ul-Fitri, OPM, 37/742 18 February 1961*, Freetown.
[89] S.P.P. *Sesay to Madam Mamawa Sama, Paramount Chief Gorahun Tunkia Chiefdom,
ASGS/12/1959*, Freetown.

This speaks to Sesay's national appeal and gravitas as a Temne Muslim elite; that is, he did not limit his proselytizing activities to Temne communities in the colony. The invitation extended to him by Mende Muslims in the protectorate indicates that he was revered by Muslims in the colony and the protectorate. Sesay also served as guest of honor of the Sierra Leone Muslim Brotherhood in Magburaka, in the north of the protectorate, with a high concentration of Temne Muslims. In the sermon he gave to the host community, he implored them to be "devoted followers of Islam as the salvation to human depravation and evanescent materialism."[90] He encouraged Muslims particularly to keep the faith and observe the religion's fundamental pillars, such as "Friday worship, zakat, fasting and performing the hajj."[91]

Quite apart from the above, in 1959, during the International Labor Organization Day celebrations, the organizing committee asked Sesay to organize a religious ceremony as part of the program. The letter sent to him states that: "the local committee has accepted a proposal from the African Field Office of the International Labour Organization to include religious services among its celebrations and I have been asked to write to you asking you in what way you can help in the fulfillment of the proposal."[92] The composition of the group and why the group specifically chose Sesay to organize the national event remained unclear. It is reasonable to assume that they chose him because he served as secretary of the national board of imams, or as the chief imam of *Jam ul-Jaleel*, at the time. In spite of this, the invitation of Sesay speaks to his reputation as a charismatic and influential religious leader. Though an imam, he performed other duties outside the province of his religious responsibilities; he arbitrated disputes between Temne and non-Temne politicians. In 1959, the Islamic community asked him to intervene in an altercation between "Honorable Kande Bureh" and "Honorable M.S. Mustapha," a renowned Aku Muslim and politician. A founding member of the SLPP and the SLMC, Mustapha became a Government Minister of Works and Transportation in 1953.[93] Two years after his appointment as minister, in 1955, he became a victim of vandalism during the nationwide riots.[94] Bumptious rioters attacked and looted his property because they perceived him as part of the government establishment. Mustapha's

[90] S.P.P. S.I. *Kanu to Alhaji Sheik Gibril Sesay, Invitation As Guest Speaker, July 2, 1959*, Freetown.
[91] S.P.P. S. I. *Kanu to Alhaji Sheik Gibril Sesay.*
[92] S.P.P. S. J. A. *Short to Alhaji Gibril Sesay, I.L.O. Celebrations- Religious Services, 16th July 1959.* Freetown.
[93] *West Africa*, June 25, 1960.
[94] *Daily Mail*, February 15, 1955.

continued loyalty to the SLPP earned him additional responsibilities in government, when the Prime Minister appointed him deputy premier in 1960.[95] Supporters of Mustapha and Bureh perceived the two political heavyweights as rivals. A disagreement between the two honorable men quickly degenerated into an exchange of insults, which prompted the Islamic community to intervene. Asked to mediate, Sesay invited the two men and other senior members of the Islamic community, including imams and politicians to a "special meeting at the Temne School ... to settle a dispute which took place between the Honourable Kande Bureh and the Honourable M. S. Mustapha."[96] It is not clear how Sesay resolved the dispute between the two men. However, he received a note of appreciation for his peace efforts from Kande Bureh. Additionally, when Maigore Kallon, a distinguished founding member of the SLPP, relinquished his party membership, the SLPP again called on Sesay and Bureh to persuade Kallon to return to the SLPP. It remains unclear why the SLPP chose Sesay to intervene, since he never officially joined the SLPP. It may be argued that the SLPP asked him to prevail on Kallon in his capacity as chief imam of one of the largest Islamic communities, or because he was a venerable Islamic missionary. Kallon, identified as a Mende-speaking politician and Muslim, felt disillusioned and unhappy with the leadership of the SLPP, led by Sir Milton Margai, and hence resigned his membership. Kallon eventually withdrew his resignation and returned to the party; Sesay's intervention at least partially influenced his decision.[97]

Though he was a revered and admired missionary, controversy surrounded Sesay's leadership of the *Jam ul-Jaleel*. Disgruntled members of the Temne mosque accused him of nepotism and corruption. The first major controversy, which occurred in 1958–59, resulted in a fissure among congregants of the *Jam ul-Jaleel*, and outlasted Sesay's tenure as chief imam. This happened when one of the imams at the mosque, popularly known as Imam Bashr, clashed with Sesay and his supporters over ideology. After Sesay returned from his studies at Al Azhar University in Egypt, he became a practitioner of Sufism and a sympathizer of the Tijaniyya Brotherhood, based in northern Nigeria. As a Sufi scholar, Sesay believed in mysticism through personal experience and connection with God. His deputy, Imam Bashr, rejected and bashed

---

[95] *West Africa*, June 25, 1960.
[96] S.P.P *Sesay to Chiefs Imams in Freetown, 27th April 1959*. (Freetown). According to the documents, the imams of the Aku, Mandingo, Fula and Limba Muslim Communities were copied and apparently invited to this meeting.
[97] *Shekpendeh*, August–September, 1958.

Sufi doctrine; this led to a division in the Temne Central Mosque. In the end, Bashr and his supporters abandoned the mosque and started a new Temne Muslim movement – the Bashr movement. Supporters of the new movement raised funds and constructed a brand new mosque in the neighborhood of the Temne Central Mosque.[98] In short, Sesay became Bashr's sworn enemy and bitter rival in the Temne Muslim community.

Informants for this study also noted that Bashr abandoned the Temne Central Mosque because he did not have the credentials to be imam, since he failed his final exams at Al Azhar University. They noted that before the controversy came to the fore, rumors of Imam Bashr's lack of credentials gripped regular attendees at the mosque. Some sheiks claimed that Imam Bashr lied when he claimed to have a Diploma in Islamic Studies, because he failed his final exams. The information came to light when an official, a professor from Al Azhar University, where Bashr purportedly studied, revealed the information during a visit to his former student, Gibril Sesay. The visiting professor particularly objected to the fact that the executive of the *Jam ul-Jaleel* allowed Bashr to serve as a senior imam, and was allowed to lead Friday prayers. The professor argued that Bashr did not have the credentials to serve as imam, because he had failed his final exams, and that the university never certified him as an Islamic scholar with the requisite training to be an imam. The executives of the mosque, led by Sesay, confronted Bashr with the information; Bashr felt cornered and cried foul. He told his supporters that Sesay wanted to get rid of him "because congregants preferred his sermons over those of Sesay."[99] In short, the controversy forced Bashr to give up his membership of the *Jam ul-Jaleel* and establish his mosque not too far from the *Jam ul-Jaleel*. Because of this, Sesay became a target of scorn and vituperative attacks by Bashr and his supporters.

The government intermittently intervened to separate the two camps, particularly after Friday prayers. Sesay's supporters accused Bashr of peddling lies and propaganda, given that he did not have the qualification to be an imam. Sources show that the wider Temne Islamic Community in the colony never recovered from this caustic schism.

[98] Macksoud Sesay, telephone interview, by Joseph J. Bangura, Kalamazoo, January 10, 2016.
[99] Interview, Hajj Bangurah, Freetown.

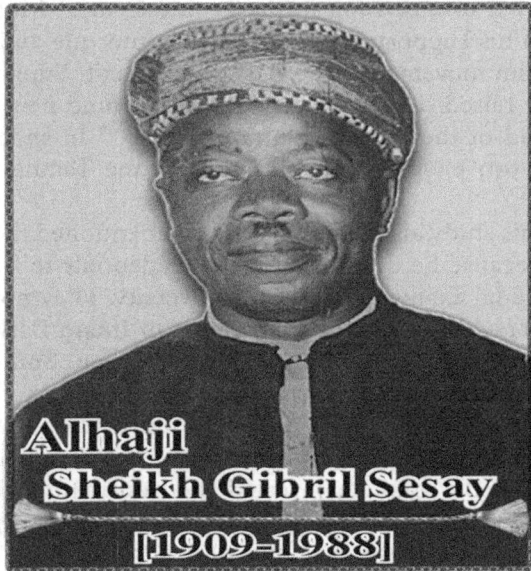

Alhaji Gibril Sesay

Sesay's critics also accused him of religious bigotry, while others described him as practicing political Islam. His public appeals to his congregants and supporters to "vote for Temne candidates in the municipal elections" in 1957 drew the ire of his critics.[100] In a public reprimand, a critic observed, "Alhaji Sesay in a campaign mood told Muslims in the Temne school that under no circumstances a Muslim should support a Christian against another Muslim."[101] The critic complained that Sesay used his coveted status as a national religious figure to meddle in national and local politics. Not only did Sesay instruct Temne Muslims to vote for Muslim candidates, he himself vied for a parliamentary seat as an independent candidate. His candidacy posed a huge challenge to the incumbent SLPP candidate, which made Sesay a target of the government. Although he lost the election, his candidacy jeopardized his position as a revered Islamic missionary, and a magnifico. The SLPP lost confidence in his neutrality, and went after him through the Municipal City Council. The City Council took Sesay to court for an unpaid loan he had borrowed to expand the Temne school. A court ordered his arrest

---

[100] *Shekpendeh*, October 29, 1958.
[101] *Shekpendeh*, October 29, 1958.

for corruption, because he refused to pay the loan, and eventually, he served time in prison. The above account is in contrast to the narrative offered by Lamin Sanneh, in his terse assessment of Sesay's stewardship of the Islamic community in Sierra Leone.

Despite his troubles, Sesay remained the recognized leader of the Temne Islamic Community; he regularly "spoke on behalf of the Temne Community" at official ceremonies.[102] The management of the broadcasting corporation, the Sierra Leone Broadcasting Service (SLBS), periodically asked him to chair roundtable discussions on national radio on multiple themes relating to Islam.[103] In spite of his imprisonment, the Freetown City Council nominated Sesay as a representative of the Islamic Community on the Council in 1957. As a member of the Council, he occasionally accompanied the mayor on official visits abroad.[104] When Her Majesty Queen Elizabeth II paid her first visit to Sierra Leone in 1961, Sesay became a member of the delegation that welcomed the Queen. Sesay's delegation traveled with the Queen on several visits around the country.[105] In 1961, after serving out his term as counselor, the town clerk asked Sesay to serve on the council's Board of Education.[106] However, shortly before his term came to an end, the government asked him to take up appointment as Sierra Leone's Ambassador and Plenipotentiary to the Arab Republic of Egypt; he accepted the position and served as Ambassador in the country of his alma mater.[107]

Alhaji Gibril Sesay's legacy as a missionary and an admired teacher is insufficiently recognized in Sierra Leone historiography. Historical documents reveal that, like others lauded in the historiography, Sesay immensely contributed to the development of a strong Islamic tradition in the Sierra Leone colony and beyond. Informants for this study stress that Sesay was one of the most important Islamists in Sierra Leone as a whole. He used his status as chief imam of one of the largest Islamic communities in the colony to shape, radicalize, or revolutionize the practice of Islam. In fact, the colonial administration regarded Sesay as a national leader, who introduced a new form of religious expression in the Islamic Community. In all, he led his Temne Islamic Community in propagating Islam in the Sierra Leone colony and beyond.

[102] *SLWN*, February 25, 1950.
[103] S.P.P. *Leslie A. Perowne to Gibril Sesay, SLBS/14/1/175 27th December 1959*. (Freetown). Perowne was Director of the Sierra Leone Broadcasting Service.
[104] S.P.P. *Sesay to the Education Officer, Colony Office, 14/4/1959*, Freetown.
[105] S.P.P. *J. B. Jenkins-Johnston to Alhaji G. Sesay: Re Visit of Her Majesty, 4566/FC/292 10/10/61*. (Freetown: 1961).
[106] S.P.P. *J. B. Jenkins-Johnston, Town Clerk to Councillor Alhaji G. Sesay, Board of Education, 1896/ED/4/38 19/4/61*. (Freetown: 1961).
[107] Interview, Hajj Bangurah, Freetown.

In sum, the Islamic Community venerated Moyi-Dean Kamara and Alhaji Gibril Sesay as Islamic elites. Simply put, Moyi-Dean and Alhaji Gibril Sesay increased the profile of Islam and the Temne community in a colony established as an experiment in Christian evangelism in Africa. The national profiles of these men not only injected new expressions of Islam, they also broadened the concepts of "being" Muslim and "being" a Temne Muslim in the colony.

Temne Muslims and the Sierra Leonization of Islam, 1920–1961

In the 1950s, the Temne surpassed the Freetonians, Mende-, Limba-, Mandingo-, and Fula-speakers as the largest ethnic group in the colony.[108] Furthermore, Temne Muslims not only owned the largest mosque and the highest number of mosques in the colony, they constituted the largest conglomeration of Muslims in the colony and arguably in the protectorate. Therefore, Temne Muslims and lustrous highbrows such as Alhaji Gibril Sesay, Haja Sukainatu Bangura, Kande Bureh (though he was more of a secular pseudointellectual), and Moyi-Dean promoted a new dimension of Islamic practice in the colony. Put another way, Temne Muslims contributed to the Sierra Leonization of Islam: that is, the appropriation and integration of Islam into indigenous Temne contexts – a multilayered process which simplified the practice of Islam. This paradigmatic form of Islam gave the religion a boost among many agnostic Temnes, as many empiricists or unbelievers within the Temne community chose it as their preferred religion. In fact, the Sierra Leonization of Islam paradigm can be situated in the Africanization of Islam concept propounded by David Robinson, Nehemia Levtzion, Roman Loimeier, and Sean Hanretta, among others.

Robinson, Levtzion and others argue that Africans embraced Islam since the seventh century because of its flexibility and adaptation to the continent's cultural milieu. Levtzion states that "indeed the Islamization of Africa became more successful because of the Africanization of Islam. Islam proved its vitality because of its rational basis and simplicity and adaptability on the one hand and its tradition of scholarship on the other."[109] Robinson also addresses the significance of this concept in one of his signal works. A leading authority on the subject, Robinson defines

---

[108] Lamin Sanneh, *The Crown and the Turban: Muslims and West African Pluralism* (Boulder, Colorado: Westview Press, 1997), p. 175.

[109] Nehemia Levtzion, *Islam in West Africa: Religion, Society and Politics to 1800* (Vermont and Great Britain: Ashgate Publishing Ltd., 1994), p. 208; see also, Nehemia Levtzion and Pouwells Randall, *The History of Islam in Africa* (Athens, Ohio: Ohio University Press, 2000).

the Africanization of Islam as "the various ways that, at different times over the past 1,400 years, Islam has been appropriated or articulated in particular societies ... African groups created 'Muslim' space or made Islam their own."[110]

Robinson's concept of the Africanization of Islam has been challenged by other scholars, including Rudolph T. Ware III, Loimeier, and others. Ware III argues that the application of the concept undermines the immense and quintessential contributions of Africa in the spread and growth of Islam in the world. He states that "the dynamics of Africanization and Islamization is still a discussion of syncretism and assimilation" and that such narratives and categorizations indicate that "Arab Muslims are in positions of perpetual tutelage over non-Arabs"; based on such framings of "syncretism and assimilation, it is difficult for the periphery to provide meaningful insight on the center."[111] Succinctly put, Ware III states that the concept of the Africanization of Islam and its application are deprecating to African Islam. He states that such rhetoric is reminiscent of the colonial-versus-colonized binary deployed in racist literature.

Roman Loimeier also excoriates the concept of the Africanization of Islam in his major work. Like Ware III, Loimeier argues that it is impossible to talk about the Africanization of Islam, because of the vastness and heterogeneity of the African continent: "African historical experiences with Islam have also been much too diverse to support the notion of a single, African Islam."[112] He states that many African Muslims appropriated Islam, and lived Islam in multiple ways that reformists condemned as "un-Islamic." In lieu of the concept of the Africanization of Islam, Loimeier states that "Islam could thus acquire a distinct Moroccan, Senegalese or Somaal notion but not an African character," as Robinson and Levitzon posit.[113]

In analyzing the activities of Temne Muslims in the Sierra Leone Colony, this study also challenges the notion of the Africanization of Islam. Using Loimeier's hypothesis about distinct notions of Islam, this volume argues that Temne Muslims engaged in religious syncretism by introducing a new expression of Islam in the colony. As already mentioned, oral data show that Temne Muslims took advantage of the complaisant nature of

---

[110] David Robinson, *Muslim Societies in African History* (New York: Cambridge University Press, 2004), p. 42.
[111] Rudolph T. Ware III, *The Walking Qur'an: Islamic Education, Embodied Knowledge and History in West Africa* (Chapel Hill, North Carolina: University of North Carolina Press), p. 22.
[112] Loimeier, *Muslim Societies in Africa*, p. 11.
[113] Loimeier, *Muslim Societies in Africa*, p. 18.

Islam, and appropriated it to suit local traditional values and culture. Specifically, many radical Temne Muslims used commercial goods from the Mediterranean (discerned as Islamic because of the origin of these goods) as a sign of their devotion to Islam and their unique way of practicing its principles. The use of amulets and/or talismans, for example, became widespread among Muslims in the Sierra Leone Colony, particularly among Temne Muslims. Beyond this, many of the costumes put on by performers of Temne cultural associations had amulets and talismans imbedded in them. Members and performers who wore the costumes believed the amulets and talismans, embedded with Qur'anic verses and cowrie shells, protected them from evil. They also used these objects to launch sometimes deadly or life-altering preemptive attacks on perceived enemies and rivals. During public performances, singers and dancers of the *Alimania, Nuru Jinati,* and *Ariah* courted perceived heretical onlookers and coaxed them to convert to Islam as their only ticket to heaven. They used the allure of their performances to proselytize to agnostic bystanders. On other occasions, members of these associations sang songs in *Theimne* and Arabic, accompanied by melodious drumming, and playing sonorous fiddles, to induce spectating greenhorns into accepting the Islamic religion as the source of eternal salvation. Haja Sukainatu, *Mammy Queen* of the *Alimania* and a devout Muslim woman, organized the dance troupes and the choir.[114] Such unconventional approaches to spreading the Islamic religion and/or courting proselytes deviated from orthodox Islam. Conservative Islamists railed against such heterodox forms of practicing Islam or winning converts over to Islam.[115] Nonetheless, the approach proved successful in the Temne community. Oral data show that the glamor of *Alimania, Ariah,* and *Nuru Jinati* influenced some apostate Temne and non-Temne to convert to Islam, particularly those who had hitherto feigned disinterest in Islamic expositions. The unconventional use of cultural groups or dance groups to convert neophytes to the Islamic religion was a marked feature of the Sierra Leonization of Islam.

Parallel to the above, the use of *Theimne* as medium of communication during Islamic enunciations, committee meetings, official weddings, and business transactions in the numerous Temne mosques is testament to the contributions of Temne Muslims in giving Islam a distinct Sierra

[114] Interview, Haja Sukainatu Bangura, Freetown, September 29–30, 2003.
[115] See Tilman Nagel, *The History of Islamic Theology: From Muhammad to the Present* (Princeton, New Jersey: Markus Wiener Publishers, 2000). See also Beverley Mack and Jean Boyd, *One Woman's Jihad: Nana Asma'U, Scholar and Scribe* (Bloomington: Indiana University Press, 2000).

Leonean character. Informants for this study recalled that the translation of Qur'anic verses into *Theimne* by imams, sheiks, and others during prayers on Fridays enhanced the comprehensibility of Islamic sermons, which otherwise would have been difficult for some congregants to comprehend. The use of the *Theimne* lingua franca highlights the grasp and knowledgeability of the principles of the Qur'an by Temne Imams. It also illustrates the growing prestige and status of Temneness, and the confidence it gave those who openly flaunted Temne identity as a badge of honor. On top of using *Theimne* as medium of communication, officiants at Temne mosques occasionally translated some sermons from *Theimne* into Krio to accommodate non-Temne visiting Muslim worshipers in the various mosques.

Furthermore, the Sierra Leone Reformation Council's idea of urging Muslims to process on the streets of the colony while exhibiting exuberant handiworks (lanterns) in celebration of *Eid al-Fitri* and *Eid al-adha* was considered heterodox by conservative and immutable clerics. As a matter of fact, Sufi Islam rejects dancing and drumming in social settings, because they interfere with the "meditation on God and the word of God as conveyed in the Qur'an."[116] In spite of this, though scholars note that the Qur'an negates such practices, highly revered Sufis such as Alhaji Gibril Sesay, and others, encouraged the practices as effective means of recruiting non-Muslims to Islam. Clearly, Muslims and non-Muslims participated in the yearly lantern parades, and looked forward to them with alacrity. This eccentric approach to proselytization remained popular throughout the colonial period.

Observation of the "Fortieth Day" ceremony after the death of a Muslim or non-Muslim in the Temne Islamic Community also constituted another layer of the Sierra Leonization of Islam as practiced by Temne Muslims. Upon the death of a Temne Muslim, a big feast accompanied the pouring of libations on the fortieth day following the burial rites. Imams and sheiks presided over such rituals; they led the recitation of Qur'anic verses for several hours in supplication to God for the forgiveness of the sins of the dead. Oral data indicate that even though the tradition became commonplace in the Temne Islamic Community, it sharply conflicted with the Qur'an and its teachings.[117] Temne culture compels the living to honor the dead through rituals followed by singing, dancing, and prolonged revelry. It can be assumed that other ethnic groups in Sierra Leone practiced similar customs in honor of the dead. It

[116] Beverley and Boyd, *Nana Asma'U*, p. 15.
[117] Interview, Atou Diagne, Touba, Senegal May 10, 2006; also, interview, Mohamed Kuyateh, Kalamazoo, April 14, 2006.

is evident that, over time, Temne Muslim leaders wittingly Islamized this aspect of their culture. Consequently, many in the Temne community saw a thin line between such a celebratory culture and Islam.

Aside from the Fortieth Day tradition, there is another layer of celebratory tradition practiced by Temne Muslims at the passing of Temne Muslim men. That is, at the death of a Temne Muslim man, the family of the deceased required the widow or widows to be confined to a designated space within the home during the long mourning period – which lasted for "three months and ten days."[118] During this grieving process, a widow or widows wore white traditional garb, and routinely observed *Salat*, defined as "formal worship or prayer, which is performed five times a day."[119] If the widow or one of the widows was not a Muslim, tradition required her to convert to Islam on the death of her husband. The couple's children surrounded the immured widow, accompanied by subdued festivities. Apparently, this practice of confining widows and forcing non-Muslim women to convert to Islam at the death of their husbands belied Islamic orthodoxy.[120] Informants for this study stated that gatekeepers of Temne traditions originally introduced the long period of lamentation for two principal reasons. First, close observers of the confined widow watched for signs of pregnancy, to corroborate any such claims she might make. In addition to this, the long period of mourning gave traditional executors time to discuss the hereditary rights of the family, especially if the deceased did not have a formal will. Members of both families invoked sharia and Temne customs and traditions to guide their deliberations and final resolutions. Decisions reached on such occasions were not subject to further appeal, since the Qur'an served as the basis of the deliberations. The above account shows that this aspect of the Sierra Leonization of Islam proved androcentric, especially when informants for this study failed to demystify a contrary scenario.

The use of compellations constitutes the final element of the Sierra Leonization of Islam practiced by Temne Muslims in the Sierra Leone Colony. One of the five pillars of Islam states that all able-bodied Muslims must undertake a pilgrimage to Mecca at least once in their lifetime, if they can afford to do so.[121] Temne Muslim men and women in the colony, particularly *alfas*, *sheiks* and imams, used noms de guerre such as "*Alhaji*," and "*Haja*," to address Sierra Leonean pilgrims returning from the pilgrimage, or *hajj*, performed in Mecca – one of the sacred places of Islam. Though the titles broadly refer to a "returnee" or a "stranger,"

[118] Personal observation, November 1996.
[119] Badru and Sackey, *Islam in Africa*, p. 28.
[120] Interview, Gibril Kamara, Freetown, November 4, 2003.
[121] Nagel, *The History of Islamic Theology*, pp. 2–17.

many used the compellations generally to heap reverence on pilgrims who had successfully completed this quintessential obligation in Islam. In fact, the Temne Islamic Community gave the term a new meaning, and broadened its functional dimension to mean "a powerful person with ostensible wealth, sanctimonious status and head of a big household."[122] As returnees from Mecca, many Muslims in the Islamic community deified the *Alhajis* and *Hajas* because they equated the titles with "socio-economic and political power."[123] Multiple sources reveal that the contextual misapplication of *Alhaji* and *Haja* defied Islamic orthodoxy. Nonetheless, the application of the compellations remained popular in the Temne Islamic Community, and in the Islamic community as a whole.[124] Thus, the Sierra Leonization of Islam by Temne Muslims shows the flexibility and adaptability of the Islamic religion. *Sheiks, Alfas* and imams in the Temne Islamic Community created the context for adherents to appropriate the religion in terms of space and visual culture, and in terms of belief in the power of charms, sorcery, and other practices frowned upon by conservative Islamic scholars. In short, Temne Muslim men and women catapulted Islam into a momentous position in a colony founded on Judeo-Christian principles.

Overall, then, though Temne Muslims successfully syncretized, and to some extent conflated, indigenous traditions with aspects of Islamic principles, "this did not undermine the basic institutions and obligations of Islam."[125] In light of this, it is evident that the Sierra Leonization of Islam practiced by Temne Muslims contributed to a widespread appreciation and entrenchment of the teachings of the religion among neophytes and proselytes. Fyfe reinforces this perspective, when he states, "if some European observers noted the West African Muslims' deviations from strict orthodoxy, their disregarding the restrictions on plurality of wives, their using magic to exploit the credulous, Winterbottom observed how strictly they kept their times of prayer and the Ramadan fast."[126] Expressed differently, though Temne Muslims practiced Islam in a contrarian fashion, relative to orthodox Islam as proclaimed by the Wahhabis, they however continuously upheld the basic institutions of the religion.

[122] Interview, Alhaji Sheik Gibril Kamara, Freetown, November 4, 2003; this was also corroborated in a separate interview with Mohammed Kuyateh, Kalamazoo, April 14, 2006.
[123] Interview, Alhaji Sheik Gibril Kamara, Freetown, November 4, 2003; this was also corroborated in a separate interview with Mohammed Kuyateh, Kalamazoo, April 14, 2006.
[124] Personal observation; author has observed this practice for over 25 years.
[125] Alhaji Sheik Gibril Kamara, Freetown, November 5, 2003.
[126] Christopher Fyfe, *A History of Sierra Leone* (London: Oxford University Press, 1962), p.66.

The mosque of Sheik Amadou Bamba in Touba, Senegal
Source: Author's personal collections during a visit to Touba, May 2007.
Author's permission needed for reproduction or use of these photographs and images in published works or public fora.

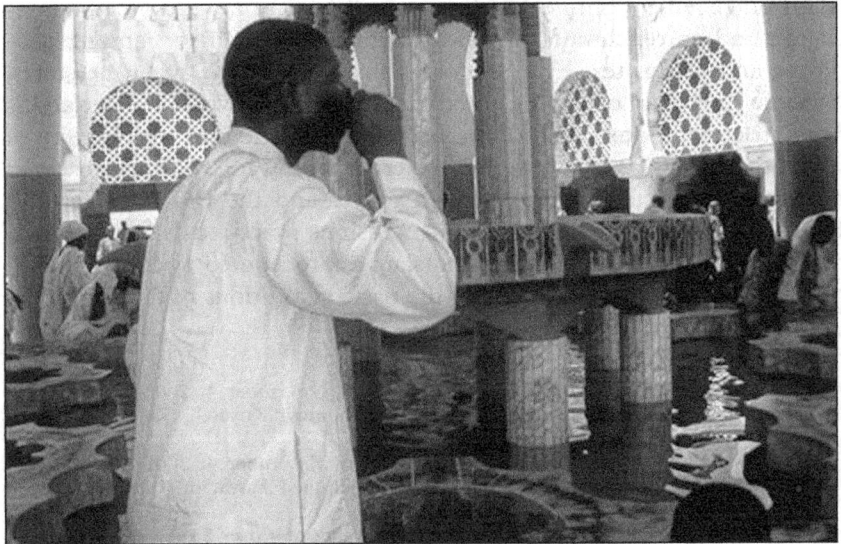

Mosque in Touba Senegal; author visited mosque

Conclusion

In light of the foregoing analysis, the settlement founded in Sierra Leone in 1787 with Christianity at its core became a multireligious enterprise by the close of the nineteenth century. The British philanthropists who founded the settlement envisaged a free society anchored in Westphalian democratic principles. Though Christianity thrived throughout the colony's history, Islam proved to be a forceful alternative in the beginning of the nineteenth century. In other words, despite its bumpy path, Islam became a resilient force; it gave adherents hope, prestige, and status in a colony dominated by Victorian traditions and values. Islamic institutions also served as alternatives to British institutions largely staffed by Western-educated elites. That is, Muslim leaders with large followings assisted the colonial establishment in upholding the rule of law.

The adoption of Islam as a religion by many in the Temne Islamic Community enhanced the influence of Temneness in the Sierra Leone Colony. In succinct terms, on one level, Temneness became manifestly associated with Islam and it appurtenances. This is because Temne and non-Temne Muslims on numerous occasions linked Temne traditions, culture, and customs with Islamic principles. Additionally, Temne Muslims also linked the mission and activities of Muslim leaders, such as Muyu-Deen Kamara, Alhaji Gibril Sesay, and to some extent, Kande Bureh, Sukainatu Bangura, and others, with Temneness. While such conflations helped propagate Islam among agnostic Temne and Temne apologists, it also exposed Temne Muslims to criticism from conservative Islamic clerics.

All in all, this chapter shows that Temne Muslims played a great role in the propagation, popularization, and transmogrification of Islam in the Sierra Leone Colony, contrary to the assertions of the extant historiography. In a nutshell, Temne Muslims gave Islam a differentiable attribution and attraction, which enhanced its growth and profundity.

The ensuing chapter focuses on the role of Temne women, marketers, and leaders of the proletarian class, retail politicians, and grassroots ethnonationalists in the social formation of the Sierra Leone Colony. Historical documents show that non-Western-educated Temne, and non-Temne female activities, formed the bedrock of the highly recognized women's movements in this British colonial space.

7   From the Margins to the Center: The Role of Temne Market Women Traders

This chapter explores the role of non-Western-educated Temne market women in shaping the social and economic history of the colony. It addresses the neglect of women's participation in the economy, and highlights the cultural foundations of Temne women's activism. The previous chapters note that the Temne organized around various institutions to strengthen their influence in the colony. This chapter shows that Temne women traders organized around commercial institutions, the leadership of powerful market women, and the TTA. In conjunction with women's groups, Temne women used commercial institutions to simultaneously enhance their profile and Temne influence in this British colony.

The historical literature concerning the colony makes sparse reference to the activities of non-Western-educated women, particularly Temne women's roles in the economic and social life of the colony. The conventional history of the colony emphasizes the role of men, and to some extent, Western-educated women, especially Freetonian women. Feminist scholars such as Emily Lynn Osborn, Gracia Clark, and Susan Geiger, working in other African contexts, have drawn attention to the androcentric biases in the historical literature of colonial Africa, and the strategies for uncovering the history of illiterate subjects. Geiger makes reference to "the accumulation of androcentric bias in written records both primary (produced by colonial officials, missionaries and travelers) and more recently, secondary (produced by Western as well as African scholars) ... in African history."[1] It is remarkable to observe that, where the androcentric literature references women's role in shaping the social formation of societies in Africa, they are portrayed as powerless. As Andrea Cornwall notes, African women are usually and easily portrayed as "powerless, inviting intervention on their behalf."[2] Osborn refers to this

---

[1] Susan Geiger, "Tanganyikan Nationalism as 'Women's Work': Life Histories, Collective Biography and Changing Historiography." *The Journal of African History* 37, no. 3, 1996, pp. 465–466.

[2] Andrea Cornwall, "Perspectives on Gender in Africa" in *Readings in Gender in Africa*, ed. Andrea Cornwall (Bloomington: Indiana University Press, 2005), p.1. See also Michael

as the "masculinization of the historical records."[3] Other scholars, such as Frances White, LaRay Denzer, and Catherine Coquery-Vidrovitch, also draw attention to the fact that Sierra Leone historiography downplays the economic and political activities of Sierra Leonean women. In their works, many of these scholars highlight the contributions of women in shaping the political, social and economic history of the colony. White's works analyze the role of Freetonian women she describes as settler women in developing the microeconomy of the protectorate. She highlights the activities of these women in making essential commodities available and accessible to rural markets in the protectorate. Though such undertakings helped Freetonian women traders accumulate wealth, which increased their economic standing in a male-dominated society, it also improved the standard of living of protectorate women and men.[4] In fact, in the peninsula villages of York, Regent, Gloucester, and Leicester, Freetonian women accumulated wealth from trading in raw produce, which in turn strengthened their hands to act independently on a wide range of issues. The Big Market, established as a trading center for residents, served as a major center for commercial activity that brought together Freetonian and non-Freetonian women traders in an interactive mode.[5] In brief, the Big Market formed an important core of colonial Freetown, where Freetonian and non-Freetonian women crossed paths.[6]

Aside from White, Coquery-Vidrovitch mentions the presence of Temne- and Mende-speaking women traders in her work, though her principal focus is on the superior position of Freetonian women traders. She stresses the point that Freetonian women contributed significantly to shaping the history of the colony.[7] As an additional example, in her assessment of the Sierra Leone Women's Movement (SLWM), one of Sierra Leone's foremost women's organizations, Denzer touts the leadership of a distinguished Freetonian woman, Agatha Cummings-John, as chairwoman. A careful reading of the diary of the SLWM and other historical sources reveals that Temne women, such as Haja Sukainatu Bangura in her capacity as vice chairwoman of the women's movement,

---

Kevane, *Women and Development in Africa: How Gender Works* (Boulder, Colorado: Lynne Rienner Publishers, 2004).
[3] Emily Lynn Osborn, *Our New Husbands Are Here: Household, Gender, and Politics in a West African State from the Slave Trade to Colonial Rule* (Athens, Ohio: Ohio University Press, 2011), p. 3.
[4] Frances White, *Sierra Leone Settler Women Traders: Women on the Afro-European Frontier* (Ann Arbor, Michigan: University of Michigan Press, 1987), p.6.
[5] Frances White, "The Big Market in Freetown: A Case Study of Women's Work Place," *Journal of the Historical Society of Sierra Leone*, 4, (December 1980), p.22.
[6] White, "The Big Market," pp. 29–30.
[7] Coquery-Vidrovitch, *African Women*, p. 175.

served as a trusted lieutenant of Cummings-John, at least for a decade.[8]
In all, White, Denzer, and others discredit the idea that women played a
lesser or an insignificant role in the social or economic formation of the
Sierra Leone Colony. They argue eloquently that the commercial activities of women helped shape the colony's economy. Yet, the contributions of this non-Western-educated woman feature little in the feminist
literature. Added to this, the activities and significant contributions of
other non-Freetonian and illiterate women feature less prominently in
the works of Denzer, White, and others.

Notwithstanding the efforts of these scholars to correct this lacuna
in the historiography, their works do not fully appreciate the contributions of non-Freetonian women, especially Temne women, who formed
the preponderant portion of the population of women in the colony's
commercial and sociopolitical landscape. Put differently, the big picture
that emerges from the works of these scholars shows that women mattered, and Freetonian women better represented this agency. However,
privileging Freetonian women over Temne-, Mende-, Loko-, and Limba-
speaking women narrates an incomplete story. A careful examination of
the historical records indicates that women traders from the Temne community significantly contributed to shaping the colony's history.

Historical sources show that many of the women traders, particularly Temne women traders despite their illiteracy, engaged in various
commercial activities, and used commercial spaces for "information
exchange, social interactions, social control, influence building and net-
working."[9] This means the very nature of the spaces market women controlled empowered them in society, because it gave them a certain voice
and leverage. Despite the lack of resources and/or opportunities, many of
the market women worked very hard, and became successful and powerful. As Teresa Barnes argues with respect to women traders in colonial
Harare, women devised various methods of survival despite the many
restrictions they suffered from the colonial authorities: they cooked,
sold handicrafts, and hawked crocheted doilies and other cloths.[10]
Although Barnes's work focuses on how gender and class intertwined

---

[8] *Diary of the Sierra Leone Women's Movement, 1951–1981* (Freetown: 1981), p.8.

[9] Toyin Falola, "Gender, Business, and Space Control: Yoruba Market Women and
Power" in Bessie House-Midamba and Felix K. Ekechi, eds., *African Market Women
and Economic Power: The Role of Women in African Economic Development* (Westport,
Connecticut: Greenwood Press, 1995), p. 24.

[10] Teresa A. Barnes, *"We Women Worked So Hard": Gender, Urbanization, And Social
Reproduction in Colonial Harare, Zimbabwe, 1930–1956* (Portsmouth, New Hampshire:
Heinemann, 1999), p. 31. See also Barry LaMont Isaac, *Traders in Pendembu: A Case
Study of Entrepreneurship* (Chicago: University of Chicago Press, 1969).

in colonial Zimbabwe, her analysis of the contributions of women to the Zimbabwean economy is analogous to how Temne women traders worked so hard and became influential in the economic development of the colony. Whether they resided in the peninsula towns or in the colony proper, many of the traders organized around strong feminist leaders they admired and revered. Some of the leaders include Haja Sukainatu Bangura, Mbalu Conteh, Yankaday Kargbo, and Adama Kamara.[11] Bangura became active in promoting credit unions among those in her employ, and created job opportunities for others.[12]

By focusing on the role of these illiterate women and their leadership, this study embraces the new social history approach advocated by Teresa Barnes, Susan Geiger, Elizabeth Schmidt, Emily Lynn Osborn, Jane Parpart, and Sharon B. Stichter, among many others. Geiger, for example, argues that Western education was not an absolute variable in assessing the importance of women in colonial Tanganyika in the 1950s. She contends that women with little or no Western education contributed immensely to Tanganyikan nationalism.[13] She also highlights the energy and enthusiasm injected into TANU by an illiterate activist, Bibi Titi Mohammed. Bibi Titi drove TANU to higher heights during the nationalist struggles; she mobilized men, and illiterate as well as literate women, in challenging the colonial administration in Tanganyika, now Tanzania. In other words, women such as Bibi Titi Mohammed proved to be prime movers and shakers in TANU.[14] Schmidt uses the same approach in assessing the role of Guinean women in fighting colonialism in Guinea. She asserts that women from all walks of life, both illiterate and literate, participated in the *Rassemblement Democratique Africain* (RDA), which helped secure Guinean independence in 1958. Schmidt attributes this achievement to the collective efforts of women, especially market women.[15] She believes that the agency of women in African historiography is better appreciated when both literate and illiterate female

[11] Interview, Sukainatu Bangura, September 15, 2003. The author is not related to the interviewee, though they share the same last name – a name widely used in northwestern Sierra Leone. Sukainatu Bangura died a few years after this extensive interview. All interviews in this paper were conducted in Temne and Krio. All translations, unless otherwise indicated, are mine.

[12] Interview, Sukainatu Bangura Freetown, September 16, 2003.

[13] Geiger, "Tanganyikan Nationalism." See also Jane L. Parpart and Sharon B. Stichter, eds., *African Women in the Home and the Workforce* (Boulder, Colorado: Westview Press, 1988).

[14] Susan Geiger, *TANU Women: Gender and Culture in the Making of Tanganyikan Nationalism, 1955–1965* (Portsmouth: Heinemann, 1997), pp. 48–52.

[15] Elizabeth Schmidt, "'Emancipate Your Husbands!' Women and Nationalism in Guinea, 1953–1958," in Jean Allman, Susan Geiger and Nakanyike Musisi eds., *Women in African Colonial Histories* (Bloomington: Indiana University Press, 2002), pp. 284–289.

players are included in the master narrative. Similarly, in the Sierra Leone Colony, illiterate Temne women not only played a role in promoting the informal economy, they engaged in other activities that promoted the cause of women.

Economic Networks and Temne Women's Entrepreneurship, 1900–1961

Historical sources show that women engaged in various socioeconomic activities in the colony and protectorate. In fact, in the nineteenth and twentieth centuries, non-Freetonian women principally engaged in retail business, as well as in wholesale commerce. Kenneth Little argues that members of the Temne- and Fula-speaking communities dominated this occupation.[16] In conjunction with this, many of the traders from the hinterland who anchored at Susan's Bay in the nineteenth century spoke *Theimne* and some form of Bullom.[17] Apparently, *Theimne* not only served as their medium of communication, it became the language of trade as well. Though the analyzes of the authors are not gender specific, it is obvious from their accounts that women proved to be more active in these kinds of trade. These traders frequently operated between the colony and the hinterland.

It should be pointed out that the colony did not have an agro-based economy; that is, residents in the colony imported food and raw products from the peninsula towns and/or from the protectorate. Temne women became notably involved in this type of trade – many shuttled to and from the peninsula to trade in raw produce. In reinforcing this point, Vernon Dorjahn points out that Temne traders played effective roles in promoting a successful trade network between western and northern Sierra Leone in the colonial period: "[M]any staple foods were shipped from Mayoso to Freetown ... for sale – oranges, bananas, peppers, kola nuts, coffee and so on."[18] Freetonian women traders unable to travel to the protectorate to buy these products relied on the supply they received from their Temne, Mende and Loko colleagues. In addition, Temne-,

[16] Kenneth Little, "The West African Town: Its Social Basis." *Diogenes: The International Council for Philosophy and Humanistic Studies* (March 1960) 8, p. 20.

[17] Allen Howard, "The Role of Freetown in the Commercial Life of Sierra Leone" in Christopher Fyfe and Eldred Jones, eds., *Freetown: A Symposium* (Freetown: Sierra Leone University Press, 1968), p. 47.

[18] Vernon Dorjahn, "African Traders in Central Sierra Leone" in Paul Bohannan and George Dalton, eds., *Markets in Africa* (Evanston, Illinois: Northwestern University Press, 1962), p. 81. Mayoso was a Temne stronghold based in northern Sierra Leone.

Mende-, and Limba-speaking women based in the colony engaged in agricultural activities at the micro level, particularly residents in rural areas: Rokel, Gloucester, Leicester, York, and Rogbarie. An observer noted in 1926 that the "Timne clean rice per kettle [was] better and lower in price than the Mendi rice per kettle."[19] The report indicates that, in the 1920s, the rice grown and sold by Temne- and Mende-speaking market women contributed to the flow of rice in the economy of the rural areas and, to some extent, in the colony.

Apart from engaging in low-scale farming, Temne women also participated in fishing, gardening, and trade activities. These women in turn sold harvested produce to colony markets. As the population figures in this volume show, the Temne constituted the bulk of the population, while the Freetonians and others remained in the minority in many of the rural communities between 1890 and 1961. (See Figure 2.) Richardson and Collins, authors of the research done on behalf of the colonial administration in Sierra Leone, did not analyze how people were assigned into ethnic categories. They state, however, that the composition of ethnic groups living in the rural areas comprised fishermen, farmers, and traders, who took their goods to Freetown markets, where they accrued big profits.[20] They also point out that Temne women traders dominated the rural economy of these peninsula towns.

The various markets in the colony served as shared economic spaces that brought traders from diverse ethnic backgrounds together. The principal colony markets included the Big Market, King Jimmy, Bombay Street and others. Temne women traded in these markets and constituted the largest single group in some of the markets, where they remained regular suppliers of fish, vegetables, and other garden products.[21] In writing about the role of markets in the economy, Osman Newland vividly states that:

Freetown has five public markets: the Vegetable Market in the Water Street, called in native parlance 'Big Market', and dating back to 1861; the Meat Market, called Garrison Street, colloquially named 'Grain Market', opened in 1862; the

---

[19] *West Africa Mail and Trade Gazette*, April 26, 1926. This was a widely circulated newspaper in colonial Freetown in the early 20th century.

[20] E. M. Richardson, and G. R. Collins, *Economic and Social Survey of the Rural Areas of the Colony of Sierra Leone* (London: Colonial Office Research Department, Unpublished Report, 1951), p. 396.

[21] Richardson and Collins, *Economic and Social Survey*, p. 396. Haja Sukainatu Bangura, who owned stalls in the market, also corroborated this information. The number of stalls she owned increased in the 1950s. She claimed to have inherited some of her business assets from relatives who traded in the Big and King Jimmy markets before her.

City Market in Kroo Town Road, erected in 1899, at a cost of £2, 000, by the late Sir Samuel Lewis; the King Jimmy Market in King Jimmy Wharf in Rock Street. There was also a slaughterhouse in King Jimmy Wharf, Water Street.[22]

Newland highlights the strategic location of King Jimmy Market, known for selling a variety of vegetables and other essential produce, in his work. The proximity of the market to the government wharf and/or port and to Susan's Bay made it easily accessible to local residents and visitors from the protectorate. In addition to this, "the market at King Jimmy handle[d] fresh fruit and vegetables" brought from the Bullom shore and other areas within the colony.[23] In her analysis of the Big Market, White overlooks the centrality of King Jimmy and its role in the colony's economy. Because of the focus of her work, she also overlooks the competitive spirit which developed between traders based at King Jimmy Market and those of the Big Market. At the King Jimmy Market in the 1950s, Temne women rallied around the leadership of Sukainatu Bangura and Adama Kamara. Bangura and Kamara held bi-weekly meetings with other women traders, where they discussed key economic matters and "pledges of assistance to any colleague hit with low returns during unforeseen economic emergencies."[24] Additionally, Temne women traders also had significant presences in the various markets in the peninsula towns. Figure 3 in Part II shows that Temne women outnumbered other women in the peninsula towns between 1947 and 1950; that is, the number of Temne women exceeded Freetonian, Mende-, Limba-, and Loko-speaking women traders.[25] It is evident that many of the Temne women in the rural towns engaged in commercial transactions, and worked together on numerous economic projects and entrepreneurial ventures.[26]

To foster micro-agricultural activities among rural women, the colonial administration established a fairly well financed scheme, the Agricultural and Commercial Society. The Society helped market women in the peninsula districts "sell agricultural produce" to residents of the colony and protectorate.[27] The hierarchical structure of the society is not clear; however, the colonial administration appointed a chairman of the society

---

[22] H. Osman Newland, *Sierra Leone: Its People, Products, and Secret Societies* (New York: Negro Universities Press, 1969), p. 17.

[23] J. McKay, "Commercial Life in Freetown" in Christopher Fyfe and Eldred Jones, eds., *Freetown: A Symposium* (Freetown: University of Sierra Leone Press, 1968), p. 74.

[24] Interview, Adama Kamara, Freetown, November 5, 2003.

[25] Richardson and Collins, *Economic and Social Survey*, pp. 82–85. The report was completed in 1950.

[26] Interview, Sukainatu Bangura Freetown, October 4, 2003; interview, Adama Kamara, Freetown, October 4, 2003. Though both women were interviewed on the same day they were interviewed separately.

[27] *Sierra Leone Weekly News*, Freetown, July 25, 1931.

charged with the responsibility of "granting seedlings" to rural women engaged in farming and gardening. The society also helped stabilize agricultural prices through an office created to coordinate the purchase and distribution of raw produce. This action undertaken by colonial authorities helped promote commercial activities among Temne, Freetonian and other women traders. Despite the availability of funding for mid-level commercial activities, many Temne women continued to engage in petty trading by peddling their commodities in Leicester, York, and Gloucester. Though many retailed their goods, few prosperous Temne women traders sold their goods wholesale to their Freetonian counterparts in colonial Freetown. In the case of rice, one of the principal staple foods, "the Temne and Mende rice were often highly consumed," compared to rice produced by other ethnic communities.[28]

In their joint report on the state of commerce in the rural areas of the colony, Richardson and Collins state that, from 1947 to 1951, Temne women dominated trade in vegetables and other produce.[29] Sukainatu Bangura, one of the lead marketers and a feminist in her own right, recalled that this trend continued in the 1950s and the early part of the 1960s.[30] She stated that she and other Temne women traders served as major suppliers of raw commodities to traders in the Big Market, King Jimmy and other markets in the colony. It is difficult to determine the extent of the economic power the traders commanded; however, it is clear that their commercial activities contributed to the informal economy of the colony.

Historical sources also indicate that Temne women organized small loan schemes meant to help each other during bad harvests or poor returns from sales, especially in fairly remote sections of the colony.[31] The modus operandi of the scheme involved women in the retail business obtaining loans from established Market women like Sukainatu Bangura, Adama Kamara, and Ya Bom Posseh, among numerous others. The recipients of such loans agreed to repay the loans at specific dates, barring unforeseen circumstances. The loans helped some Temne women start their own businesses. Mammy Fatu, a former Temne trader at Bombay Street Market, whose relatives migrated from Leicester Peak to Freetown in the 1920s, states that Ya Bom Posseh headed one of the microcredit schemes, and taught some of her peers small-scale entrepreneurship. She recalls

[28] SLWN, September 12, 1931.
[29] West Africa Mail and Trade Gazette, Freetown, April–June 1930.
[30] Interview, Sukainatu Bangura, October 5, 2003.
[31] Interview, Mammy Fatu, Freetown, October 16, 2003. This scheme differed from Esusu, a scheme that was popularly used in colonial Sierra Leone.

that, in the 1940s, when she started her own business at the Bombay Street Market, she engaged in similar practices by pulling together her resources with those of other Temne and non-Temne colleagues. Nonetheless, in the 1950s, she dissolved the scheme to join a much bigger one run by Sukainatu Bangura.[32] The scheme offered larger sums of money and longer repayment periods. It also expanded its pool of participants; that is Mende-, Limba-, and Loko-speaking women joined the scheme.

Furthermore, Figure 3 shows that, contrary to some of the views expressed in the established literature, Freetonian women living in rural towns depended on the cooperation, agricultural capability, and business acumen of Temne women traders. The 1947 census in Rokel, one of the strategic commercial towns, indicates that Temne women traders dominated retail trade in this locale. The census report reveals that the population of Rokel constituted the following in 1947: 20 Freetonian women, 9 girls, and 28 boys, 40 Mende-speaking women, 10 girls, and 20 boys, 175 Temne women, 56 girls, and 118 boys.[33] The report shows that a majority of Temne women in Rokel engaged in petty trading and small-scale farming. Because of its strategic location, residents of Rokel had easier access to colony markets, compared to residents in Waterloo. Such access guaranteed Temne women high income levels as they sold much of their produce, especially those who engaged in the wholesale business directly in the colony.[34] Freetonian women in Rokel also served as markets for Temne women, because they bought many of the goods they could have bought from the Big Market in colonial Freetown, from Temne women traders based in Rokel. Quite apart from Rokel, Temne women traders engaged in commercial activities in Gloucester, Leicester, Regent, York, and Lakkah.[35] Those who did not engage in commerce undertook other ventures, such as low-scale farming and gardening. Richardson and Collins state that, in the mid-1950s, Temne women in particular did not rely on their spouses for financial support because of the success of their entrepreneurial activities.[36] This suggests that trade proved helpful to the women, and they presumably led better and independent financial lives. Sukainatu Bangura stressed that she depended less on her husband's

[32] Interview, Mammy Fatu, Freetown, November 10, 2003. There is no archival or documentary evidence to support Mamy Fatu's claim. The author heavily relied on her recollection of the implementation of the scheme. Richardson and Collins, however, alluded to the existence of similar schemes among peninsula residents.

[33] Richardson and Collins, *Economic and Social Survey*, p. 330.

[34] Richardson and Collins, *Economic and Social Survey*, p. 395.

[35] *West Africa Mail and Trade Gazette*, Freetown, April–June 1930.

[36] Richardson and Collins, *Economic and Social Survey*, p. 428.

income as her business network grew and expanded. She recalled that due to her economic success and the level of income generated from her enterprises, her husband, a janitor in the colonial administration, largely relied on her for financial support; she provided food and other groceries for her household. She recollects that she did fewer chores at home, since she employed maids and utilized the services of relatives under her care to help take care of her home. Mammy Fatu, who corroborated some of Bangura's claims, also affirmed that her husband, Pa Momodu Sankoh, a court messenger, also relied on her for provision of victuals and other domestic essentials, including groceries. She reminisced that, at the passing of her husband in the mid-1960s, she singlehandedly ran her large household. Being the sole breadwinner of her large household, Mammy Fatu stated that she had a significant number of foster children she adopted from relatives and friends to care for and support. Both Bangura and Fatu stated that, despite their prosperous economic stature and independence, their husbands remained the heads of their households. The two women revealed that, though sex-segregated budgets formed part of the core of their households, they absorbed a large part of the school expenses for their children.[37] In sum, in the 1940s and mid-1950s, Bangura and a few of her colleagues continuously displayed financial independence from their menfolk. The economic independence of Bangura, Mammy Fatu, and others indicates that "women put to various uses the proceeds that they accumulated from selling foodstuffs, dyeing cloth, spinning cotton, and making woven mats."[38] Osborn maintains that, in Guinea, the notion that wives relied on their husbands for support did not ring true in the case of the hard working market women in the Kankan market.

The Historical Context for Temne Women's Activism, 1920s–1960s

To thoroughly understand the significant social and economic contributions of non-Western-educated or illiterate women traders in the Sierra Leone Colony, it is useful to analyze the activities of a few prominent women, such as Sukainatu Bangura, also known as Kai Bangura, and Yankaday Kargbo, among others. Though there are numerous book-length biographies of Western-educated Freetonian men and women, there are few such projects on illiterate non-Freetonian women. To date, there is no major study on illiterate or lowly-educated non-Freetonian women and their socioeconomic contributions in the formation of the

[37] Both women observed that this episode characterized the androcentric environment that prevailed in the colony.
[38] Osborn, *Our New Husbands*, p. 169.

Sierra Leone Colony. This study is one of the first to write some of these women into the historical literature of Sierra Leone. It should be pointed out that much of the data used in assessing the careers and life histories of these women came from lots of interview sessions held with these women and/or their associates. As a matter of fact, there are no archival data on the activities of many non-Western-educated women, especially Bangura and Kargbo. It is significant that their life histories are analyzed because "life histories preserve and highlight the uniqueness of individual perspectives and personal agency as these interact with the wider sweep of historical events and social structures."[39] Aside from the lack of archival information on the life histories of illiterate women in the colony, in 1999, the Revolutionary United Front (RUF) rebels invaded the capital city of Sierra Leone, Freetown, formerly the Sierra Leone Colony, causing massive damage to the Freetown City Council library. The library had held numerous documents on the history of the city since it became a British Crown Colony in the nineteenth century. Consequently, this study relied heavily on testimonies of informants who participated in some of the historical events assessed. In spite of the dearth of documentary information, in 1961, the SLWM established a newspaper to cover the activities of its membership. Despite its ephemerality, the paper provided valuable information on the activities of some market women in colonial Freetown.

Haja Sukainatu Bangura, or Kai Bangura, was born in northern Sierra Leone in 1901 to Temne parents, before she migrated to the colony in 1911.[40] She started her economic life at the age of eighteen at sea, where she engaged in the fishing business. In 1925, she bought and rented canoes over a period of time, and used the proceeds to start a farming business. She bought husked and cleaned rice, vegetables, fruits, and palm oil from the protectorate for sale at the King Jimmy Market.[41] In 1929, Bangura began trading at the King Jimmy Market, where she quickly became famous and "well liked" by her colleagues and numerous customers.[42] With the increase in her fortunes, accompanied by an expansion of her multifarious businesses, Bangura employed the services of young Temne-, Loko-, and Limba-speaking women in the agriculturally fertile rural areas, where the women farmed much of the produce they sold to her at low cost. She sold these goods "on a cost recovery basis" to her colleagues, regular customers, and friends and relations.[43] This account

---

[39] Gracia Clark, *African Market Women: Seven Life Stories from Ghana* (Bloomington: Indiana University Press, 2010), p. 22.
[40] Interview, Haja Sukainatu Bangura.
[41] Interview, Haja Sukainatu Bangura.
[42] Interview, Pa Alimamy Yenki Kamara.
[43] Interview, Sukainatu Bangura.

suggests that Bangura sold her produce at relatively affordable prices to different markets. Added to this, she funded some of the gardening activities of the market women in Rokel and Lakkah. By employing Temne-, Loko-, and Limba-speaking women as farm hands and vendors, Bangura replenished her stock with a regular supply of vegetable goods. Through this method, she provided a regular supply of goods and services to her customers, mostly Freetonian, Temne-, Mende-, and Loko-speaking women at the King Jimmy and Bombay Street markets.[44]

Closely related to the above, Kai became an activist in her own right, as she played a highly influential role in the socioeconomic and political life of the colony. Her activities clearly reveal that non-Western-educated women played important roles in shaping African societies. The stories of Kai and Kamara prove that powerful women existed with large followings among non-Freetonian market women.

In the 1940s, Kai Bangura returned to the fishing business after a few years' intermission. She used her growing income to purchase additional fishing boats and rented them to men and women of diverse ethnic backgrounds. Between 1945 and 1948, she owned and rented five fishing boats to Temne- and Bullom-speaking men in particular. She recalls that renters paid her weekly dues for the use of each vessel.[45] The proceeds from the rented boats contributed to the expansion of the frontier of her business, as she bought additional stalls at the King Jimmy and Bombay Street markets.

Over and above this, Bangura also tried her hand at the weaving of local fabric popularly referred to as *Gara* in *Theimne*. Woven and sometimes embroidered by skilled employees, the fabrics were sold to a wide variety of customers in the colony and protectorate. The diversification of her business encouraged her to increase the size of her labor force. Bangura's senior employees and business partners included Mbalu Conteh, Fatu Bangura, Rukor Koroma, Gbassay Sesay, and many others, although some of the women later started and established their own small businesses.[46] Aside from employing young women and men, Bangura also gave out personal loans to colleagues to help them start businesses of their own. The major beneficiaries of this scheme proved to be women with low incomes and low business returns. She granted the loans on an interest-free basis, with acceptable short-term payment plans. Kai Bangura cited the case of Adama Kamara, a friend she bailed out of a financial abyss when her business

[44] Interview, Sukainatu Bangura.
[45] Interview, Sukainatu Bangura, Freetown, November 1, 2003. The name Gbassay is interchangeably used with Gbessay; the variation in spelling is based on the source of information.
[46] Interview, Rukor Koroma, Freetown, September 12, 2003.

plunged due to a risky investment she undertook. Through Bangura's help, Kamara became an active feminist and in fact undertook a pilgrimage to Mecca, which increased her stature within and outside the Temne Islamic Community.[47] Furthermore, Nana Turay, a Susu-speaking feminist and a social and political activist, also benefited from Bangura's economic scheme. Because of her fair exposure to Western education, Turay's activism and popularity made her one of the most respected and recognized feminists in the colony. She became a staunch member of the SLWM, and served as one of its chairpersons and occasionally represented the movement at international conferences and symposia.[48] As with Bangura, the dominant literature overlooks the activities of Turay and other women. Because of the scope of this study, Turay's biographical activities have not been fully analyzed and discussed in this volume. Suffice it to state, however, that Mammy Nana, as many of her fans fondly referred to Nana Turay, became an important ally of Kai Bangura's in the 1950s.[49] As close allies, both women fought strongly for women's rights and gender equality in the colony. Both women also "spoke with one voice during SLWM meetings" on numerous issues "concerning the welfare of women in the colony and they won on several instances."[50] Although Mammy Nana and Kai came from different ethnic backgrounds, they both strongly worked together and passionately promoted women's interests in a masculinized environment. Historical sources show that Mammy Nana had the added advantage of being moderately educated, which allowed her to represent Sierra Leone women at local and international women's leadership fora.

In 1952, Bangura and Yankaday Kargbo established an informal microlending cooperative at the King Jimmy and Kissy Road markets.[51] Bangura recollected that the cooperative served as an informal mini-bank for both parties during financial emergencies. The cooperative mainly offered financial assistance to young market women employed by the two

[47] Interview, Abdul Bangura, Freetown, October 9, 2003. Abdul is the eldest surviving son of Sukainatu Bangura. Like his mum, Abdul Bangura is not related to the author. He was seventy years old when the author interviewed him. He is a retired sailor. Abdul informed the author that, as a young man in colonial Freetown, he actually wrote some informal loan agreements between his mother and her debtors. He has no records of these receipts he wrote over forty-five years ago.

[48] *Diary of the SLWM*, p. 9. See also *Madora*, February 16, 1961. *Madora* was a newspaper established by the SLWM to cover its activities, because the male dominated press was biased in its coverage of the activities of women in the colony.

[49] Turay is deceased and could not be interviewed for this study.

[50] Interview, Sukainatu Bangura, Freetown, October 9, 2003.

[51] See *Daily Mail*, Freetown, December 27, 1952.

partners – Bangura and Kargbo. Over and beyond this, the cooperative
also made loans accessible to credit- worthy customers and colleagues,
with strict repayment plans. She observed that the loans proved beneficial to several young women traders who otherwise would have remained
unemployed. Other informants for this study pointed out that, though
the cooperative proved useful to the informal economy, young Temne
women traders at the King Jimmy, Kissy Road and Bombay Street markets disproportionately benefited from it. Some informants familiar
with the operation of the scheme observed that the loans alleviated the
economic situation of recipients, but that the returns on the loans also
benefited the shareholders. Nonetheless, Bangura noted that, albeit she
accrued some profits from this, the enterprise largely served as a solidarity gesture to many women traders as a whole, and Temne market women
in particular.[52]

In recognition of her contribution to the development of commerce
in the colony, the Freetown City Council appointed Sukainatu Bangura
coordinator of Temne market women at the King Jimmy Market in
1949.[53] As head trader, she used her leverage with the council to advocate better amenities for traders. In her new role, she regularly arbitrated
altercations, and referred criminal cases to the council, or the TTA, as
she deemed necessary. The structure of the market meant that Temne
women traders occupied a section of the market assigned to them,
where they sold various goods and ingredients, including condiments
"used to prepare specialized Temne dishes."[54] When the taps or wash-
rooms in the Temne section of the market broke down, the head trader
sought resolution of the problem by calling on the relevant department
at the city council. The government also appointed coordinators among
Freetonian, Mandingo-, and Mende-speaking women traders at the King
Jimmy Market as well. Gbessay Sesay noted that the government initially
extended this opportunity to Temne and Freetonian market women,
because they constituted the largest number of traders. In addition to her
role as market coordinator, the government contracted Kai Bangura as a

[52] Interview, Sukainatu Bangura, Freetown, November, 2, 2003. Bangura stated that she
and Kargbo were close allies. However, Kargbo is deceased and could not be reached for
an interview to ascertain her recollection of the event. Also, Ambassador Sorsoh Conteh
recalled that he knew Yankaday Kargbo very well; he claimed that Kargbo was a senior
colleague to him in the *Alimania* association. The *Alimania* was a dance society formed
by Alhaji Gibril Sesay to bolster Temne pride and identity in colonial Freetown.
[53] Interview, Abdul Bangura, Freetown, October 10, 2003. Chief Alimamy Yenki Kamara
and Sukainatu Bangura corroborated this claim in separate interviews with them. The
author found no archival document or press reports to verify this claim.
[54] Abdul Bangura, interviewed by Joseph J. Bangura, tape recording, Freetown, October
10, 2003.

regular supplier of food to the Police and Prisons' departments located in close proximity to the King Jimmy Market. She recalled that the government paid for these services on a monthly basis.[55]

The foregoing analysis suggests that, in addition to shaping the economy, Temne and non-Temne market women clearly played a prominent role in the administration of local markets in the colony. The activities of market women affected economic policies far more than is acknowledged in the dominant narrative. The contributions of these non-Western-educated women traders illumine the fact that "African women were not simply creatures of the domestic sphere."[56] An analysis of Osborn's work shows that the manifold activities of non-Western-educated and/or lowly educated female elites underpinned the economic success of many rural and urban African societies, including the Sierra Leone Colony.[57] The coordinating role of Bangura made her a prominent Temne trader; her activities directly or indirectly bolstered Temneness. Moreover, many of her employees perceived her as a prominent Temne woman "who fought for the interests of Temne women."[58] Oral sources also show that some women assumed Temne identity in order to be in Bangura's employ. Thus, it is justifiable to argue that some of Kai's employees passed themselves off as Temne for instrumental purposes. Kai recollects that, though many observers and friends viewed her as a Temne merchant or a Temne chauvinist, she always "fought for the interests of all women regardless of their ethnic background."[59] Nonetheless, oral data reveal that Bangura employed far more young Temne women, in comparison to the number of non-Temne employees she hired. Furthermore, oral data suggest that, though Bangura became popular among grassroots women of all ethnic backgrounds, some of her staunch allies identified themselves as Temne. In spite of this, in 1951, when Agatha Constance Cummings-John nursed the idea of forming the SLWM, Kai Bangura became one of the first women trader's at the King Jimmy Market to be contacted.[60] This is how

---

[55] Interviews, Gbessay Sesay, Freetown, October 6, 2003, and Pa Alimamy Yenki Kamara, Freetown, October 8, 2003. Like other events described above, there is no archival evidence or coverage of the event in any of the major colonial newspapers to support the information. The arrangement may have been a low level or an ad hoc one. I suspect the head of a sub-department within the police and prison systems may have entered into this agreement with Bangura. Abdul Bangura claimed that he kept records of some of these transactions.

[56] Osborn, *Our New Husbands*, p. 166.

[57] See Gracia Clark, *African Market Women: Seven Life Stories* (Bloomington: Indiana University Press, 2010).

[58] Interview, Haja Sukainatu Bangura, Freetown, September 10, 2003.

[59] Interview, Sukainatu Bangura, Freetown, September 10, 2003.

[60] Interview, Sukainatu Bangura Freetown, September 11, 2003.

she recalled the episode: "[W]hen Mammy Constance wanted support for the formation of a women's movement she came to me at King Jimmy Market to elicit my opinion. I supported the idea and she invited and asked me to take along as many ladies as I can to the inaugural meeting."[61] Kai Bangura attended the maiden meeting together with other Temne women, including Mbalu Conteh, Gbessay Sesay, Adama Kamara, and the Susu-speaking Nana Turay. All attendees at the meeting agreed to pay a registration fee of ten cents per head. In the end, the meeting reached consensus on establishing the SLWM. The SLWM became the core of LaRay Denzer's major work.[62] The movement's aims and objectives broadly included the improvement of the status of women, seeking broad representation for women on government bureaus, and forging a sense of unity among women regardless of "tribe" or religion. The SLWM also aimed at eradicating ethnic prejudice and religious bigotry within its ranks.[63] This is evident in the fact that the initiator of the women's movement, Cummings-John, professed to be a practicing Christian, while many of the grassroots membership of the movement professed to be Muslims.

Denzer states in her work that Cummings-John and some Freetonian colleagues founded and comprised the executives of the SLWM.[64] However, the available historical evidence reveals that Temne and other non-Freetonian women became an integral part of the association. Though Cummings-John remained the undisputed leader of the movement, Bangura served as one of the deputy chairs and leader of the grassroots wing of the movement. Historical sources also indicate that Cummings-John acted in concert with other members of the executive, and did not take arbitrary decisions. That is, executive members collectively adopted decisions and strategies, and each member of the executive "reserved the right to veto or object to any decision contrary to the spirit of the organization."[65] For instance, Bangura and Adama Kamara

---

[61] Interview, Sukainatu Bangura, Freetown, November 2, 2003. Bangura noted that "Mammy" was a title bestowed on Cummings-John by those who respected and admired her. The title is generally used to confer reverence on older women or women with financial clout in society.

[62] Interview, Sukainatu Bangura, Freetown, November 2, 2003.

[63] Interview, Mbalu Conteh Freetown, November 5, 2003.

[64] LaRay Denzer, *Constance Cummings-John: Memoirs of a Krio Leader with Introduction and Annotation By LaRay Denzer* (Ibadan: Sam Bookman for Humanities and Research Centre, 1995), p. ixl; see also her work on "Women in Freetown Politics, 1914–61: A Preliminary Study." *Africa: Journal of the International African Institute*, 57, no. 4, Sierra Leone, 1787–1987 (1987), p. 449.

[65] Interview, Sukainatu Bangura, Freetown, November 2, 2003. See also *The Diary of the SLWM*, pp. 8–10.

recount that, when Cummings-John introduced the idea of forming a "women's [political] party" in 1953, barely two years after the formation of the SLWM, "we opposed the idea and she accepted our opposition. We made it clear to her that the movement was too young to take on such a big political role."[66] Denzer and others did not acknowledge the input of women like Sukainatu Bangura and Mbalu Conteh in founding this quintessential women's movement. In fact, Conteh represented the SLWM at international conferences like Nana Turay. Due to the scope of this study, Conteh's activities are not fully addressed here.[67]

As one of the vice or deputy chairwomen of the SLWM, Bangura liaised between the executive and other market women who did not formally join the SLWM. She addressed misgivings brought to her attention by disgruntled grassroots members of the movement, and referred complex disputations to the executive committee. In 1954, when the colonial government closed the Princess Christian Maternity Hospital and Children's Clinic, Bangura claimed to have persuaded the executive of the SLWM to protest against the decision. She averred that "though the government refused to back down immediately, they heard us loud and clear through our street demonstration."[68] Similarly, in 1955, when the Artisans and Allied Workers Union went on a nation-wide strike, Marcus Grant, the head of the striking workers, asked the executive of the SLWM to join them. This is how Cummings-John recollects the episode:

Grant requested a meeting with the executive of the SLWM to discuss the situation and ask us to support the workers in their struggle ... Grant and others complained to us that too much capitalism existed in the country ... we women did not create the strike, but it became necessary to back our husbands, sons and brothers. The men provided the organization.[69]

Bangura posits that when the SLWM executive received the request from the head of the striking workers, she initially rejected the idea of joining the strikers, fearing police brutality. Cummings-John assured her that members of the SLWM would merely play a moderate role; this assurance persuaded Bangura and other skeptical women to support the striking workers. Thus, the SLWM membership agreed to support the striking workers with the assurance that their demonstration would be peaceful and non-violent. Based on the assurances from Cummings-John, Bangura supported and joined the strike. The executive of the

---

[66] Interviews, Sukainatu Bangura, Freetown, November 2, 2003, and Adama Kamara, Freetown, November 5, 2003.
[67] *Madora*, Freetown, February 16, 1961.
[68] Interview, Sukainatu Bangura, Freetown, November 2, 2003.
[69] Cited in Denzer, *Cummings-John*, p. 104.

SLWM asked Bangura to urge her colleagues at the King Jimmy and Bombay Street markets to join the strike. In the end, women of all backgrounds – Freetonian, Temne-, Limba-, Loko-, and Mandingo-speaking women – participated in and supported the strike action.[70] Though the SLWM membership avoided rambunctious behavior, it emerged that the strike took a bumptious turn. The striking workers took to the streets and prevented government officials, private citizens, Lebanese residents, and onlookers from conducting their business.[71] Cummings-John states that the SLWM protected some Lebanese women and children, because they considered them friendly to her movement:

> My executive did what it could to help alleviate the situation, particularly with the Lebanese. Many of them went into hiding because the looters attacked their shops. Because so many of them had helped the SLWM, we now wanted to return the favor by bringing water and food to them. We escorted their women and children to our secretariat where we had established a rudimentary refugee camp.[72]

She maintains that Freetonian elites impugned the SLWM and its leadership for participating in the strike. Mbalu Conteh contends that the support of the SLWM proved crucial to the strike's success even though it remain unclear what success of the strike meant.[73] However, the *Daily Guardian* also corroborates this account noting that the support of the SLWM gave the strike a timely boost.[74]

Bangura recalls that though the grassroots membership of the SLWM showed revulsion at the idea of forming a political party, Cummings-John persisted in her endeavor to get the "women to support the idea."[75] In a closed-door meeting, Cummings-John summoned Kai Bangura, Mammy Nana, Mrs. Magba-Kamara, and Mrs. Marie Tucker to discuss politics. Bangura maintains that Cummings-John again raised the issue of women's participation in national politics. Saddened by the indifference women demonstrated toward party politics, Cummings-John argued that women should be politically active to secure the gains of the SLWM. At the conclusion of the meeting, Cummings-John and her

---

[70] Interviews, Sukainatu Bangura, Freetown, November 2–5, 2003, and Adama Kamara, Freetown, November 5, 2003. Both women were interviewed separately on the same day.

[71] *The Daily Guardian*, Freetown, February 14, 1955.

[72] Cited in Denzer, *Cummings-John*, p. 106.

[73] Interview, Mbalu Conteh, Freetown, November, 2003; see *Diary of SLWM*, pp. 8–9. See also Denzer, *Cummings-John*, pp. 105–106.

[74] *The Daily Guardian*, Freetown, April 17, 1955.

[75] Haja Sukainatu Bangura, interviewed by Joseph J. Bangura, tape recording, Freetown, November 4, 2003.

colleagues agreed to form an association that would be affiliated with the ruling SLPP.[76] Consequently, the SLWM established a women's wing of the SLPP with Cummings-John serving as chair, Nana Turay and Mrs. Magba-Kamara as Secretaries, while Sukainatu Bangura served as Mammy Queen.[77] Referring to this account, Cummings-John stated, "On August 25, 1955, we formally announced the formation of the women's section of the SLPP."[78] Unity within and outside the SLWM proved momentous in successfully pursuing their interests. At the official launch of the organization, Kai coordinated plans for SLWM members at the King Jimmy and Bombay Street markets to participate in the proceedings. Bangura noted a flash of disagreement in the newly formed SLWM branch of the SLPP when Cummings-John suggested the idea of weekly subscriptions, an idea she opposed: "I argued against the idea because it would have been too much on women with low income at King Jimmy and Bombay Street Markets ... the idea was dropped and we all agreed to stick to the usual monthly subscriptions."[79] The claim above suggests that other executive members of the SLWM influenced Cummings-John and the direction of the women's movement. As Mammy Queen, she collected the monthly subscriptions from SLWM members based at the King Jimmy and Bombay Street markets, and apprised them of decisions reached at executive meetings, held every fortnight. Bangura's account depicted that she played a central role in the success of the SLWM and a lot of the grassroots membership "looked up to her for guidance."[80] This speaks to Schmidt's point on the relevance of market women in colonial cities in Africa. Schmidt argues that in Guinea, Conakry market women formed the bedrock of the RDA.[81] Despite the fact that elite and educated women joined the RDA struggle, market women, cloth-dyers, and seamstresses violated gender norms by embarking on anti-colonial activities. The activities of the women left an indelible imprint on the "RDA, its methods, programs" and general objectives.[82]

Similarly, Osborn's emphasis on the role of Kankan market women in developing the local economy in Guinea reinforces this point. In the case of the Sierra Leone Colony, the appeal of the SLPP broadened when the

[76] Interview, Sukainatu Bangura, Freetown, November 2, 2003. See also Denzer, "Women in Politics."
[77] The African Vanguard, August 1955.
[78] Cited in Denzer, Cummings-John, p. 114.
[79] Interview, Adama Kamara, Freetown, November 5, 2003.
[80] Interview, Adama Kamara, Freetown, November 5, 2003. She was also a member of the executive.
[81] Schmidt, "Emancipate Your Husbands!", p. 283.
[82] Schmidt, "Emancipate Your Husbands!", p. 283.

SLWM joined its ranks. As a matter of fact, when the SLPP went out to campaign, women led such campaigns; they sang and taunted men and women who stayed at home, and others who refused to join their ranks out of fear. At speech-giving ceremonies where political parties courted the support of undecided voters, the women sang to persuade these voters. When SLWM members went on the campaign trail, Bangura and Mammy Musu cooked and served food to the women. They also coordinated dress codes at such campaign gatherings – they ensured that all female members wore identical dresses, also known as *Ashobie*.[83] The support the SLPP enjoyed from the SLWM tipped the balance in its favor in the 1957 and subsequent national elections. In other words, the women's wing of the SLPP delivered a majority of the female votes to the SLPP. As Geiger argues in the case of Tanzania, women proved useful in mobilizing TANU as it eventually led Tanganyika to independence.[84] Osborn stresses the important role women played in nationalist struggles in Africa, and observes that "studying the relationship of the household to statecraft, and its implications for gender roles, might usefully illuminate, for example, the dynamics of nationalist movements and political and social structures of independent African states."[85]

In the 1957 general elections, the two political parties – the SLPP and NCSL – headed by Drs. Sir Milton Margai and Bankole-Bright, fielded candidates.[86] Cummings-John contested the general elections as an SLPP candidate in the Colony. Her SLWM colleagues passionately campaigned for her, and she won by an impressive margin. Her unique victory made her the first woman in Sierra Leone, and arguably in West Africa, to defeat a male candidate and the head of a political party in national elections. Cummings-John attributed her success to the support she received from friends and SLWM colleagues.[87] Bangura believed in Cummings-John both as colleague and a friend; she attributed Mammy Nancy's victory at the polls as a symbol of success for women in Sierra Leone and the SLWM in particular.[88] The success of Cummings-John at the polls speaks to the inclusive politics of the SLWM, and the unity it promoted among its membership and among women as a whole. The fact that the candidate of the SLPP, also a member of the SLWM, defeated the leader of an elitist, Freetonian, male-dominated party shows the reach of the SLWM, and the degree of unity in the women's movement.

---

[83] Interview, Mammy Fatu, Freetown, November 5, 2003.
[84] Geiger, *TANU Women*, pp. 66–68.
[85] Osborn, *Our New Husbands*, p. 186.
[86] *The African Standard*, August 16, 1955.
[87] Denzer, *Cummings-John*, pp. 114–116.
[88] Interview, Sukainatu Bangura, Freetown, November 2003.

It also reveals that, when women came together to break ethnic barriers, they made remarkable gains in an androcentric environment. Kai and her allies proved to be movers and shakers in the SLWM; she mobilized women during mass rallies.[89] Not only that, she taught some of her SLWM colleagues the value of mutual benefit schemes and savings clubs. Bangura "represented the voice of the unheard in the SLWM and in the *Alimania*, particularly the shy and inarticulate ones."[90] As a strong feminist and social activist, she forged and organized marriages among young Temne men and women. She also brokered peace between Temne-, Limba-, and Loko-speaking couples when they asked for her intervention. She stated, "Young boys and girls always approached me for advice on marital affairs and frequently asked me to serve as their god parents."[91]

In the cultural sphere, Temne women contributed to the development of popular culture in the colony.[92] Little pays tribute to women like Sukainatu Bangura when he argues that the role women played in running voluntary associations encouraged and enabled women to act more independently than was customary under the traditional system.[93] In underscoring this point, he limns that "the Temne Dancing Compin helped women to get to know young men personally in a way that might ordinarily be difficult. Through the numerous recreational activities, weekly gatherings, excursions to another town, dancing together, brought the sexes together and enabled courtships to start in an easier atmosphere."[94] Little also argues that "the fact that in the mixed associations women frequently shared administrative responsibilities with men is equally important for female morale, particularly in an urban environment."[95] As Mammy Queen of the *Alimania*, Sukainatu became part of the executive that helped build the *Jam ul-Jaleel* or Temne Central Mosque in the 1940s. She provided free food and drinks to the men and women who constructed the mosque. In the course of completing the Temne mosque, she suggested that official quarters be built for the imams and other officials. To that end, the committee in charge of constructing the mosque partially implemented her suggestion when it

---

[89] Interviews, Memunatu Koroma, Freetown, October 14–15 and November 3, 2003, and Kadiatu Turay, Freetown, October 30, 2003.

[90] Interview, Sukainatu Bangura, Freetown, November 2, 2003.

[91] Interview, Sukainatu Bangura, Freetown, November 2, 2003.

[92] Interview, Salamatu Sesay, Freetown, September 8, 2003.

[93] Kenneth Little, *West African Urbanization: A Study of Voluntary Associations in Social Change* (London: Cambridge University Press, 1965), p. 137.

[94] Little, *West African Urbanization*, pp. 134–135.

[95] Little, *West African Urbanization*, pp. 135–136.

modified its plans by constructing a parish for the chief imam of the mosque as his official residence.[96] Assigning an official residence to the imam gave the office honor, special prestige, and a boost within the Temne Islamic Community.

Like Bangura, other women, such as Yankaday Kargbo, also contributed to the economic formation of the colony. The extant historiography overlooks Kargbo's contribution as an established Temne woman trader at the King Jimmy and Kissy Road markets in the 1950s. Though illiterate and lacking Western education, she became an enterprising and industrious activist and feminist. Kargbo became one of Kai Bangura's confidantes, and a close friend and ally of Mammy Nana. As a close confidante of Bangura, Kargbo was a strong founding member of the SLWM since the establishment of the movement. Born in 1920 in the colony to a Temne father and a Bullom mother, Kargbo became a trader at the tender age of fourteen, after the death of her mother. She quickly formed a partnership with Kai Bangura, due to the latter's "fame and socio-economic stature" at the time.[97] A member of the *Alimania*, Kargbo employed many Temne-, Mandingo-, Mende-, and Loko-speaking women; these employees assisted her in coordinating her multiple businesses. Ambassador Sorsoh Conteh described Kargbo as a "prominent Temne business woman dealing in 'Garrah' dyeing with several apprentices from all parts of the city of Freetown" in 1952.[98] She travelled the length and breadth of the colony to trade in assorted goods. Like Bangura, Kargbo also forged partnerships with women traders in different parts of the protectorate. In short, although Kargbo lacked the big name recognition and financial gravitas Sukainatu Bangura enjoyed among women traders, she proved to be a commercial force among her constituents and devotees. Unlike Bangura, however, Kargbo did not wear her ethnic or religious badge on her sleeve. She did not openly identify herself as a Temne, nor did she regularly communicate with customers in *Theimne*. Several informants for this study lauded Kargbo's fierce sense of neutrality, openness, and affability to her sundry acquaintances and customers. Many of her employees and colleagues saw her as a "strong and a no-nonsense Temne woman" who worked in the interest of all women, regardless of ethnic or religious background.

---

[96] Interview, Sheik Gibril Kamara, Freetown, November 2, 2003. All three senior officials of the Temne Central Mosque corroborated this claim.
[97] Interview, Ambassador Sorsoh Conteh, Freetown, November 3, 2003.
[98] Interview, Ambassador Sorsoh Conteh, Freetown November 3, 2003.

Conclusion

This study foregrounds the silent voices of unrecognized agents, including market women traders and grassroots, illiterate women in Sierra Leone historiography. It shows that, contrary to the received wisdom, no particular ethnic group absolutely dominated the economic and political landscape of the colony from the 1890 onwards. Historical evidence indicates that Freetonian women traders alone did not dominate market spaces in the colony, as some feminist scholars argue. The organization of Temne market women around their microlending schemes made them influential, and a force to reckon with, not least in the produce business, and in commodities such as fish and rice. The leverage Bangura, Kargbo, and others exercised over market women convinced some of them to support Temne candidates in municipal elections in 1957. On numerous occasions, politicians like Kande Bureh, a former deputy Prime Minister in Sierra Leone, addressed Temne women traders and canvassed "their support for the SLPP."[99] Oral data indicates that, though Kai Bangura promoted the interests of women traders, her accounts suggest that she promoted Temneness. She did not reject and/or disavow the notion that she used her leverage in commerce to portray Temneness as having a certain cachet and power. Though she joined the SLPP through the SLWM, she eventually supported the Temne- and Limba-dominated All Peoples Congress in the 1960s.

All in all, the economic history of the Sierra Leone Colony is better understood when we widen the bounds of those who mattered. The dominant literature is to a large extent androcentric and Freetonian-centered. Writing the actions of literate Freetonian women, as well as illiterate or non-Western-educated non-Freetonian women, such as Bangura, Kargbo, Turay, Conteh, Mammy Fatu, and others into the prevailing narrative will present a more vivid picture of how various historical actors and actresses shaped the social and economic formation of the Sierra Leone Colony. By focusing on the activities of illiterate Temne women, this study is a major step in achieving this goal.

[99] Interview, Mammy Fatu, Freetown, November 5, 2003.

8   Conclusion: Nexus of Microhistory – New Perspective on the Colony's Historical Landscape

The initial impetus in the historiography of the colony was national-ist. Fyfe, Porter, Spitzer, Wyse, White, Denzer, and others focused on Freetonian accomplishments to make the case that African agency, as well as colonial initiative, became important in the making of the British colony. The extant historiography consigned non-Freetonian groups to the background and grouped them as "non-colony peoples" or "interior peoples."[1] Even when other groups came under inquiry, such as women, non-Freetonians, and Muslims, the Freetonian focus remained. But colo-nial censuses identify a Temne population that matched the Freetonian populace, and the colonial government recognized and entrenched the Temne Tribal Authority in its structure. The study demonstrates that the history of the Sierra Leone Colony is much more complex than the reductionist rendition accorded it in the historiography. In other words, the study shows that a diverse cast of historical figures shaped the social history of the colony. That is, multifarious dance societies, mosques, and other socio-cultural associations presenting themselves as Temne were, as shown in this study, prominent in the social landscape of the colony, especially from the late 1920s onward. Further, individuals recognized as Temne, such as Sukainatu Bangura, Yankaday Kargbo, Mbalu Conteh, Alhaji Gibril Sesay, and Kande Bureh, became prominent leaders among market women and Muslims. The study also shows that the social history

---

[1] Akintola J. G. Wyse, *H.C. Bankole-Bright and Politics in Colonial Sierra Leone, 1919–1958* (Cambridge: Cambridge University Press, 1990), p. 17. See also Christopher Fyfe, *A History of Sierra Leone* (London: Oxford University Press, 1962); Arthur Porter, *Creoledom: A Study of the Development of Freetown Society* (London: Oxford University Press, 1963); Leo Spitzer, *The Freetonians of Sierra Leone: Responses to Colonialism, 1870–1945* (Madison, Wisconsin: University of Wisconsin Press, 1974), Frances White, *Sierra Leone's Settler Women Traders: Women on the Afro-European Frontier* (Ann Arbor, Michigan: University of Michigan Press, 1987), with her other work, "The Big Market in Freetown: A Case Study of Women's Workplace," *Journal of the Historical Society of Sierra Leone* 4, nos. 1 and 2 (December 1980); and LaRay Denzer, *Constance Cummings-John: Memoirs of a Krio Leader* (Ibadan: Sam Bookman for Humanities Research Center, 1995).

of the colony can be fully appreciated when these various strands of history are integrated in the prevalent literature.

Closely related to the above, the study aims at analyzing this case of Temne agency, and promotes an alternative view on the social history of the colony. It illustrates that no single ethnic group dominated cultural organizations, politics, religion, and commerce. As a matter of fact, across a variety of social spaces – mosques, cultural associations, and local administration – the idea of being Temne not only mattered, it also clearly grew in profile and importance in the colonial period, especially in the early twentieth century. As already mentioned in Part II, with the passing of the 1905 and 1906 ordinances, the Temne Tribal Authority became entrenched and fully operational, thus providing various services for its community. It succeeded in organizing the Temne community as a force to contend with in this mélange of a British colony. This is evident in the support the TTA gave to prominent Temne social activists in forming and establishing the *Alimania* and the Temne Progressive Union in the 1930s, the *Ambas Geda* and *Jam ul-Jaleel* in the 1940s and Boys London and *Ariah* in the 1950s. These institutions gave a stamp of importance to Temneness in the colony.

Though the study focuses on the factors that stimulated the emergence of Temne institutions, and their significant role in the social formation of the colony, these observations highlight a number of themes worth studying in future work. Historical documents indicate that Temneness became an attractive identity in the mid-twentieth century. This was true not only for Temne migrants from Temne strongholds in the protectorate, but among some Mandingo-, Loko-, Limba-, Mende-, and Fula-speaking groups, and also the colonial administration and the SLPP as well. Temne identity became a symbol of prestige; it proved important because it strengthened what Frederick Cooper calls "commonality," "groupness," and "connectedness."[2] Thus, those who publicly flaunted Temneness and became Temne showed group boundedness by drawing, again as Cooper argues, a sharp distinctiveness from non-Temne-speaking groups, and a clear boundary between insiders and outsiders. Once they became members of Temne associations, they acted collectively to attain the aims and objectives of these groups. In short, those who publicly adopted Temne identity to make them eligible to join Temne associations exercised due diligence in boosting Temne pride and prestige in public. They worked hard to show that Temneness commanded influence in a competitively complex political space. Withal, it is reasonable to argue

[2] Frederick Cooper, *Colonialism in Question: Theory, Knowledge, History* (Berkeley, California: University of California Press, 2005), p. 75.

that Temne identity proved important and attractive to non-Temne communities, which made them apply to become members of Temne cultural associations. Clearly, the attraction of the associations could be found in the services they provided for their immediate communities. The *Alimania*, for example, built a school for the Temne community in 1943 and contributed to the war efforts during World War II. The *Alimania* and other Temne cultural associations also helped raise funds for the building of the Temne Central Mosque and other community mosques for their worshippers.[3] The associations also served the larger community by promoting, organizing, and arranging marriage ceremonies for Mandingo-, Fula-, and Limba-speakers. Finally, the associations helped shape the mores of their members in public, created intercommunity interactions, and organized sports tournaments and lantern parades; they also helped found the All Peoples Congress (political party) in 1960.

Temneness also proved important to the SLPP, which used it as a political and demographic asset at convenient intervals. During the political confrontation between Freetonian and non-Freetonian groups, for example, the SLPP, particularly its leader Sir Milton Margai, identified as a Mende-speaker, used Temne historical claims to the colony to thwack Freetonian cultural and political arrogance. As noted in this study, Margai impugned Freetonians as a bunch of ingrates who failed to appreciate the generosity of indigenous groups, especially the Temne, for accommodating them in the territory that became the Sierra Leone Colony. Historical records show that the Freetonians found it challenging to fend off such unalloyed obloquy. It is tenable to argue that this line of attack proved effective in demoralizing the Freetonian establishment, and in convincing the colonial authorities to allow majority rule as the true form of representative democracy in Sierra Leone. At the dawn of independence, protectorate politicians led by Sir Milton Margai assumed the mantle of leadership from the departing colonial authorities.

In the sphere of local administration, Temneness played an underlying role in upholding the principle of indirect rule. One of the most prominent leaders of the TTA, Kande Bureh, played a key role in challenging unremitting Freetonian vilification of local administration. Though colonial authorities eventually abolished local administration, the system lasted longer than the Freetown Municipal Council craved. Since the recognition of a Temne Tribal Headman in the 1890s, the Temne community and the Freetonian establishment disagreed over the need for the existence of local authorities. While the Temne "never fully forgot

---

[3] *SLWN*, May 14, 1949.

that the land which served as the colony settlement originally belonged to them," the Freetonian elite believed otherwise, and in fact perceived them and other non-Freetonians as "undesirable elements in their community."[4] The rivalry between the two communities – Freetonian and Temne – played out in other arenas, such as control of markets, necropolises, and other public spaces. Clearly, since the early 1940s, overbearing leaders of the Temne community had refused to give in to Freetonian assertions of authority. In all this, the colonial administration ensured that the Freetonian establishment respected the existence of non-Freetonian institutions, including Temne institutions, which by far posed the greatest challenge to Freetonian ambitions and aspirations and what they represented.

On the basis of the above, it is evident that the colonial administration's support for the Temne Tribal Authority and other Temne groups empowered non-Freetonian groups, and at the same time limited the power and reach of Freetonians. Put another way, colonial authorities facilitated the process that created effective tribal institutions in a Christian colony dominated by highly anglicized Africans. The alternative institutions in turn boosted the colonial enterprise and its appurtenance.

Temneness also became expedient to notable Freetonian politicians, such as I.T.A. Wallace-Johnson. Wallace-Johnson adopted a popular Temne epigrammatic expression *sabbanoh*, which means, "We own this place," as his maxim, to demonstrate the inclusive and all-embracing nature of his organization.

In congruence with the analysis above, provincial migrants recognized the importance of Temne identity when they migrated to different sections of the Temne community between the 1920s and 1950s. By associating with Temneness and openly exhibiting its values, the migrants received a variety of benefits from Temne institutions. It is clear that migration to the colony from Temne strongholds in the protectorate increased steadily in the beginning of the 1920s for several reasons. Barry Riddell points out that "a desire by many, especially the young, to break from traditional authority or discipline," in addition to the "quest for higher standard of living," inspired some immigrants to migrate to the colony.[5] When Temne migrants visited the colony, many of them first called on officials of the Temne Authority, or the various heads of the cultural associations. Officials of these institutions provided a wide range of assistance

---

[4] Gershon Collier, *Experiment in Democracy in an African Nation* (New York: New York University Press, 1970), pp. 48–55.

[5] Barry Riddell, *The Spatial Dynamics of Modernization in Sierra Leone: Structure, Diffusion and Response* (Evanston, Illinois: Northwestern University Press, 1970), p. 106.

to the migrants, including burying those who died as paupers or debtors. Temne local elites, such as Sukainatu Bangura, provided job training for protectorate migrants and other residents. The cooperative society and microcredit scheme Bangura organized privileged Temne girls over many non-Temne girls. More importantly, the microcredit scheme served as a vehicle of social welfare by encouraging community action, particularly among traders at the King Jimmy, Bombay, and Kissy Road Street markets. These facilities provided by Temne institutions for the members of its community may have served as a magnetic force, which possibly encouraged individuals and groups to identify with Temneness.

Over and above this, it is reasonable to observe that the overt adoption of Temne identity by others had a tremendous impact on the social history of the colony. First, it shows that Freetonians had company, and thus interacted with indigenous groups in the colony, even though they continuously detested the idea of sharing the same political space with indigenous representatives. Second, it also reveals the difference between being Temne and being Freetonian. In other words, Temneness meant not being Freetonian, and vice-versa. Residents of the colony, including -, Mandingo-, Limba-, Loko-, and Mende-speakers, among others, at some point or another confronted the option of maintaining their primordial identity, passing themselves off as Freetonian, or adopting Temne identity. It is therefore fair to reckon that Temneness served as a useful alternative to the Freetonian way of life, contrary to the assertions made by Fyfe and Porter.

Notwithstanding the foregoing, it should be noted that, though the need to show group boundedness and sameness made Temne identity distinct, the concept itself proved fluid, shifty, and malleable. This is because those who became attracted to Temne institutions did what was required to identify with Temneness, even when some carried other identities. This indicates that the TTA and the leaders of the cultural associations became gatekeepers of Temne identity. Expressed differently, local intellectuals, elites, leaders of cultural associations, and gatekeepers identified, determined, and endorsed who became Temne via the provision of different services and privileges. The variables used to make such determinations proved circumstantial and multi-dimensional. By admitting non-Temne members who passed off as Temne, executive members of the cultural associations showed unadulterated devotion to the idea of uplifting and coruscating Temne ethnic pride. Such burly avidity made the leaders admit people who engaged in activities that gave Temneness an incandescent outlook and portrait.

The malleability of Temneness and its institutions raises intriguing questions. An examination of the oral data reveals that prominent Temne activists, such as Bangura, Bureh, and Sesay, carried two closely intertwined identities in public. Sesay performed many functions as a missionary and chief Imam of *Jam ul-Jaleel*. The various accounts in this study indicate that though Kai Bangura portrayed herself as a nationalist and promoter of women's interests, her activities show that she favored Temne young women and men over others in her employ. Thus, her numerous supporters widely perceived her as a Temne elite and influential Temne advocate. A careful analysis of the accounts of informants for this study show that apologists for Kai Bangura as celebrated women's leader and Temne icon conflated her role as an active feminist with her role as an influential Temne entrepreneur in the colony. In numerous interview sessions with her, Bangura insisted that she represented the course of "women in Sierra Leone and not just Temne women."[6] It is also valid to observe that Temne market women, and officials of the TTA, obsessively branded prominent Temne officials as Temne agents and/or elites, rather than as nationalist leaders in their own right. More research needs to be done to further probe questions relating to how identities based on religion, or social function in the marketplace, intertwined with ideas of ethnic identification, such as Temneness.

This study has not provided a complete analysis of the contributions of Temne and other non-Freetonian groups and their institutions in the historical development of Britain's oldest overseas territory in colonial West Africa. However, it is a major step in drawing attention to the lacuna in the dominant literature on the contributions of non-Freetonian groups in the making of the Sierra Leone Colony. In spite of the instrumentality of Temne identity, it is apparent that the adoption of Temne identity in certain contexts provided people with access to urban services, vocations, and activities that proved beneficial to them. On account of the questions raised in this study, more research needs to be done to probe the relationship between other non-Temne indigenous institutions and Freetonian institutions. Not only that, it will be useful to undertake research that will probe the meaning of "being Mende," "being Limba," or "being Fula," in the Sierra Leone Colony. What significant role did these indigenous ethnic communities play in the social formation of this archetypal British colony? How did these communities evolve over time? How were the ethnic categories of these communities determined? Did the identities of the groups outlined above proved to be primordial, or largely instrumental in the Sierra Leone Colony? It will be very useful and timely to address these questions in future research projects.

[6] Interview, Haja Sukainatu Bangura, Freetown, November 5, 2003.

From the preceding analysis, this avant-garde study offers a foundation for a new approach to understand the history of the Sierra Leone Colony, given the social history agenda advocated by Frederick Cooper, Bill Bravman, Jane Parpart, Thomas Spear, Jonathon Glassman, and Philip Zachernuk, among many others. These scholars advocate examining historical issues that go beyond nationalist questions. The approach adopted in the various works of these scholars in probing the activities of diverse historical actors in colonial West Africa offers a trenchant methodological blueprint in anatomizing the contributions of various agents in the formation of the Sierra Leone Colony. The numerous voices of local intellectuals, ethnonationalists, marketers, religious entrepreneurs, and non-Western-educated elites remain silent in the historiography. These scholars argue that colonial questions are complex, and cannot be reduced to simple interpretations. In his major work, *Colonial Subjects: An African Intelligentsia and Atlantic Ideas*, Zachernuk argues that the motives and activities of colonial subjects and intellectuals in southern Nigeria were not merely nationalist, as some argue.[7] He asserts that economic factors, power politics, and self-aggrandizement influenced the behavior and activities of these subjects. In other words, Zachernuk argues that, to situate the activities of the colonial intelligentsia in southern Nigeria within the colonizer and colonized model glosses over complex questions. Like Cooper and others, Zachernuk believes that African history is not all about the European-versus-African model.

Quite apart from Zachernuck, Parpart, Osborn, Cornwell, Geiger, Coquery-Vidrovitch, and others show in many of their works that African history cannot be understood through the lens of the tension that characterized the colonial moment; rather, other questions, such as feminism, complex social issues, and the development discourse also matter. These scholars state that African history is richer in content and methodology when other strands of history that go beyond the nationalist discourse are integrated in the dominant literature. In his numerous works, Howard also aligns with the view that African history is more than the transcendent tension between the colonizer versus the colonized. His argument meshes well with the questions Cooper and others raise in their study about "who shaped the city, in what image, by what means and against what resistance." In tandem, the authors advocate a new approach, which investigates the "details of life in the workplace, the marketplace and the residence."[8] In light of this, it is clear that the

---

[7] See Philip S. Zachernuk, *Colonial Subjects: An African Intelligentsia and Atlantic Ideas* (Charlottesville, Virginia: University of Virginia Press, 2000).

[8] Frederick Cooper, ed., *Struggle for the City: Migrant Labor, Capital and the State in Urban Africa* (London: Sage Publications, 1983), p. 10.

history of the Sierra Leone Colony did not merely constitute European denigration of Africans; the history of this British sphere of influence goes way beyond the recurrent tension between the British colonial authorities and the Freetonian establishment, or the predominance of Black Englishmen in the governance of the colony. This study highlights that the history of the colony can be fully appreciated when the bounds of history are expanded to include silent voices, and illiterate grassroot-market women traders. Riddell underscores the significance of this point when he observes that the colony that later became known as Freetown was not only a Freetonian town, but also the largest Temne, Mende, and Limba town.[9]

This means the history of this multiethnic colony cannot be thoroughly understood until the activities and contributions of commercial and various political institutions, spaces, and residents in the full complexity of their identities are wholly incorporated in the historical narrative. This study shows that the history of the colony can no longer be presented as a story centered on Freetonians or "Creoledom" or on the "Krios of Sierra Leone" or on "Creolization." Many different, organized, vital, and influential groups formed part of the core of the story. Locating the rise and influence of groups and people marked as Temne is one step toward achieving a more satisfactory account of Britain's first and oldest colony in West Africa.

[9] Riddell, *Spatial Dynamics*, p. 104.

Bibliography

Primary Source Materials

Colonial Secretary's Office. *Sierra Leone Blue Books, 1901.* Freetown: Government Printing Office, 1901.

Colonial Secretary's Office. *An Ordinance for the Development and Expression of Education on Western Lines among the Mohammedans of the Colony of Sierra Leone and Protectorate.* Freetown: Government Printing Office, 1902.

Colonial Secretary's Office. *An Ordinance to Promote a System of Administration by Tribal Authority among the Tribes Settled in Freetown, No. 19 of 1905.* Freetown: Government Printing Office, 1905a.

Colonial Secretary's Office. *Returns of Mohammedan Schools, 1905,* Freetown: Government Printing office, 1905b.

Colonial Secretary's Office. *An Ordinance to Confer Certain Powers on the Headmen of Towns in the Colony of Sierra Leone, No. 31 of 1906.* Freetown: Government Printing Office, 1906a.

Colonial Secretary's Office. *Regulation Made by the Headman of Adonkia Under Section 4 of "the Headman Ordinance 1905" (No. 38 of 1906).* Freetown: Government Printing Office, 1906b.

Colonial Secretary's Office. *Appointment of Kandeh as Timni Alikali of Waterloo, MP 1681/21 LM 34 3/11 109/23.* Freetown: Government Printing Office, 1911a.

Colonial Secretary's Office. *Commissioner of Police to District Commissioner, Head Quarter District, Waterloo, MP/F No. 238, 1911.* Freetown: Government Printing Office, 1911b.

Colonial Secretary's Office. *Local Administration in Waterloo District, MP 234/18 PC 22 1/18 112/10.* Freetown: Government Printing Office, 1911c.

Colonial Secretary's Office. *Report on Mohammedan Education, 1912.* Freetown: Government Printing Office, 1912.

Colonial Secretary's Office. *Notes on Tribal Administration in Freetown M P/170/ 39: Tribal Rule 48/1915.* Freetown: National Archives, 1917.

Colonial Secretary's Office. *Report and Summary of the Census of 1921.* Freetown: Government Printing Office, 1922.

Colonial Secretary's Office. *Alimamy Suri, Tribal Ruler of the Timnies, Minute Paper 107/2211/1923.* Freetown: Government Printing Office, 1923.

Colonial Secretary's Office. *Employment and Administrative Report, 1923.* Freetown: Government Printing Office, 1924.

Colonial Secretary's Office. *Laws of the Colony and Protectorate of Sierra Leone. Revised Edition, January 1, 1925*. Freetown: Government Printing Office, 1925.

Colonial Secretary's Office. *The Laws of the Colony and Protectorate of Sierra Leone. Revised Edition, January 1, 1946*. Freetown: Government Printing Office, 1946.

Colonial Secretary's Office. *Complaints against the Temne Tribal Headman, T2/6/ 5, MP 1158/1/1/16, 4/10/49*. Freetown: Government Printing Office, 1949a.

Colonial Secretary's Office. *Report of 1947 Population Census*. Freetown: Government Printing Office, 1949b.

Colonial Secretary's Office. *Treaty between the Governor of Sierra Leone and King Tom, 1801*. London: UK National Archives, 1801.

Colonial Secretary's Office. *Proceedings of the Seventh Meeting*. Freetown: Government Printer, 1950.

Colonial Secretary's Office. *Report of Commission of Inquiry into the Strike and Riots in Freetown, Sierra Leone During February 1955*. Freetown: Government Printing Office, 1955.

Colonial Secretary's Office. *Review of Government During the Year From November 1952 to November 1953*. Freetown: Government Printing Office, 1953.

Colonial Secretary's Office. *Ministry of Internal Affairs and Development 137/64/ 23/1/52*. Freetown: Elections Organ Office, 1957.

Colonial Secretary's Office. *An Ordinance to make Provision with respect to Municipal City of Freetown No. 1 of 1945*. Freetown: Government Printing Office, 1945.

Colonial Secretary's Office. *The Rural Area Council Ordinance No. 11 of 1949 MP 13764/23*, Freetown: Government Printing Office, 1949.

Colonial Secretary's Office. *Complaint from I.T.A.Wallace-Johnson About the Temne Tribal Ruler to the Governor, 134/11, 1957*. Freetown: Government Printing Office, 1957.

Colonial Secretary's Office. *Colonial Secretary to Isaac T.A.Wallace-Johnson, March 25, 1957*. Freetown: Government Printing Office, 1957.

Colonial Secretary's Office. *Legislative Council Debates, Sessions 1925–1926*. Freetown, 1956.

Colonial Secretary's Office. *An Ordinance for the Development and Expression of Education on Western Lines Among the Mohammedans of the Colony of Sierra Leone and Protectorate*. Freetown: Government Printing Office, 1902.

Colonial Secretary's Office. *Legislative Council Debates, Sessions 1925–1926*. Freetown: 1926.

Colonial Office 267/683 6/21/1941 32336. London: National Archives.

Colonial Office 267/683, 32375/1943. London: National Archives.

Colonial Office 267/698, 32810/9/4/51. London: National Archives.

Colonial Office 267/698 1950.

Colonial Office 267/683 1941.

COLONIAL SECRETARY'S OFFICE. *Sierra Leone Blue Book, 1901*. Freetown: Government Printing Office, 1901.

COLONIAL SECRETARY'S OFFICE. *Sierra Leone Blue Book, 1910*. Freetown: Government Printing Office, 1910.

COLONIAL SECRETARY'S OFFICE.*Sierra Leone Blue Book 1913*. Freetown: Government Printing Office, 1913.

COLONIAL SECRETARY'S OFFICE. *Sierra Leone Blue Book, 1928*. London: National Archives, 1928.

COLONIAL SECRETARY'S OFFICE. *Sierra Leone Blue Book, 1911*. Freetown: Government Printing Office, 1914.

Colonial-Era Newspapers

Daily Mail, Freetown, February 15, 1955.

Sierra Leone Daily Mail, Freetown, November 11, 1952.

Sierra Leone Daily Mail, Freetown, November 25, 1952.

Daily Mail, Freetown, May 23, 1952.

Daily Mail, Freetown, February 15, 1955.

Daily Mail, Freetown, April 7, 1955.

Daily Mail, Freetown, October and November, 1953.

Madora, Freetown, February 16, 1961.

Shekpendeh, Freetown, August–September 1958.

Shekpendeh, Freetown, October 20, 1958.

Shekpendeh, Freetown, September 29, 1958.

Shekependeh, Freetown, October 29, 1958.

Sierra Leone Mail and Guardian, Freetown, September 1912.

Sierra Leone Observer, Freetown, May 6, 1950.

Sierra Leone Times, Freetown, June 18, 1892.

Sierra Leone Times, Freetown, August 24, 1895.

Sierra Leone Times, Freetown, March 12, 1892.

Sierra Leone Times, Freetown, January 23, 1897.

Sierra Leone Times, Freetown, February 17, 1900.

Sierra Leone Times, Freetown, May 20, 1893.

Sierra Leone Times, Freetown, June 17, 1893.

Sierra Leone Times, Freetown, February 2, 1895.

Sierra Leone Times, Freetown, September 29, 1900.

Sierra Leone Weekly News, Freetown, January–April, 1892.

Sierra Leone Weekly News, Freetown, September–November 1892.

Sierra Leone Weekly News, January 17, 1892.

Sierra Leone Weekly News, Freetown, June 15, 1895.

Sierra Leone Weekly News, Freetown, April 9, 1951.

Sierra Leone Weekly News, Freetown, April 8, 1893.

SLWN, Freetown, October 10, 1893.

Sierra Leone Weekly News, Freetown, January–March 1887.

Sierra Leone Weekly News, Freetown, June and September, 1893.

Sierra Leone Weekly News, Freetown, September 20, 1884.

Sierra Leone Weekly News, Freetown, August 13, 1887.

Sierra Leone Weekly News, Freetown, April 20, 1889.

Sierra Leone Weekly News, Freetown, February 5, 1898.

Sierra Leone Weekly News, Freetown, October 18, 1890.

Sierra Leone Weekly News, Freetown, May 10, 1890.

Sierra Leone Weekly News, Freetown, May 7, 1898.
Sierra Leone Weekly News, Freetown, June 18, 1898.
Sierra Leone Weekly News, Freetown, June 6, 1885.
Sierra Leone Weekly News, Freetown, August 13, 1887.
Sierra Leone Weekly News, Freetown, September 24, 1887.
Sierra Leone Weekly News, Freetown, April 22, 1893.
Sierra Leone Weekly News, Freetown, December 16, 1895.
Sierra Leone Weekly News, Freetown, January 4, 1902.
Sierra Leone Weekly News, Freetown, October 30, 1909.
Sierra Leone Weekly News, Freetown, December 23, 1911.
Sierra Leone Weekly News, Freetown, August 24, 1924.
Sierra Leone Weekly News, Freetown, June 24, 1939.
Sierra Leone Weekly News, Freetown, August 24, 1924.
Sierra Leone Weekly News, Freetown, August 23, 1924.
Sierra Leone Weekly News, Freetown, October 9, 1948.
Sierra Leone Weekly News, Freetown, August 3, 1950.
Sierra Leone Weekly News, Freetown, April 5, 1947.
Sierra Leone Weekly News, Freetown, August 2, 1947.
Sierra Leone Weekly News, Freetown, November 26, 1946.
Sierra Leone Weekly News, Freetown, September 11, 1948.
Sierra Leone Weekly News, Freetown, May 14, 1949.
Sierra Leone Weekly News, Freetown, November 5, 1949.
Sierra Leone Weekly News, Freetown, August 5, 1950.
Sierra Leone Weekly News, Freetown, October–November 1950.
Sierra Leone Weekly News, Freetown, February 25, 1950.
Sierra Leone Weekly News, Freetown, January 24, 1951.
Sierra Leone Weekly News, Freetown, July 7, 1951.
Sierra Leone Weekly News, Freetown, April 20, 1892.
Sierra Leone Weekly News, April 16, 1890.
Sierra Leone Weekly News, Freetown, April–June, 1893.
Sierra Leone Weekly News, Freetown, March 15, 1894.
The Sierra Leone Weekly News, Freetown, August 26, 1899.
Sierra Leone Weekly News, Freetown, July 25, 1931.
Sierra Leone Weekly News, Freetown, September 12, 1931.
Sierra Leone Weekly News, Freetown, June 14, 1942.
Sierra Leone Weekly News, Freetown, September 9, 1943.
The Sierra Leone Daily Mail, Freetown, March 21, 1953.
The Agency, Freetown, January 8, 1887.
The *African Standard*, Freetown, August 12, 1949.
The *African Vanguard*, Freetown, February 25, 1955.
The *African Standard*, Freetown, August 19, 1945.
The African Standard, August 16, 1955.
The African Vanguard, Freetown, August 19, 1955.
The Daily Guardian, Freetown, February 14, 1955.
The Daily Guardian, Freetown, April 17, 1955.
The Sierra Leone Guardian, Freetown, August 18, 1919.
West Africa Mail and Trade Gazette, Freetown, January 30, 1926.
West Africa Mail *and Trade Gazette*, January 2, 1926.

West Africa Mail and Trade Gazette, Freetown, January 9, 1926.
West Africa Mail and Trade Gazette, Freetown, April 10, 1926.
West Africa Mail and Trade Gazette, Freetown, April 26, 1926.
West Africa Mail and Trade Gazette, Freetown, April–June, 1930.
West Africa, June 11, 1960.
West Africa, June 25, 1960.
West Africa, September 24, 1960.
West Africa, June 25, 1960.

Audiotaped Interviews

Abdul Bangura, interviewed by Joseph J. Bangura, Freetown, October 9–10, 2003.
Alhaji Sheik Gibril Kamara, interviewed by Joseph J. Bangura, Freetown, November 5, 2003.
Alhaji Usman Sillah, interviewed by Joseph J. Bangura, Freetown, November 4, 2003.
Hassan Bangura, interviewed by Joseph J. Bangura, Freetown, November 4 and 10, 2003.
Hajj Bangurah, interviewed by Joseph J. Bangura, Freetown, November 1–5, 2003.
Ambassador Sorsoh Conteh, interviewed by Rahman M. Bangura, Freetown, December 1–10, 2003.
Chief Adikalie Gbonko, interviewed by Joseph J. Bangura, Freetown, October-November, 2003.
Alhaji Usman Sillah, interviewed by Joseph J. Bangura, Freetown, November 10, 2003.
Atou Diagne, interviewed by Joseph J. Bangura, Touba, Senegal, May 10, 2006.
Yamba Kalie, interviewed by Joseph J. Bangura, Freetown, September 30, 2003.
Gibril Kamara, interviewed by Joseph J. Bangura, Freetown, November 4, 2003.
Haja Sukainatu Bangura, interviewed by Joseph J. Bangura, Freetown, September 29–30 and November 1–5, 2003.
Mbalu Conteh, interviewed by Joseph J. Bangura, Freetown, November 5, 2003.
George Caulker, interviewed by Joseph J. Bangura, Freetown, November 4–5, 2003.
Pa Alimamy Yenki Kamara, interviewed by Joseph J. Bangura, Freetown, November 2–4, 2003.
Adama Kamara, interviewed by Joseph J. Bangura, Freetown, October 5 and November 5, 2003.
Mohamed Sorie Kamara, interviewed by Joseph J. Bangura, Freetown, November 2, 2003.
Lamin Kamara, interviewed by Joseph J. Bangura, Freetown, November 3, 2003.
Hassan Kamara, interviewed by Joseph J. Bangura, Freetown, October 5, 2003.
Rukor Koroma, interviewed by Joseph J. Bangura, Freetown, September 12, 2003.
Memunatu Koroma, interviewed by Joseph J. Bangura, Freetown, October 14–15 and November 3, 2003.

Ansumana Koroma, interviewed by Joseph J. Bangura, Freetown, September 5, 2003.

Kadiatu Turay, interviewed by Joseph J. Bangura, Freetown, October 30, 2003.

Pa Dumbuya, interviewed by Joseph J. Bangura, Freetown, November 1–3, 2003.

Pa Sorie Dumbuya, interviewed by Joseph J. Bangura, Freetown, November 10, 2003.

Mohammed Kallay, interviewed by Joseph J. Bangura, Freetown, November 2, 2003.

Brima Sesay, interviewed by Joseph J. Bangura, Freetown, November 10, 2003.

Mammy Fatu, interviewed by Joseph J. Bangura, Freetown, November 10, 2003.

Santigie Turay, interviewed by Joseph J. Bangura, Freetown, November 3, 2003.

Ibrahim Fadika, interviewed by Joseph J. Bangura, Freetown, November 4, 2003.

Gbessay Sesay, interviewed by Joseph J. Bangura, Freetown, October 6, 2003.

Salieu Jalloh, interviewed by Joseph J. Bangura, Freetown, November 1, 2003.

Imam Sillah, interviewed by Joseph J. Bangura, Freetown, November 2, 2003.

Mohamed Turay, interviewed by Rahman Bangura, Freetown, December 4, 2003.

Morlai Kamara, interviewed by Joseph J. Bangura, Freetown, November 10, 2003.

Macksoud Sesay, interviewed by Joseph J Bangura, Kalamazoo, January 10, 2016.

Mohammed Kuyateh, interviewed by Joseph J. Bangura, Kalamazoo, April 14, 2006.

Sheik Gibril Kamara, interviewed by Joseph J. Bangura, Freetown, November 6, 2003.

Salamatu Sesay, interviewed by Joseph J. Bangura, Freetown, September 8, 2003.

Private Papers: Alhaji Gibril Sesay

Sesay Private Papers, *"Notes on Islamic Teachings"* (Freetown: 1951).

Sesay Private Papers, *"The Alimania"* (Freetown: 1951), p. 10.

Sesay Private Papers, *"The Temne Mosque Project,"* p. 15.

Sesay Private Papers, *J. B. Jenkins-Johnston to Alhaji G. Sesay: Re. Visit of Her Majesty, 4566/FC/292 10/10/61.* (Freetown: 1961).

Sesay Private Papers, *J. B. Jenkins-Johnston, Town Clerk to Councillor Alhaji G. Sesay, Board of Education, 1896/ED/4/38 19/4/61.* (Freetown: 1961).

Sesay Private Papers, *Leslie A. Perowne to Gibril Sesay, SLBS/14/1/175 27th December 1959.* (Freetown).

Sesay Private Papers, *Permanent Secretary to Sesay, Lantern Procession, 22 July 1959,* (Freetown).

Sesay Private Papers, *Prime Minister to Sesay: Eid-ul-Fitri, OPM, 37/742 18 February 1961* (Freetown).

Sesay Private Papers, *Proudfoot to Sesay, September 9 1958* (Freetown).

Sesay Private Papers, *S. I. Kanu to Alhaji Sheik Gibril Sesay, Invitation As Guest Speaker, July 2 1959* (Freetown).

Sesay Private Papers, *S. J. A. Short to Alhaji Gibril Sesay, I.L.O. Celebrations-Religious Services, 16th July 1959* (Freetown).

Sesay Private Papers, *Sesay to Chief Imams In Freetown, 27th April 1959.* (Freetown).

Sesay Private Papers, *Sesay to His Excellency the Governor, Eid-ul-Fitri Celebrations in Sierra Leone, April 1958* (Freetown).

Sesay Private Papers, *Sesay to Imams in Freetown Moulid Nabi's Celebrations August 12 1958* (Freetown).

Sesay Private Papers, *Sesay to Imams in Sierra Leone, July 1959* (Freetown).

Sesay Private Papers, *Sesay to Madam Mamawa Sama, Paramount Chief Gorahun Tunkia Chiefdom, ASGS/12/1959* (Freetown).

Sesay Private Papers, *Sesay to Members of the Sierra Leone Pilgrims Association, May 28 1957* (Freetown).

Sesay Private Papers, *Sesay to Ministry of Trade and Industry 22 February 1960* (Freetown: 1960).

Sesay Private Papers, *Sesay to the Education Officer, Colony Office, 14/4/1959* (Freetown).

Sesay Private Papers, *Sesay to the Mayor, Freetown City Council, August 19, 1958* (Freetown).

Sesay Private Papers, *Sesay to the Temne Congregation, General Meeting, 11 May 1959* (Freetown).

Sesay Private Papers. *Proudfoot to Sesay, June 1, 1960.* (Freetown: 1960).

Secondary Sources

Books, Dissertations, Articles And Unpublished Reports

Abdulkader, Tayob. *Islam in South Africa: Mosques, Imams and Sermons.* Gainesville: University Press of Florida, 1999.

Alhadi, Ahmed. *The Re-Emancipation of the Colony of Sierra Leone.* Freetown: 1956.

Alharazim, M. Saif'ud Deen. "The Origin and Progress of Islam in Sierra Leone" *Sierra Leone Studies* 21 (January 1939): 13–26.

Alldridge, Thomas J. *A Transformed Colony. Sierra Leone: As It Was, and As It Is, Its Progress, Peoples, Native Customs and Underdeveloped Wealth.* London: Seeley, 1910.

Badru, Pade and Brigid Maa Sackey, eds. *Islam in Africa South of the Sahara: Essays in Gender Relations and Political Reform.* Lanham: The Scarecrow Press, Inc., 2013.

Badru, Pade. "Basic Doctrines of Islam and Colonialism in Africa." In Pade Badru and Brigid Maa Sackey, eds. *Islam in Africa South of the Sahara: Essays in Gender Relations and Political Reform.* Lanham: The Scarecrow Press, Inc., 2013:27–46.

Bangura, Joseph J. "Constitutional Development and Ethnic Entrepreneurism in Sierra Leone: A Metahistorical Analysis." In Marda Mustapha and Joseph J. Bangura, *Democratization and Human Security in Postwar Sierra Leone.* New York: Palgrave Macmillan, 2016: 13–34.

Identity Formation and Ethnic Invention: A Case Study of the Creoles, 1870–1961 Dalhousie University, Unpublished MA thesis, 2001.

"Gender and Ethnic Relations in Colonial Freetown: Temne Women in Colonial Freetown, *History in Africa,* 39 (2012):267–292.

Banton Michael, *West African City: A Study of Tribal Life in Freetown*. London: Oxford University, 1957.
"Adaptation and Integration in the Social System of Temne Immigrants in Freetown" *Africa* 26, 4 (October 1956):354–368.
Barnes, Teresa A. "We Women Worked So Hard." *Gender, Urbanization, and Social Reproduction in Colonial Harare, Zimbabwe, 1930–1956*. Portsmouth, NH: Heinemann, 1999.
Beverley Mack and Jean Boyd, *One Woman's Jihad: Nana Asma'U, Scholar and Scribe* Bloomington: Indiana University, 2000.
Blyden, Edward III. *Sierra Leone: The Pattern of Constitutional Change, 1924–1951*. PhD Dissertation, Harvard University, 1959.
Bravman, Bill. *Making Ethnic Ways: Communities and their Transformations in Kenya, 1800–1950*. Portsmouth: Heinemann, 1998.
Buxton, T.F.V. "The Creole in West Africa," *Journal of the African Society* (1912–1913): 385–394.
Cameron, Donald. "Native Administration in Nigeria and Tanganyika," cited in Thomas Spear, "Neo-Traditionalism and the Limits of Invention in British Colonial Africa," *Journal of African History* 44 (2003):3–27.
Cartwright, John. *Politics in Sierra Leone, 1947–1967*. Toronto: University of Toronto Press, 1970.
Clark, Gracia. *African Market Women: Seven Life Stories from Ghana* Bloomington: Indiana University Press, 2010.
Clarke, John I. *Sierra Leone in Maps*. London: University of London, 1969.
Cohen, Abner. *The Politics of Elite Culture: Explorations in the Dramaturgy of Power in a Modern African Society*. Oakland: University of California Press, 1981.
Collier, Gershon. *Experiment in Democracy in an African Nation*. New York: New York University, 1970.
Cooper, Frederick. *Africa Since 1940: The Past of the Present*. Cambridge: Cambridge University, 2002.
    Struggle for the City: Migrant Labor, Capital and the State in Urban Africa Beverly Hills, London and New Delhi: Sage Publications, 1983, p. 10
Cole, Gibril. *The Krio of West Africa: Islam, Creolization, and Colonialism in the Nineteenth Century*. Athens, Ohio: Ohio University Press, 2013.
Cornwall, Andrea. "Perspective on Gender in Africa." In Andrea, Cornwall, ed. *Readings in Gender in Africa*. Bloomington: Indiana University Press, 2005:1–19.
Coquery-Vidrovitch, Catherine. *African Women: A Modern History*. Boulder, Colorado: Westview Press, 1997.
Cromwell, Adelaide. *An African Victorian Feminist: The Life and Times of Adelaide Casely Hayford 1868–1960*. Washington, D.C.: Howard University Press, 1992.
Crooks, J. J. *History of the Colony*, p. 30; *Sierra Leone Weekly News*, April 16, 1890.
Dorjahn, Vernon R. "The Changing Political System of the Temne" *Africa* 30, 2 (1960):110:140.
"African Traders in Central Sierra Leone." In Paul Bohannan and George Dalton, eds., *Markets in Africa*. Evanston, Illinois: Northwestern University Press, 1962:61–88.

Falola, Toyin. "Gender, Business, and Space Control: Yoruba Market Women and Power." In Bessie House-Midamba and Felix K. Ekechi, eds. *African Market Women and Economic Power: The Role of Women in African Economic Development.* Westport, Connecticut: Greenwood Press, 1995:23–40.

Goodwin, Stefan. *Africa's Legacy of Urbanization: Unfolding Saga of A Continent.* Lanham: Lexington Books, 2006.

Fyfe, Christopher. "1787-1887-1987, Reflections on A Bicentenary." In Murray Last and Paul Richards. *Two Centuries of Intellectual Life.* Manchester: Manchester University Press, 1988. pp. 411–421.

"European and Creole Influence in the Interior of Sierra Leone before 1896" *Sierra Leone Studies* 6 (1956), pp. 113–115.

A History of Sierra Leone. London: Oxford University Press, 1962.

Sierra Leone Inheritance. London: Oxford University Press, 1964.

"The Term 'Creole': A Footnote to History" *Africa* 50, 4, (1980): 422.

"A. B. C. Sibthorpe: A Tribute," *Sierra Leone Studies ns 10* (1958): 99–109.

"Akintola Wyse: Creator of the Krio Myth." In Mac Dixon Fyle and Gibril Cole, *New Perspectives on the Sierra Leone Krio.* Baltimore: Peter Lang Inc., 2005.

Geiger, Susan, *TANU Women: Gender and Culture in the Making of Tanganyika Nationalism, 1955–1965.* Portsmouth: Heinemann, 1997.

"Tanganyika Nationalism as 'Women's Work': Life Histories, Collective Biography and Changing Historiography" *The Journal of African History* 37 3 (1996):465–478.

Glassman, Jonathon. *War of Words, War of Stones, Racial Thought and Violence in Colonia Zanzibar.* Bloomington: Indiana University Press, 2011.

Goodwin, Stefan. *Africa's Legacy of Urbanization: Unfolding Saga of A Continent.* Lanham: Lexington Books, 2006.

Hailey, Lord. *Native Administration in the British Territories.* London: His Majesty's Stationery Office, 1951.

Harrell-Bond, Barbara, Allen M. Howard and David E. Skinner, *Community Leadership and the Transformation of Freetown (1801–1976).* The Hague: Mouton Publishers, 1978.

Hanretta, Sean. *Islam and Social Change in French West Africa: History of An Emancipatory Community.* New York: Cambridge University Press, 2009.

Hargreaves, J. D. "Sir Samuel Lewis and the Legislative Council" *Sierra Leone Studies,* n.s., 6 (June 1956):40–52.

"The Establishment of the Sierra Leone Protectorate and the Insurrection of 1898" *Cambridge Historical Journal* 12, 1 (1956):56–80.

"Western Democracy and African Society: Some Reflections from Sierra Leone," *International Affairs (Royal Institute of International Affairs 1944)* 31, 3 (July, 1955): 327–334.

Harrell-Bond, Barbara, Allen M. Howard and David E. Skinner, *Community Leadership and the Transformation of Freetown (1801–1976).* The Hague: Mouton Publishers, 1978.

Harris, David John. *Sierra Leone: A Political History.* London: Oxford University Press, 2014.

Harvey, Milton. "Implications of Migrations to Freetown: A Study of the Relationships Between Migrants, Housing and Occupation" *Civilisations* 18, 2 (1968):247–269.

Horton, James Beale Africanus. *West African Countries and Peoples, British and Native* Switzerland: Kraus-Thomson, 1970.

Howard, Allen M. "Mande Identity Formation in the Economic and Political Context of North-West Sierra Leone, 1750–1900" *Padeuma* 46 (2000): 13–35.

"Contesting Commercial Space in Freetown, 1869–1930: Traders, Merchants and Officials" *Canadian Journal of African Studies* 37 (2003): 236–268.

Howard, Allen M. and Richard M. Shain, eds., *The African Spatial Factor in African History: The Relationship of the Social, Material, and Perceptual.* Leiden and Boston: Brill, 2005.

"Pawning in Coastal Northwest Sierra Leone, 1870–1910." In Toyin Falola and Paul E. Lovejoy, eds., *Pawnship in Africa: debt bondage in historical perspective.* Boulder and San Francisco: Westview Press, 1994:267–283.

Howard, Allen. "The Role of Freetown in the Commercial Life of Sierra Leone." In Christopher Fyfe and Eldred Jones, eds., *Freetown: A Symposium.* Freetown: Sierra Leone University, 1968:38–64.

Ijagbami, Adeleye. "The Kossoh War 1838–41: A Study in Temne/Colony Relations in the Nineteenth Century" *Journal of the Historical Society of Nigeria* 1, 4 (June 1971).

The History of the Temne in the 19th Century. PhD Dissertation, Edinburgh University, 1968.

Naimbana of Sierra Leone. London: Heinemann, 1976.

Ingham, Ernest G. *Sierra Leone after a Hundred Years.* London: Cass Library of African Studies, 1968.

Insoll, Timothy. *The Archaeology of Islam in Sub-Saharan Africa.* Cambridge: Cambridge University Press, 2003.

Isaac, Barry LaMont, *Traders in Pendembu: A Case Study of Entrepreneurship.* Chicago: University of Chicago Press, 1969.

Jalloh, Alusine. *African Entrepreneurship: Muslim Fula Merchants in Sierra Leone.* Athens, Ohio: Ohio University Center for International Studies, 1999.

Kevane, Michael. *Women and Development in Africa: How Gender Works.* Boulder and London: Lynne Rienner Publishers, 2004.

Kilson, Martin. *Political Change in a West African State: A Study of the Modernization Process in Sierra Leone.* Cambridge: Harvard University Press, 1966.

Kuczynski, R. R. *Demographic Survey of the British Colonial Empire.* London and New York: Oxford University Press, 1948.

Kup, A. P. "An Account of the Tribal Distribution of Sierra Leone," *Man* (August 1960).

Little, Kenneth. *Africa Women in Towns: An Aspect of Africa's Social Revolution.* London: Cambridge University Press, 1973.

West African Urbanization: A Study of Voluntary Associations in Social Change. Cambridge: Cambridge University Press, 1970.

"Structural Change in the Sierra Leone Protectorate" *Africa* 25, 3 (1955): 217–234.

Loimeier, Roman. *Muslim Societies in Africa: A Historical Anthropology.* Bloomington: Indiana University Press, 2013.

Lewis, Roy. *Sierra Leone: A Modern Portrait.* London: Her Majesty's Stationery Office, 1954.

Last, Murray and Paul Richards, *Sierra Leone, 1787–1987: Two Centuries of Intellectual Life.* Manchester: Manchester University Press, 1988.

Levtzion, Nehemia. *Islam in West Africa: Religion, Society and Politics to 1800.* Vermont and Great Britain: Ashgate Publishing Ltd., 1994.

Levtzion, Nehemia. and Pouwells Randall, *The History of Islam in Africa.* Athens, Ohio: Ohio University Press, 2000.

Luke, T. C. "Some Notes on the Creoles and their Land" *Sierra Leone Studies* 21 (1939), 53–66.

McCaskie, T. C. *History and Modernity in an African, Village, 1850–1950.* Athens, Ohio: Ohio University Press, 2001.

Migeod, F. W. H. *A View of Sierra Leone.* New York: Brentano's, 1927. Cited in Lewis, *Sierra Leone*, p. 33.

Moore, Moses N. *Orishatukeh Faduma: Liberal Theology and Evangelical Pan-Africanism, 1857–1946.* London: Scarecrow Press, 1996.

Miller, Joseph C. *The Problem of Slavery As History: A Global Approach.* New Haven: Yale University Press, 2012.

Morgan, Kenneth. *Slavery and the British Empire: From Africa to America* Oxford: Oxford University Press, 2007.

Newland H, Osman. *Sierra Leone: Its People, Products and Secret Societies.* New York: Negro Universities Press, 1969.

Moraes, P. F. de and Karin Berber, eds., *Self-Assertion and Brokerage: Early Cultural Nationalism in West Africa.* Birmingham: University of Birmingham Center for West African Studies, 1990.

Osborn, Emily Lynn. *Our New Husbands Are Here: Household, Gender, and Politics in a West African State from the Slave Trade to Colonial Rule.* Athens, Ohio: Ohio University Press, 2011.

Parpart, Jane L. and Sharon B. Stichter, eds., *African Women in the Home and the Workforce.* Boulder: Westview Press, 1988.

Pen Portrait of Muslims in Sierra Leone. Freetown: Unpublished Pamphlet, n.d.

Peel, J. D. Y. *Religious Encounter and the Making of the Yoruba.* Bloomington: Indiana University Press, 1999.

Peterson, John. "*A Study of the Dynamics of Liberated African Society, 1807–1870.*" Northwestern University, PhD Dissertation, 1963.

Province of Freedom: A History of Sierra Leone 1787–1870. London: Faber and Faber, 1969.

Phillips, Anne. *The Enigma of Colonialism: British Policy in West Africa.* Bloomington and Indianapolis: Indiana University Press, 1989.

Porter, Arthur. *Creoledom: A Study of the Development of Freetown Society.* London: Oxford University Press, 1963.

Proudfoot, L. "Mosque Building and Tribal Separatism in Freetown East" *Africa* 29 (1959).

"Towards A Muslim Solidarity in Freetown" *Africa* 31 (1961).

Rashid, Ismail and Sylvia Ojukutu-Macauley. *Paradoxes of History and Memory in Post-Colonial Sierra Leone.* Lanham: Lexington Books, 2013.

Riddell, Barry. *The Spatial Dynamics of Modernization in Sierra Leone: Structure, Diffusion and Response.* Evanston: Northwestern University Press, 1970.

Robinson, David. *Muslim Societies in African History.* New York: Cambridge University Press, 2004.

Sanneh, Lamin. *"Islamic Consciousness and the African Society: An Essay in Historical Interaction"* Freetown: Unpublished Paper, Institute of African Studies, University of Sierra Leone, 1975, pp. 4–7.

The Crown and the Turban: Muslims and West African Pluralism. Boulder, Colorado: Westview Press, 1997.

Schmidt, Elizabeth. "'Emancipate Your Husbands!' Women and Nationalism in Guinea, 1953–1958." In Jean Allman, Susan Geiger and Nakanyike Musisi eds., *Women in African Colonial Histories.* Bloomington: Indiana University Press, 2002:282–304.

Sierra Leonean Heroes: Fifty Great Men and Women Who Helped Build Our Nation. London: Commonwealth Printers Ltd., 1988.

Sitwell, Sean. *Slavery and Slaving in African History.* New York: Cambridge University Press, 2014.

Skinner, David, Barbara Harrell-Bond, Allen M. Howard, "A Profile of Urban Leaders in Freetown, Sierra Leone (1905–1945)" *Tarikh* 7, 1 (1981):11–19.

"Mande Settlement and the Development of Islamic Institutions in Sierra Leone" *International Journal of African Historical Studies* 11 (1978).

"Islam and Education in the Colony and Hinterland of Sierra Leone (1750–1914)" *Canadian Journal of African Studies* 3 (1976), p. 503.

Islam in Sierra Leone During the 19th Century. Unpublished PhD Dissertation, University of California, 1971.

Spear, Thomas and Richard Waller, eds., *Being Massai: Ethnicity and Identity in East Africa.* Athens, Ohio: Ohio University Press, 1993.

Spear, Thomas. "Neo-Traditionalism and the Limits of Invention in British Colonial Africa" *Journal of African History,* 44 (2003): 3–27.

Spitzer, Leo. "The Sierra Leone Creoles, 1870–1900." In Philip D. Curtin, ed., *Africa and the West: Intellectual Responses to European Culture* Madison: The University of Wisconsin Press, 1972.

The Creoles of Sierra Leone: Responses to Colonialism, 1870–1945. Madison: University of Wisconsin Press, 1974.

Sierra Leone Creole Reactions to Westernization, 1870–1925. Unpublished PhD Dissertation, University of Wisconsin, 1969.

Thayer, James Steel. "A Dissenting View of Creole Culture in Sierra Leone" *Cahiers d'Etudes Africaines* 121–122 31 1–2 (1991), p. 251.

Tilman Nagel, *The History of Islamic Theology: From Muhammad to the Present.* Princeton: Markus Wiener Publishers, 2000.

Ware III, Rudolph. *The Walking Qur'an: Islamic Education, Embodied Knowledge and History in West Africa.* Chapel Hill: University of North Carolina Press, 2014.

White, E. Frances. "The Big Market in Freetown: A Case Study of Women's Workplace" *Journal of the Historical Society of Sierra Leone* 4, 1&2 (December 1980), p. 22.

Sierra Leone's Settler Women Traders: Women on the Afro-European Frontier (Ann Arbor: University of Michigan Press, 1987).

Wyse, Akintola. *H. C. Bankole-Bright and Politics in Colonial Sierra Leone, 1919–1958* Cambridge: Cambridge University Press, 1990.

The Krio of Sierra Leone: An Interpretive History. Freetown: Hurst and International African Institute, 1989.

"The Krio of Sierra Leone: Perspectives and West African Historiography." In McGrath, Simon et al., eds. *Rethinking African History*. Edinburgh: University of Edinburgh Press, 1997.

Wilmsen, Edward and Patrick McAlister. *The Politics of Difference: Ethnic Premises in a World of Power*. Chicago: University of Chicago Press, 1996.

Zachernuk, Philip S. *Colonial Subjects: An African Intelligentsia and Atlantic Ideas*. Charlottesville: University of Virginia Press, 2000.

Index

Bombali, 80
Bombay Street, 97
Bombay Street Market, 173, 174
Boys London, 25, 64, 115, 190
Bravman, Bill, 55, 195
Britain
  abolition of the slave trade, 5
British
  born subject, 41
  government, 3
  colony, 16, 29, 166, 189
  Constitution, 51
  Crown Colony, 176
  philanthropists, 4
  subjects, 22, 44, 60
  territory, 18
  West Africa, 95
Bureh, Kande, 82, 83, 88, 89, 91, 96, 98,
    108, 117, 125, 141, 142, 188, 189
Buxton, T. F. V., 35, 35n22, 38, 204

Casely-Hayford, Adelaide
  women, traders, Sierra Leone Women's
    Movement, 28
census data, 42, 44
Central Temne Mosque, 109
Chief Adikalie Gbonko, 91, 118, 119, 123
Chief George Caulker, 124
chief imam, 145
Children's Clinic, 182
Christian, 127, 128, 129
  city, 130
  colony, 26
  Creoles, 131
  evangelism, 158
  missionaries, 98
  schools, 137
  tradition, 26
Circular Road, 101
City Corporation, 24
City Council, 94
Clapham Sect, 5
Clark, Gracia, 166
Cline Town, 143
coastal territory
  Bullom-speakers, 3, 64
  Sherbro-speakers, 64
Cohen, Abner, 11, 29
colonial
  Sierra Leone, Freetown, 26
colonizer, 4
Conteh, 188
Conteh, Ahmed, 94
Conteh, Mbalu, 113, 169, 177, 181,
    182, 189

Cooper, Frederick, 59, 190, 195
Coquery-Vidrovitch, Catherine, 167
Cornwall, Andrea, 166
Cornwell, 195
Creole, 15, 22, 24, 34, 57, 79
  Creoledom, 15
  identity, 22, 23
  Krio, 8, 22, 30
  Mohammedans, 130
  of Sierra Leone, 54
cultural associations, 105, 127
Cummings-John, 181, 183, 185
Cummings-John, Constance Agatha, 28,
    180

Daily Guardian, 183
dance associations, 15
Dar al-Islam, 147
Denzer, LaRay, 13, 167, 182, 189
Department of Extra-Mural
    Studies, 148
Diarra, Fatou, 114
District Commissioner, 51, 77, 110
Dorjahn, Vernon, 170
Dress Reform Society, 47
Dubai, Sheik Al Hassan, 137
Dumbuya, 123

East End Political Group (EEPG), 89
Eid al-adha, 151, 152, 161
Eid al-fitr, 115, 150, 151, 152, 161
Elections Before Independence Movement
    (EBIM), 117
Emily Lynn Osborn, 166, 169
Endeavor, 105, 115, 116
Ethnicity, 58
ethnonationalists, 101, 195
Europe, 3, 12, 30, 117n53
European, 4, 26, 196
Europeanized African, 34

Fadika, Ibrahim, 121
Faduma, Orishatukeh, 47
female elites, 180
feminism, 195
Fortieth Day, 161, 162
Foud, Sheik, 148
Fourah Bay College, 149
freemason, 25, 48
Freetonian, 23, 60, 71, 75, 85, 87, 96, 136,
    188, 189, 192
  intelligentsia, 90, 94
  women, 166, 167, 174
Freetown City Corporation, 24
Freetown City Council, 63, 95, 179